English-Arabic Business Dictionary

English-Arabic Business Dictionary

M.A. ABDEL HALEEM
and
ERNEST KAY

Graham & Trotman

First published in 1984 by

Graham & Trotman Limited
Sterling House
66 Wilton Road
London SW1V 1DE

British Library Cataloguing in Publication Data

Haleem, M. A. Abdel
English - Arabic business dictionary.
1. Business — Dictionaries — English
2. English language — Dictionaries — Arabic
I. Title II. Kay, Ernest, 1929-
338.7'0321 HF1002

ISBN 0-86010-448-6

Whilst every effort has been made to ensure that the material used in this Dictionary is accurate, neither the publishers nor the compilers can accept any responsibility for any errors or inaccuracies.

Printed in Great Britain by Billing & Sons Limited, London and Worcester.

CONTENTS

PREFACE

This dictionary has been compiled to fulfil the linguistic needs of English speaking business people visiting or doing business with countries of the Middle East area. Frequently, during discussions and negotiations, the Arabic equivalent of a key word is required to avoid misunderstanding or to effect an agreement in precise terms. Not only will this dictionary provide such an equivalent; it will go further and will enable the Arabic word to be pronounced with sufficient accuracy that it will be clearly understood. One of the major problems non-Arab speaking people experience in their dealings with the Middle East is avoided by the use of the unique transliteration script appearing side-by-side with every Arabic word. A few minutes perusal of the first few pages will make the use of the transliteration very easy. Arab businessmen, translators, lawyers and students, will also find the book useful for ascertaining the Arabic equivalents of English terms.

The terms have been very carefully selected during the compilation of the dictionary to ensure that the main ones used during general business discussions are included. Because of the need to provide a dictionary which is compact and convenient to carry – yet with sufficient clarity of print as to be easily read – the number of terms had to be restricted to around 5000.

Nevertheless, because of the business expertise of the authors and their experience in so many disciplines, the dictionary gives adequate coverage to the most important commercial areas. Included are terms often used in discussions concerning accountancy, banking, investment, insurance, office management, business law, transport, communications, chemical, petrochemical, oil and gas industries, and various branches of construction work and engineering.

At the beginning of the book are some basic grammatical points, a few basic phrases for everyday use, and a listing of Arabic numerals. A section at the end lists the currencies of the major countries of the world with Arabic equivalents and transliteration for ease of pronunciation.

We would like to acknowledge the help of Foster Wheeler Corporation, especially that of Mr.K.A. De Ghetto and Mr.W.C. Chatman, who helped during the compilation of the dictionary.

M.A. Abdel Haleem
Ernest Kay

London, 1984

INTRODUCTION

An important feature of this dictionary is the provision of transliterations of the Arabic words for those who do not read Arabic. However, even a brief acquaintance with the Arabic letters themselves will also assist users to pronounce the words correctly, and the following remarks can be borne in mind:

The Arabic alphabet

The Arabic alphabet consists of 29 letters, written from right to left, written in the following order:

ا	*a*	ط	*ṭ*
ب	*b*	ظ	*ẓ*
ت	*t*	ع	c
ث	*th*	غ	*gh*
ج	*j*	ف	*f*

ح	*ḥ*	ق	*q*
خ	*kh*	ك	*k*
د	*d*	ل	*l*
ذ	*dh*	م	*m*
ر	*r*	ن	*n*
ز	*z*	ه	*h*
س	*s*	و	*w*
ش	*sh*	ى	*y*
ص	*ṣ*	ء	'
ض	*ḍ*		

With the exception of the first (ا), all these letters are consonants. These are the shapes of the letters when they stand alone. As a simplification, we can say that when letters are joined, they lose their final flourish (if they have one), whether it goes upwards (بـ تـ ثـ فـ قـ لـ نـ and يـ for ى), or downwards (جـ حـ خـ سـ شـ صـ ضـ عـ غـ مـ): otherwise the main base of the letter remains the same. ا د ذ ر ز may not be joined to a following letter at all, but they, as well as all the other letters may be joined to a letter coming before them.

Note that the following groups of letters differ only in the dots that go with them. Care should thus be taken with them:

b	*t*	*th*	*n*	*y*	*j*	*ḥ*	*kh*
بـ	تـ	ثـ	نـ	يـ	جـ	حـ	خـ

s	*sh*	*ṣ*	*ḍ*	*ṭ*	*ẓ*	^{c}	*gh*	*f*	*q*
سـ	شـ	صـ	ضـ	ط	ظ	عـ	غـ	فـ	قـ

d	*dh*	*r*	*z*
د	ذ	ر	ز

There are no capital letters in Arabic.

Roughly speaking, the following letters are pronounced like their English equivalents:

ب = *b*, ت = *t*, ث = *th* (as in thin), ج = *j*

د = *d*, ر = *r*, ز = *z*, س = *s*, ذ = *dh* (as in the)

ش = *sh*, ف = *f*, ك = *k*, ل = *l*, م = *m*

ن = *n*, ه = *h*, و = *w*, ي = *y*.

However, the following sounds need special attention:

ح transliterated (*ḥ*), is a gutteral *h* heard with a hissing sound as when you sigh with exasperation. It should not be confused with

خ which is another gutteral, sounded as in the Scottish word *loch*.

ص *(ṣ)*, ض *(ḍ)*, ط *(ṭ)*, and ظ *(ẓ)* are emphatic counterparts of:

س *(s)*, د *(d)*, ت *(t)*, and ذ *(dh)*.

To give them their emphatic value, try to pronounce each of them as if it were accompanied by the sound *w* said at the same moment, thus *swa* for ص, *dwa* for ض, etc.

ء transliterated (') as in the word *ta'mīn* (insurance) and *dā'in* (creditor). This is a glottal stop. It appears in English with the Cockney accent (*I 'aven't 'ad an 'orse*).

ع transliterated (c) as in *caqd* (contract). This is a gutteral sound. Listen to the Arabs when they pronounce the name *cAlī* . To produce it, make a long sound *aaa* and placing the tips of your fourth finger and thumb above the Adam's apple, press down and the sound will emerge.

With practice, your throat muscles will develop to do it for you, but it takes practice.

غ transliterated (*gh*) is a gargling sound as in the French *r* in *Paris* .

ق transliterated (*q*). Listen to the Arabs when they say *Qaṭar*. It sounds like a *k* pronounced in the throat where you pronounce غ .

There are only three vowels in Arabic: *a* as in *fat* , *i* as in *fit* and *u* as in *put*. They can be lengthened to double their length by adding ا for long *a* , ي for long *i* and و for long *u*.

With the exception of texts written for teaching beginners and religious texts like the *Qur'ān*, short vowels are not usually written in Arabic words. Written Arabic is thus similar to shorthand. Short vowels, however, appear in the pronunciation and hence in the transliteration. The long vowels are indicated in the transliteration by a dash placed above the vowels. Thus *bayān* = *bayaan* (a statement), *wakīl* = *wakiil* (agent), and *sūq* = *suuq* (market).

There are two diphthongs in literary (or written) Arabic: *ay* as in *bayt* (house) and *aw* as in *yawm* (day).

Note the absence in literary Arabic of the English consonants *g*, *v* and *p*, and of the English vowels *e* and *o* and of a number of English diphthongs.

Once again, note the difference between the sounds

ء and ع	*(' and c)*	Both are written <u>above</u> the line in transliteration
ت and ط	*(t and ṭ)*	
ه and ح	*(h and ḥ)*	
د and ض	*(d and ḍ)*	
ذ and ظ	*(dh and ẓ)*	
س and ص	*(s and ṣ)*	

Finally: in all your reading and pronunciation of Arabic, short vowels must be pronounced short, and long ones must be pronounced long, and double consonants must be emphasised as double (unlike English). This will help you to get the stress right. All Arabic *r*s must be rolled. Every letter in a word must be pronounced.

A NOTE ON GRAMMAR

The definite article (i.e. *the*)

The definite article in Arabic is (*al-*) prefixed to the noun it qualifies, as in *al-kātib* (the clerk). When the noun begins with one of certain letters of the Arabic alphabet, the *l* in *al-* is assimilated to the first letter, as in *as-sana* (the year). So if you see *a* followed by a letter which is repeated after the dash, the word is definite. If the preceding word ends in a vowel, the *a* of the definite article is elided and an apostrophe is used as in *as-sana 'l-māliyya* (the financial year).

The indefinite article (*a*, *an*) does not appear in the transliteration of terms.

Gender

There are only two genders in Arabic: masculine and feminine. Inanimate objects are either masculine or feminine. When you see a word ending in *a*, which is the most common feminine ending, you may assume it is feminine. For example, *sana* (a year, *sharika* (a company). But *īṣāl* (a receipt) and *shīk* (a cheque) are masculine.

The plural feminine ending is *-āt* as in *riyālāt* (riyals) and other currencies. Plurals of all foreign words in Arabic are formed in this way, as in *kamirāt*, *tilifyūnāt*, etc.

Adjectives

The adjective is placed after the noun it qualifies. It agrees with the noun it qualifies in gender, in being definite or indefinite. Thus: *dakhl kabīr* (a large income) and *sharika kabīra* (a large company), *mudīr jadīd* (a new director) and *al-mudīr al-jadīd* (the new director). An adjective agrees with its noun in number also; but adjectives of plural inanimate objects appear usually in the feminine singular as in *arbāḥ kabīra* (large profits).

Conventions and symbols used

1. In Arabic dictionaries verbs usually appear in the past tense of the third person masculine singular. Thus you find 'he bought', he sold', 'he came', etc. (In English dictionaries you find the infinitive: (to) buy, (to) sell, (to) come.) In this dictionary we chose to put the verbs in the present tense, which is more suitable for business. But because of certain features of Arabic, we had to keep the verbs in the third person masculine. For example, *yabīᶜ* (he sells), *yursil* (he sends). Note that you will find verbs beginning either with *ya* or *yu*. When you want to talk about yourself in the singular, substitute *a* for *ya* and

u for *yu* . Say *abīᶜ* (I sell), *ursil* (I send). When you want to talk about yourself in the plural, substitute *na* and *nu* respectively, saying *nabīᶜ* (we sell), *nursil* (we send). When you want to talk about your company, substitute *ta* and *tu* respectively, saying *sharikatnā tabīᶜ* (our company sells), and *sharikatnā tursil* (our company sends).

2. Sometimes you will find one English term transliterated by more than one Arabic term, separated by a comma in the transliteration and a full stop in the Arabic words. This could be due either to Arabic words being synonyms equally current, or the English word may have different meanings in Arabic, or a matter of usage in different geographical locations. In many cases Egypt may have one word for a concept and the countries in Arabia and the Fertile Crescent another. Both would be current and understood, but we thought it better for the user of the dictionary

to have both. Examples are:

maṣrif, bank	(bank)	مصرف ٠ بنك
nafṭ, bitrūl	(petrol)	نفط٠ بترول
ta'mīn, ḍamān	(insurance)	تأمين ٠ ضمان

3. An oblique gives an alternative to the word immediately preceding it within the phrase, for example:

yusawwī/yaḥsim nizāᶜ	(to settle a dispute)	يسوّى/يحسم نزاع
tawkīl/tafwīḍ ᶜāmm	(general power of attorney)	توكيل/تفويض عام

USEFUL PHRASES

- *ṣabāḥ al-khair!*	good morning!
- *ṣabāḥ an-nur!*	good morning!
- *ismī Richard*	my name is Richard
- *aish ismak?*	what is your name?
- *ismī John*	my name is John
- *ahlan wa sahlan!*	welcome!
- *ahlan bīk*	the same to you!
- *kaif ḥālak?*	how are you?
- *bikhair, shukran*	fine thank you
- *ana min injiltira/amrīka*	I come from England/America
- *ashtaghil fī sharikat Graham & Trotman*	I work for Graham & Trotman
- *ashtaghil mudīr sharika*	I am a company director
- *ashtaghil mudīr al-bayᶜ*	I am a sales manager

- *arīd ...*	I want/would like
- *arīd taxi, min faḍlak*	I'd like a taxi, please
- *arīd funduq min faḍlak*	I want a hotel, please
- *arīd ashrab gahwa*	I would like a coffee
- *arīd ashrab shāy*	I would like some tea
- *arīd ashrab cocacola*	I would like a Coca-cola
- *arīd ākul*	I'd like to eat
- *arīd ākul sandawitch*	I'd like to eat a sandwich
- *arīd arūḥ ilā 's-sūq*	I'd like to visit the market
- *arīd arūḥ ilā dukkān*	I'd like to go to a shop
- *arīd arūḥ ilā funduq*	I'd like to go to a hotel
- *arīd arūḥ ilā qism ash-shurṭa*	I'd like to go to the police station
- *arīd arūḥ ilā maktab al-barīd*	I'd like to go to the post office

- *arīd arūḥ ilā 'l-maṭār*	I'd like to go to the airport
- *arīd agābil al-mudīr*	I would like to meet the director/manager
- *arīd asāfir ilā Qaṭar*	I want to travel to Qatar
- *arīd ashtarī sajāyir*	I'd like to buy some cigarettes
- *arīd ashtarī film*	I'd like to buy some film
- *kam?*	how much?
- *khamsa riyāl*	5 riyals
- *itfaḍḍal*	here you are!
- *shukran*	thanks
- *maᶜ as-salāma!*	good-bye

NUMERALS

1	*wāḥid*	١
2	*ithnain*	٢
3	*thalātha*	٣
4	*arba^{c}a*	٤
5	*khamsa*	٥
6	*sitta*	٦
7	*sab^{c}a*	٧
8	*thamāniyah*	٨
9	*tis^{c}a*	٩
10	*^{c}ashara*	١٠
11	*aḥad ^{c}ashar*	١١
12	*ithna ^{c}ashar*	١٢
13	*thalāthat ^{c}ashar*	١٣

14	*arba^{c}at ^{c}ashar*	١٤
15	*khamsat ^{c}ashar*	١٥
16	*sittat ^{c}ashar*	١٦
17	*sab^{c}at ^{c}ashar*	١٧
18	*thamāniyat ^{c}ashar*	١٨
19	*tis^{c}at ^{c}ashar*	١٩
20	*^{c}ishrīn*	٢٠
21	*wāḥid wa ^{c}ishrīn*	٢١
22	*ithnain wa ^{c}ishrīn*	٢٢
23	*thalātha wa ^{c}ishrīn*	٢٣
24	*arba^{c}a wa ^{c}ishrīn*, etc.	٢٤

30	*thalāthīn*	٣٠
31, etc.	*wāḥid wa thalāthīn*, etc.	٣١
40	*arbaᶜīn*	٤٠
50	*khamsīn*	٥٠
60	*sittīn*	٦٠
70	*sabᶜīn*	٧٠
80	*thamānīn*	٨٠
90	*tisᶜīn*	٩٠
100	*miyya*	١٠٠
101	*miyya wa wāḥid*	١٠١
111	*miyya wa aḥad ᶜashar*	١١١

121	*miyyah wāḥid wa ᶜishrīn*	١٢١
200	*miyyatain*	٢٠٠
300	*thalāth miyya*	٣٠٠
400	*arbaᶜ miyya*	٤٠٠
500	*khams miyya*	٥٠٠
600	*sitt miyya*	٦٠٠
700	*sabᶜ miyya*	٧٠٠
800	*thamān miyya*	٨٠٠
900	*tis' miyya*	٩٠٠
1000	*alf*	١٠٠٠
1001	*alf wa wāḥid*, etc.	١٠٠١
1121	*alf miyya wāḥid wa ᶜishrīn*	١١٢١

2000	*alfain*	٢٠٠٠
3000	*thalāthat ālāf*	٣٠٠٠
4000, etc.	*arba^{c}at ālāf*, etc.	٤٠٠٠
10,000	*^{c}asharat ālāf*	١٠٠٠٠
11,000, etc.	*aḥad ^{c}ashar alf*, etc.	١١٠٠٠
$\frac{1}{2}$	*niṣf*	١/٢
$\frac{1}{3}$	*thulth*	١/٣
$\frac{1}{4}$	*rub^{c}*	١/٤
5%	*khamsa fi'l-miyya*	٥٪

NUMERALS

Note that Arabic numerals are written in the same direction as English numerals, reading from left to right: 1983 = ١٩٨٣

A

abandoned goods	*baḍā'iʿ matrūka*	بضائع متروكة
abnormal costs	*takālīf ghayr ʿādiyya*	تكاليف غير عادية
abnormal risk	*khaṭar ghayr ṭabīʿī*	خطر غير طبيعى
abolish	*yulghī. yubṭil*	يلغى . يبطل
abortive	*fāshil. ʿaqīm*	فاشل . عقيم
above-board	*bi ṣarāḥa. ʿalāniyatan*	بصراحة . علانية
above par	*fawq al-siʿr al-aṣlī*	فوق السعر الاصلى
abridgement	*mūjaz*	موجز
abroad	*fi 'l-khārij*	فى الخارج
absence of consideration	*ʿadam wujūd maṣlaḥa*	عدم وجود مصلحة
absenteeism	*taghayyub mutaṭāwil*	تغيّب متطاول
absolute majority	*aghlabiyya muṭlaqa*	اغلبية مطلقة
absorbed costs	*takālīf mustawʿaba*	تكاليف مستوعبة
abstain	*yamtaniʿ ʿan*	يمتنع عن
abstract of account	*mustakhraj ḥisāb*	مستخرج حساب
abuse of confidence	*isāʿat istiʿmāl thiqa*	اساءة استعمال ثقة
accelerated ageing	*inḍāj muʿajjal*	انضاج معجّل
accelerated depreciation	*naqṣ al-qīma. istihlāk muʿajjal*	نقص القيمة / استهلاك معجّل
accelerated weathering	*taʿjīl āthār aḥwāl al-jaww*	تعجيل آثار أحوال الجو
acceleration clause	*sharṭ at-taʿjīl*	شرط التعجيل

acceptance, conditional	*qabūl mashrūṭ*	قبول مشروط
acceptance of lump sum settlement	*qabūl muṣālaḥa bi mablagh ijmālī*	قبول مصالحة على مبلغ اجمالى
access time	*waqt al-isti^{c}māl*	وقت الاستعمال
accident insurance	*ta'mīn ḍidd al-ḥawādith*	تأمين ضد الحوادث
accident prevention	*man^c al-ḥawādith*	منع الحوادث
accommodation	*taswiya*	تسوية
account	*ḥisāb*	حساب
accountant, chartered	*muḥāsib qānūnī*	محاسب قانونى
account, close an	*yaqfil ḥisāb*	يقفل حسابا
account, deposit	*ḥisāb īdā^c*	حساب ايداع
accounting, mechanized	*al-muḥāsaba 'l-āliyya*	المحاسبة الآلية
account, open an	*yaftaḥ ḥisāb*	يفتح حسابا
account, overdrawn	*ḥisāb makshūf*	حساب مكشوف
account payable	*ḥisāb mustaḥiqq ad-daf^c*	حساب مستحق الدفع
accounting period	*muddat al-muḥāsaba*	مدّة المحاسبة
account, profit and loss	*ḥisāb al-arbāḥ wa 'l-khasā'ir*	حساب الأرباح والخسائر
account, sales	*ḥisāb al-mabī^{c}āt*	حساب المبيعات
account, statement of	*kashf ḥisāb*	كشف حساب
accounts, annual	*ḥisāb sanawī*	حساب سنوى
accounts, audited	*ḥisābāt murāja^{c}a*	حسابات مراجعة
accounts control	*raqābat al-ḥisābāt*	رقابة الحسابات

accounts department	*qism al-ḥisābāt*	قسم الحسابات
accounts, manufacturing	*ḥisāb at-taṣnīᶜ*	حساب التصنيع
accrued assets	*uṣūl mustaḥaqqa*	أصول مستحقة
accrued dividend	*ᶜawā'id ashum mustaḥaqqa*	عوائد أسهم مستحقة
adjournment	*ta'jīl*	تأجيل
adjustment of rate	*taswiyat al-muᶜaddal*	تسوية المعدّل
administration	*idāra*	ادارة
administration cost	*takālīf al-idāra*	تكاليف الادارة
administration expenses	*maṣārīf al-idāra*	مصاريف الادارة
administrator	*mudīr. waṣiyy*	مدير • وصى
admissible	*maqbūl. jā'iz*	مقبول • جائز
admission	*qabūl. iqrār*	قبول • اقرار
adopt	*yatabanna. yuqirr*	يتبنّى • يقرّ
adsorb	*imtazz*	امتزّ
advance payment	*dafᶜ mutaqaddam*	دفع مقدم
adverse balance of trade	*mīzān tijārī ᶜājiz*	ميزان تجارى عاجز
advertisement	*iᶜlān*	اعلان
advertising agency	*wikālat iᶜlān*	وكالة اعلان
advertising budget	*mizāniyyat al-iᶜlān*	ميزانية الاعلان
advertising campaign	*ḥamla iᶜlāniyya*	حملة اعلانية
advertising effectiveness	*faᶜāliyat al-iᶜlān*	فعالية الاعلان

advertising media	*wasā'il al-iʿlān*	وسائل الاعلان
advice note	*kitāb ishʿār*	كتاب اشعار
advice note	*waraqat ikhṭār*	ورقة اخطار
advisor	*mustashār*	مستشار
advisory committee	*lajna istishāriyya*	لجنة استشارية
affidavit	*iqrār kitābī muṣaddaq ʿalayh*	اقرار كتابى مصدق عليه
affiliated company	*sharika tābiʿa*	شركة تابعة
after-sales service	*khadamāt baʿd al-bayʿ*	خدمات بعد البيع
against all risks	*ḍidd kull 'il-akhṭār*	ضد كل الاخطار
agency	*wakāla*	وكالة
agency agreement	*muwāfaqat al-wakāla*	موافقة الوكالة
agenda	*jadwal aʿmāl. mufakkira*	جدول أعمال • مفكرة
agent	*wakīl*	وكيل
agent, local	*wakīl maḥallī*	وكيل محلّى
agreement, commercial	*ittifāq tijārī*	اتفاق تجارى
agreement, oral	*ittifāq shafawī*	اتفاق شفوى
agreement, trade	*ittifāqiyya tijāriyya*	اتفاقية تجارية
agricultural chemicals	*kīmāwiyyāt zirāʿiyya*	كيماويات زراعية
agricultural imports	*wāridāt zirāʿiyya*	واردات زراعية
agricultural machinery	*muʿiddāt makaniyya zirāʿiyya*	معدّات مكنية زراعية
air-conditioning	*takyīf al-hawā'*	تكييف الهواء
aircraft maintenance	*ṣiyānat aṭ.ṭayyārāt*	صيانة الطيارات

air duct	*maslak hawā'*	مسلك هواء
air freight paid by seller	*ujrat ash-shaḥn al-jawwī ^{c}alā 'l-bā'i^{c}*	أجرة الشحن الجوى على البائع
airline	*sharikat khuṭūṭ jawwiyya*	شركة خطوط جوية
air mail	*barīd jawwī*	بريد جوى
air pollution	*talawwuth al-hawā'*	تلوّث الهواء
airport	*maṭār*	مطار
air transport insurance	*ta'mīn an-naql al-jawwī*	تأمين النقل الجوى
air transport licensing board	*majlis at-tarkhīṣ bi 'n-naql al-jawwī*	مجلس الترخيص بالنقل الجوى
alcohol	*kuḥūl*	كحول
alien	*ajnabī*	أجنبى
alienate	*yanqul milkiyya*	ينقل ملكية
allegation	*iddi^{c}ā'*	ادّعاء
alliance	*ḥilf*	حلف
allocation of resources	*tawzī^{c} al-mawārid*	توزيع الموارد
allotment of shares	*takhṣīṣ al-ashum*	تخصيص الاسهم
allowances	*i^{c}fā'āt. ^{c}alāwāt*	اعفاءات . علاوات
allowed time	*waqt masmūḥ bihi*	وقت مسموح به
all rights reserved	*ḥuqūq aṭ-ṭab^{c} wa 'n-nashr maḥfūẓa*	حقوق الطبع والنشر محفوظة
all risks insurance	*ta'mīn jamī^{c} al-akhṭār*	تأمين جميع الأخطار
alternative contract	*^{c}aqd khiyārī*	عقد خيارى

amalgamate	*yudmij*	يدمج
ambassador	*safīr*	سفير
ambiguous	*ghāmiḍ*	غامض
amended draft	*musawwada munaqqaḥa*	مسوّدة منقحة
amendment	*taᶜdīl. tanqīḥ*	تعديل · تنقيح
amicable settlement	*taswiyya widdiyya*	تسوية ودّية
amortisation	*istihlāk ad-dayn/al-ashum*	استهلاك الدين/الأسهم
amount due	*al-mablagh al-mustaḥaqq*	المبلغ المستحق
amount insured	*al-mablagh al-mu'amman*	المبلغ المؤمّن
amount payable on settlement	*qīmat at-taswiya*	قيمة التسوية
analysis, sales	*taḥlīl al-mabīᶜāt*	تحليل المبيعات
annexed	*maḍmūm. murfaq*	مضموم · مرفق
anniversary	*ᶜīd sanawī*	عيد سنوى
announcement	*iᶜlān. naba'*	اعلان · نبأ
annual audit	*faḥṣ sanawī*	فحص سنوى
annual consumption	*istihlāk sanawī*	استهلاك سنوى
annual fees	*rusūm sanawiyya*	رسوم سنوية
Annual General Meeting (AGM)	*al-jamᶜiyya 'l-ᶜumūmiyya 's-sanawiyya*	الجمعية العمومية السنوية
annual interest	*fā'ida sanawiyya*	فائدة سنوية
annual premium	*qisṭ sanawī*	قسط سنوى
annual report	*taqrīr sanawī*	تقرير سنوى

annuities	*rawātib/aqsāt sanawiyya*	رواتب/اقساط سنوية
annuity assurance	*ta'mīn ad-dakhl as-sanawī*	تأمين الدخل السنوى
annulment	*ilghā'. faskh*	الغاء • فسخ
anticipated cost	*taklifa mutawaqqaᶜa*	تكلفة متوقعة
anticipated profit	*ribḥ mutawaqqaᶜ*	ربح متوقع
anti-dumping	*ḍidd tafrīgh an-nufāya*	ضدّ تفريغ النفاية
any other business	*ayy bunūd ukhrā*	أى بنود أخرى
appeal, court of	*maḥkamat isti'nāf*	محكمة استئناف
appendix	*zā'ida dūdiyya*	زائدة دودية
applicant	*muqaddim ṭalab*	مقدم طلب
application (for a post)	*ṭalab li waẓīfa*	طلب لوظيفة
application form	*istimārat taqdīm*	استمارة تقديم
application for shares	*ṭalab ashum*	طلب أسهم
appointment	*taᶜyīn. mawᶜid*	تعيين • موعد
appraisal of risk	*taqwīm al-khaṭar*	تقويم الخطر
appreciation value	*irtifāᶜ qīmat mumtalakāt*	ارتفاع قيمة ممتلكات
appropriation account	*ḥisāb tawzīᶜ al-arbāḥ wa 'l-khasā'ir*	حساب توزيع الارباح والخسائر
approximate cost	*taklifa taqrībiyya*	تكلفة تقريبية
approximate value	*qīma taqrībiyya*	قيمة تقريبية
arbitrage	*shirā' fī sūq wa bayᶜ fī ukhrā li-ribḥ farq as-siᶜr*	شراء فى سوق وبيع فى أخرى لربح فرق السعر

arbitrary	*taḥakkumī*	تحكمى
arbitration award	*qarār taḥkīmī*	قرار تحكيمى
arbitration board	*hay'at taḥkīm*	هيئة تحكيم
arbitration clause	*sharṭ at-taḥkīm*	شرط التحكيم
arbitration, court of	*majlis at-taḥkīm*	مجلس التحكيم
arbitration proceedings	*ijrā'āt at-taḥkīm*	اجراءات التحكيم
arbitrator	*muḥakkam*	محكّم
area manager	*mudīr iqlīmī*	مدير اقليمى
area offices	*al-makātib al-iqlīmiyya*	المكاتب الاقليمية
arm's-length transactions	*muʿāmalāt asāsha tijārī baḥt*	معاملات اساسها تجارى بحت
arrears	*duyūn muta'akhkhira*	ديون متأخرة
articles of agreement	*bunūd al-ittifāqiyya*	بنود الاتفاقية
articles of association	*niẓām ash-sharika 'l-asāsī*	نظام الشركة الأساسى
articles of partnership	*ʿaqd sharikat taḍāmun*	عقد شركة تضامن
assembly, general	*jamʿiyya ʿāmma*	جمعية عامة
assembly line	*niẓām at-tajmīʿ*	نظام التجميع
assessed taxes	*ḍarā'ib/rusūm muqaddara*	ضرائب/رسوم مقدرة
assessment of claims	*taqdīr at-taʿwīḍāt*	تقدير التعويضات
assessment of taxes	*taqdīr aḍ-ḍarā'īb*	تقدير الضرائب
assessor	*muqaddir aḍ-ḍarā'ib*	مقدر الضرائب
assets, current	*amwāl/mawjūdāt mutadāwala*	أموال/موجودات متداولة

assets, fixed	*amwāl/mawjūdāt thābita*	اموال/موجودات ثابتة
assets, liquid	*amwāl/mawjūdāt sā'ila*	أموال/موجودات سائلة
assets, wasting	*amwāl/mawjūdāt hālika*	اموال/موجودات هالكة
assign	*yukhaṣṣiṣ. yufawwid. yuḥawwil*	يخصص • يفوض • يحوّل
assignment	*taḥwīl al-ḥaqq/al-milkiyya*	تحويل الحق/الملكية
assignment of right	*ḥawālat al-ḥaqq*	حوالة الحق
associated company	*sharika murtabiṭa bi-ukhrā*	شركة مرتبطة بأخرى
associate members	*aᶜḍā' mushārikūn/muntasibūn*	اعضاء مشاركون/منتسبون
association	*jamᶜiyya. sharika*	جمعية • شركة
association, deed of	*ᶜaqd ta'sīs sharika*	عقد تأسيس شركة
assurance	*ta'mīn. tawkīd*	تأمين • توكيد
assurance, endowment	*ta'mīn li-mudda muᶜayyana*	تأمين لمدة معينة
assurance, life	*ta'mīn ᶜala 'l-ḥayāh*	تأمين على الحياة
assured capital	*mablagh at-ta'mīn*	مبلغ التأمين
at maturity	*ᶜind ḥulūl al-ajal*	عند حلول الاجل
atomic energy	*aṭ-ṭāqa 'dh-dharriyya*	الطاقة الذرّية
atomic energy commission	*lajnat aṭ-ṭāqa adh-dharriyya*	لجنة الطاقة الذرّية
attorney	*muḥāmī, wakīl*	محامى• وكيل
attorney, power of	*tawkīl/tafwīḍ qānūnī*	توكيل/تفويض قانونى
auction	*mazād*	مزاد
auctioneer	*dallāl bi'l-mazād*	دلاّل بالمزاد

auction fees	*rusūm al-mazād*	رسوم المزاد
audit, annual	*al-murājaᶜa 's-sanawiyya*	المراجعة السنوية
audit of accounts	*murājaᶜat al-ḥisābāt*	مراجعة الحسابات
auditor	*murājiᶜ/mudaqqiq ḥisābāt*	مراجع / مدقّق حسابات
audit period	*fatrat al-murājaᶜa*	فترة المراجعة
audit year	*sanat al-murājaᶜa*	سنة المراجعة
authorisation	*takhwīl*	تخويل
authorised capital	*ra's al-māl al-murakhkhaṣ bihi*	رأس المال المرخّص به
authority, legal	*sulṭa qānūniyya*	سلطة قانونية
authority, public	*as-sulṭa 'l-ᶜumūmiyya*	السلطة العمومية
automatic data processing	*iᶜdād al-bayānāt al-ūtūmātīkī*	اعداد البيانات الاوتوماتيكى
automatic machine	*āla 'utumātiyya*	آلة أوتوماتية
automation	*tashghīl 'utumātī*	تشغيل اوتوماتى
available assets	*mawjūdāt mutawaffira*	موجودات متوفرة
available time	*al-waqt al-mutayassir*	الوقت المتيسر
average cost	*muᶜaddal at-taklifa*	معدّل التكلفة
average daily output	*muᶜaddal al-intāj al-yawmī*	معدّل الانتاج اليومى
average premium	*qisṭ wasaṭ*	قسط وسط
average weekly earnings	*mutawassiṭ ad-dakhl al-usbūᶜī*	متوسّط الدخل الاسبوعى
aviation fuel	*waqūd aṭ-ṭayyārāt*	وقود الطيارات
aviation insurance	*ta'mīn jawwī*	تأمين جوّى

B

backdated	*bi-maf^{c}ūl raj^{c}ī*	بمفعول رجعى
back-door operations	*^{c}amaliyyāt al-bāb al-khalfī*	عمليات الباب الخلفى
backer	*dā^{c}im*	داعم
back flow	*dafq khalfī*	دفق خلفى
backing	*da^{c}m, taghṭiya*	دعم ، تغطية
back interest	*fā'ida muta'akhkhira*	فائدة متأخّرة
back pay	*rātib muta'akhkhir*	راتب متأخر
back pressure	*ḍaghṭ mu^{c}ākis*	ضغط معاكس
back taxes	*ḍarā'ib muta'akhkhira*	ضرائب متأخرة
back-to-work movement	*ḥarakat al-^{c}awda ila'l-^{c}amal*	حركة العودة الى العمل
backwardation	*ta'jīl at-taslīm*	تأجيل التسليم
backward integration	*takāmul khalfī*	تكامل خلفى
bad debt	*dayn ma^{c}dūm*	دين معدوم
bad faith	*dhimma sayyi'a*	ذمة سيئة

bail out	*yakful*	يكفل
balance	*mīzān, raṣīd*	ميزان، رصيد
balance carried forward	*raṣīd muraḥḥal*	رصيد مرحل
balanced economy	*iqtiṣād mutawāzin*	اقتصاد متوازن
balance deficit	^{c}*ajz mīzān al-madfū*^{c}*āt*	عجز ميزان المدفوعات
balanced growth	*numuww mutawāzin*	نموّ متوازن
balance of payments	*mīzān al-madfū*^{c}*āt*	ميزان المدفوعات
balance of trade	*al-mīzān at-tijārī*	الميزان التجارى
balance sheet	*al-mīzāniyya*	الميزانية
balance surplus	*fā'iḍ mīzān al-madfū*^{c}*āt*	فائض ميزان المدفوعات
ballot box	*ṣundūq al-iqtirā*^{c}	صندوق الاقتراع
ballot paper	*waraqat al-intikhāb*	ورقة الانتخاب
ballot, secret	*iqtirā*^{c} *sirrī*	اقتراع سري
ban	*yaḥẓur*	يحظر
bank	*maṣrif, bank*	مصرف، بنك
bank account	*ḥisāb maṣrafī*	حساب مصرفي
bank advance	*sulfa min maṣrif*	سلفة من مصرف
bank balance	*raṣid fi'l-maṣrif*	رصيد فى المصرف
bank charges	*maṣārīf al-maṣrif*	مصاريف المصرف
bank commission	^{c}*umūlat al-maṣrif*	عمولة المصرف
bank credit	*i*^{c}*timād maṣrifī*	اعتماد مصرفي

bank debits	*arṣida maṣrifiyya madīna*	ارصدة مصرفية مدنية
banker's card	*biṭāqa maṣrifiyya*	بطاقة مصرفية
banker's lien	*ḥaqq al-maṣrif fī ḥajz al-wadīᶜa*	حقّ المصرف فى حجز الوديعة
banker's reference	*marjiᶜ maṣrifī*	مرجع مصرفي
bank holiday	*yawm ᶜuṭla maṣrifiya*	يوم عطلة مصرفية
bank notes	*awrāq naqd*	اوراق نقد
bank rate	*siᶜr al-khaṣm*	سعر الخصم
bank reserves	*iḥtiyāṭāt al-maṣraf*	احتياطات المصرف
bankrupt	*muflis*	مفلس
bankruptcy	*iflās*	افلاس
bank statement	*kashf ḥisāb maṣrifī*	كشف حساب مصرفي
bank transfers	*taḥwīlāt maṣrifiyya*	تحويلات مصرفية
bare boat charter	*isti'jār markib ᶜāri*	استئجار مركب عار
bargain	*ṣafqa*	صفقة
bargaining powers	*quwwāt al-musāwama*	قوّات المساومة
bargaining rights	*ḥuqūq al-musāwama*	حقوق المساومة
barratry	*khaṭa' ar-rubbān aw al-baḥḥāra al-mutaᶜammad*	خطأ الربّان أو البحارة المتعمد
barrel	*barmīl*	برميل
barrel mile	*barmīl mīlī*	برميل ميلي
barrel per day	*barmīl fi'l-yawm*	برميل في اليوم
barrister	*muḥāmī*	محامي

barter	*muqāyaḍa*	مقايضة
base currency	*ᶜumla zā'ifa*	عملة زائفة
base level	*al-mustawa 'l-adnā*	المستوى الأدنى
base price	*as-siᶜr al-asāsī*	السعر الأساسي
base rate	*al-ajr al-asāsī*	الأجر الاساسي
base royalty	*ar-rayᶜ al-asāsī*	الريع الاساسي
basic agreement	*ittifāq asāsī*	اتّفاق اساسي
basic data	*al-bayānāt al-asāsiyya*	البيانات الأساسية
basic document	*wathīqa asāsiyya*	وثيقة أساسية
basic facts	*ḥaqā'iq asāsiyya*	حقائق أساسية
basic pay	*al-ajr al-asāsī*	الأجر الاساسي
basic premium	*al-qisṭ al-asāsī*	القسط الأساسي
basic price	*as-siᶜr al-asāsī*	السعر الأساسي
basic principle	*mabda' asāsī*	مبدأ أساسى
basic rate	*muᶜaddal asāsī*	معدّل أساسى
basic structure	*al-binya' l-asāsiyya*	البنية الاساسية
basic training	*tadrīb asāsī*	تدريب أساسى
basic wage	*al-ajr al-asāsī*	الاجر الاساسى
basis of assessment	*asās taqdīr ḍarība*	اساس تقدير ضريبة
basis of discussions	*asās al-muḥādathāt*	اساس المحادثات
bearer bond	*sanad li-ḥāmilihi*	سند لحامله

bearer certificate	*shahāda li-ḥāmilihā*	شهادة لحاملها
bearer securities	*awrāq māliyya li-ḥāmilihā*	اوراق مالية لحاملها
bearer stock	*sahm li-ḥāmilihi*	سهم لحامله
belated claim	*muṭālaba muta'akhkhira*	مطالبة متأخرة
beneficiary	*mustafīd*	مستفيد
benefit	*fā'ida, nafᶜ*	فائدة ، نفع
benefit, social	*ḍamān ijtimāᶜī*	ضمان اجتماعى
benefit, tax	*mazāya ḍarībiyya*	مزايا ضريبية
benefit, unemployment	*iᶜānat al-baṭāla*	اعانة البطالة
berthing	*irsā'*	ارساء
best bid	*afḍal ᶜaṭā'*	أفضل عطاء
best efforts	*aqṣā juhd*	أقصى جهد
best price	*aḥsan siᶜr*	احسن سعر
beyond repair	*lā yumkin iṣlāḥuh*	لا يمكن اصلاحه
bi-annual	*niṣf sanawī*	نصف سنوى
bid price	*siᶜr al-ᶜarḍ*	سعر العرض
bilateral agreement	*ittifāq thunā'ī*	اتّفاق ثنائى
bilateral trade agreements	*ittifāqiyyāt tijāriyya thunā'iyya*	اتّفاقيات تجارية ثنائية
bill of credit	*sanad iᶜtimād*	سند اعتماد
bill of entry	*bayān al-baḍā'iᶜ ad-dākhila*	بيان البضائع الداخلة
bill of exchange	*kambiyāla*	كمبيالة

bill of lading	*wathīqat shaḥn, būlīṣat shaḥn*	وثيقة شحن. بوليصة شحن
bill of rights	*wathīqat al-ḥuqūq*	وثيقة الحقوق
bill of sale	*sanad bay^c*	سند بيع
bills payable	*awrāq daf^c*	اوراق دفع
bills receivable	*awrāq qabḍ*	اوراق قبض
bi-monthly	*niṣf shahrī*	نصف شهرى
binding agreement	*ittifāq mulzim*	اتّفاق ملزم
binding force	*quwwa mulzima*	قوّة ملزمة
birth rate	*mu^{c}addal al-mawālīd*	معدّل المواليد
blackleg	*mufsid al-iḍrāb*	مفسد الاضراب
blacklist	*qā'ima sawdā'*	قائمة سوداء
blackmail	*ibtizāz bi't-tahdīd*	ابتزاز بالتهديد
black market	*as-sūq as-sawdā'*	السوق السوداء
blank cheque	*shīk ^{c}alā bayāḍ*	شيك على بياض
blended gasoline	*banzīn mu'allaf*	بنزين مؤلّف
blue chip companies	*sharikāt daraja 'ūlā*	شركات درجة أولى
blue-print	*ṣūrat at-taṣmīm al-handasī. mukhaṭṭaṭ tafṣīlī*	صورة التصميم الهندسى.مخطط تفصيلى
board meeting	*ijtimā^c al-majlis*	اجتماع المجلس
board of arbitration	*majlis taḥkīm*	مجلس تحكيم
board of directors	*majlis al-idāra*	مجلس الادارة
board of inquiry	*hay'at at-taḥqīq*	هيئة التحقيق

board of trade	*wizārat at-tijāra 'l-birīṭāniyya*	وزارة التجارة البريطانية
bonanza	*fatrat zawāj saʿīd*	فترة رواج سعيد
bonded goods	*baḍā'iʿ mūdaʿa fi'l-makhāzin*	بضائع مودعة فى المخازن
bonded warehouse	*makhzan īdāʿ*	مخزن ايداع
bonus scheme	*niẓām al-mukāfa'a*	نظام المكافأة
book-keeping	*mask ad-dafātir*	مسك الدفاتر
book profit	*ribḥ daftarī*	ربح دفترى
book value	*al-qīma 'd-daftariyya*	القيمة الدفترية
border line	*khaṭṭ al-ḥudūd*	خطّ الحدود
borehole	*thuqb al-ḥafr*	ثقب الحفر
borrow	*yaqtariḍ, yastaʿīr*	يقترض، يستعير
borrowed capital	*ra'smāl muqtaraḍ*	رأس مال مقترض
bottleneck	*maḍīq ʿā'iq*	مضيق عائق
boycott	*muqāṭaʿa*	مقاطعة
branch accounts	*ḥisābāt al-furūʿ*	حسابات الفروع
branch manager	*mudīr farʿ*	مدير فرع
branded goods	*silaʿ mawsūma*	سلع موسومة
breach of contract	*ikhlāl bi'l-ʿaqd*	اخلال بالعقد
breach of promise	*nakth al-ʿahd*	نكث العهد
breach of the peace	*kharq as-salām*	خرق السلام
break-even	*taʿādul*	تعادل

break-even point	*nuqṭat at-taᶜādul*	نقطة التعادل
break off	*yaqṭaᶜ*	يقطع
breakthrough	*taqaddum mufāji'*	تقدّم مفاجئ
bribe	*rashwa*	رشوة
broker	*simsār*	سمسار
brokerage	*ᶜumūla*	عمولة
bucket seat	*maqᶜad dalwī*	مقعد دلوى (رخيص فى الطائرة)
budget	*mīzāniyya*	ميزانية
budgetary control	*murāqabat al-mīzāniyya*	مراقبة الميزانية
budgeted capacity	*ṭāqat birnāmij al-intāj*	طاقة برنامج الانتاج
building contractor	*muqāwil mabānī*	مقاول مبانى
building licence	*rukhṣat binā'*	رخصة بناء
building materials	*mawādd al-binā'*	موادّ البناء
building permit	*rukhsat binā'*	رخصة بناء
bulk buying	*shirā' kimmiyyāt kabīra*	شراء كميات كبيرة
bulk cargo	*shuḥna kabīra sā'iba*	شحنة كبيرة سائبة
bulk sale	*bayᶜ bi 'l-jumla*	بيع بالجملة
bulk shipment	*shuḥna kabīra sā'iba*	شحنة كبيرة سائبة
bulk storage	*takhzīn sā'ib bi'l-jumla*	تخزين سائب بالجملة
bullion	*sabīka*	سبيكة
bullion market	*sūq adh-dhahab aw al-fiḍḍa*	سوق الذهب أو الفضة

burden of proof	*ʿib' al-ithbāt*	عبء الاثبات
burglary insurance	*taʾmīn ḍidd as-sariqa*	تأمين ضدّ السرقة
business administration	*idārat al-aʿmāl*	ادارة اعمال
business connections	*ʿalāqāt tijāriyya*	علاقات تجارية
business economics	*iqtiṣād al-aʿmāl*	اقتصاد الاعمال
business enterprise	*mashrūʿ tijārī*	مشروع تجارى
business hours	*sāʿāt al-ʿamal, sāʿāt ad-dawām*	ساعات العمل، ساعات الدوام
business name	*ism tijārī*	اسم تجارى
business premises	*mabāni 'l-mashrūʿ*	مبانى المشروع
buyer	*mushtarī*	مشترى
buyers' market	*sūq munāsiba li'l-mushtarīn*	سوق مناسبة للمشترين
By Appointment ...	*yaṣnaʿ lil-usra 'l-malakiyya*	يصنع للأسرة الملكية
byelaws	*qānūn/niẓām dākhilī*	قانون/ نظام داخلى
by-election	*intikhāb farʿī*	انتخاب فرعى
by-pass	*mamarr jānibī*	ممرّ جانبى
by-product	*muntaj thānawī*	منتج ثانوى

C

cable	*kabl, barqiyya*	كابل • برقية
cable transfer	*taḥwīl mālī barqiyyan*	تحويل مالى برقيا
cabotage	*al-milāḥa 's-sāḥiliyya*	لملاحة الساحلية
calculating machine	*āla ḥāsiba*	آلة حاسبة
calendar month	*shahr taqwīmī*	شهر تقويمى
calendar year	*sana taqwīmiyya*	سنة تقويمية
callable bonds	*sanadāt qābila li't-tasdīd*	سندات قابلة للتسديد
call off a deal	*yulghī ṣafqa*	يلغى صفقة
campaign	*ḥamla, ghazwa*	حملة • غزوة
cancellation	*ilghā', ibṭāl*	الغاء • ابطال
cancelled cheque	*shīk mulghā*	شيك ملغى
canning industry	*ṣināᶜat at-taᶜlīb*	صناعة التعليب
capacity	*qudra, ṭāqa, qābiliyya*	قدرة • طاقة • قابلية
capacity ratio	*nisbat aṭ-ṭāqa*	نسبة الطاقة

capital	*ra'salmāl*	رأس المال
capital asset	*aṣl ra'smālī*	أصل رأسمالى
capital budget	*mīzāniyyat ra'salmāl*	ميزانية رأس المال
capital equipment	*ra'smāl tajhīz*	رأسمال تجهيز
capital expenditure	*maṣrūfāt ra'smāliyya*	مصروفات رأسمالية
capital gain	*arbāḥ ar-ra'smāl*	أرباح الرأسمال
capital gains tax	*ḍarībat arbāḥ ar-ra'smāl*	ضريبة أرباح الرأسمال
capital goods	*ra'salmāl ᶜaynī*	رأس مال عينى
capital intensive	*bi-ra'salmal kathīf*	برأس مال كثيف
capitalism	*ra'smāliyya*	رأسمالية
capitalization	*taḥwīl ilā ra'salmāl*	تحويل الى رأس مال
capital loss	*khasā'ir ar-ra'smāl*	خسائر الرأسمال
capital outlay	*maṣrūf ra'smālī*	مصروف رأسمالى
capital reserve	*iḥtiyāṭī ra'salmāl*	احتياطى رأس المال
capital sum	*al-qīma 'l-aṣliyya*	القيمة الاصلية
capital surplus	*fā'iḍ ra's al-māl*	فائض رأس المال
capital transfers	*taḥarrukāt ra'salmāl*	تحرّكات رأس المال
carbon copy	*nuskha bi'l-karbūn, ṭibq al-aṣl*	نسخة بالكربون ، طبق الاصل
card index	*fihris al-biṭāqāt*	فهرس البطاقات
card ledger	*sijill al-biṭāqāt*	سجلّ البطاقات
career	*mihna, ᶜamal*	مهنة ، عمل

care of	*bi-ṭaraf*	بطرف
cargo	*ḥumūla*	حمولة
cargo insurance	*ta'mīn ᶜalā ḥamūlāt as-sufun*	تأمين على حمولات السفن
carload	*ḥumūlat ᶜaraba*	حمولة عربة
carriage	*ujrat an-naql*	أجرة النقل
carriage free	*khāliṣ ujrat an-naql*	خالص أجرة النقل
carriage paid	*ujrat an-naql madfūᶜa*	أجرة النقل مدفوعة
carrier	*nāqil, sharikat naql*	ناقل . شركة نقل
carry forward	*yuraḥḥil ilā*	يرحّل الى
carry-over	*ta'jīl*	تأجيل
carte blanche	*tafwīḍ muṭlaq*	تفويض مطلق
cartel	*kārtil, ittiḥād al-muntijīn*	كارتل . اتّحاد المنتجين
case of emergency	*ḥālat aṭ-ṭawāri'*	حالة الطوارئ
case study	*dirāsat al-ḥāla*	دراسة الحالة
cash	*naqd, ṣundūq*	نقد . صندوق
cash account	*ḥisāb an-naqd*	حساب النقد
cash and carry	*idfaᶜ wa'nqul*	ادفع وانقل
cash asset	*aṣl naqdī*	أصل نقدى
cash before delivery	*dafᶜ qabl at-taslīm*	دفع قبل التسليم
cash book	*daftar aṣ-ṣundūq*	دفتر الصندوق
cash budget	*mīzāniyyat an-naqd*	ميزانية النقد

cash disbursement	*madfūᶜāt naqdiyya*	مدفوعات نقدية
cash discount	*khaṣm naqdī*	خصم نقدى
cash flow	*suyūla naqdiyya*	سيولة نقدية
cash forecast	*at-tanabbu' bi-kammiyyat an-naqd*	التنبّؤ بكمية النقد
cashier	*ṣarrāf*	صرّاف
cash in advance	*ad-dafᶜ naqdan muqaddaman*	الدفع نقدا مقدّما
cash in bank	*naqd fi 'l-maṣrif*	نقد فى المصرف
cash in hand	*nuqūd ḥāḍira*	نقود حاضرة
cash items	*mufradāt naqdiyya*	مفردات نقدية
cash on delivery	*ad-dafᶜ ᶜinda 't-taslīm*	الدفع عند التسليم
cash on receipt of goods	*ad-dafᶜ ᶜinda taslīm al-biḍāᶜa*	الدفع عند تسليم البضاعة
cash payment	*dafᶜ naqdī*	دفع نقدى
cash position	*al-markaz an-naqdī*	المركز النقدى
cash purchases	*mushtarayāt naqdiyya*	مشتريات نقدية
cash register	*ālat tasjīl an-naqd*	آلة تسجيل النقد
cash reserves	*iḥtiyāṭi 'n-naqd*	احتياطى النقد
cash sale	*al-bayᶜ naqdan*	البيع نقدا
cash surplus	*fā'iḍ an-naqd*	فائض النقد
cash, to	*yaṣrif*	يصرف
cash value	*qīma naqdiyya*	قيمة نقدية
cash with order	*ad-dafᶜ ᶜinda 'ṭ-ṭalab*	الدفع عند الطلب

cast a vote	*yuṣawwit*	يصوّت
casting vote	*aṣ-ṣawt al-murajjiḥ*	الصوت المرجّح
casual labour	*ᶜamal mutaqaṭṭaᶜ/lā niẓāmī*	عمل مقطّع /لا نظامى
casualty	*ḥādith, kāritha*	حادث. كارثة
casual worker	*ᶜāmil ᶜaraḍī*	عامل عرضى
catalogue	*katālūj*	كتالوج
cattle	*māshiya*	ماشية
cattle breeding	*tarbiyat al-māshiya*	تربية الماشية
cattle market	*sūq al-māshiya*	سوق الماشية
caveat emptor	*li-yaḥtaris al-mushtarī*	ليحترس المشترى
ceiling price	*aᶜlā ḥadd li's-siᶜr*	أعلى حدّ للسعر
censor	*raqīb*	رقيب
censorship	*riqāba*	رقابة
census	*taᶜdād, iḥṣā'*	تعداد. احصاء
centigrade	*mi'awī*	مئوى
central authority	*sulṭa markaziyya*	سلطة مركزية
central bank	*al-maṣrif al-markazī*	المصرف المركزى
central government	*ḥukūma markaziyya*	حكومة مركزية
centralization	*markizaiyya, tamarkuz*	مركزية . تمركز
centralization of authority	*markaziyyat as-sulṭa*	مركزية السلطة
central office	*al-maktab ar-ra'īsī*	المكتب الرئيسى

certificate	*shahāda, ijāza*	شهادة • اجازة
certificate of incorporation	*shahādat ta'sīs ash-sharika*	شهادة تأسيس الشركة
certificate of insurance	*shahādat ta'mīn*	شهادة تأمين
certificate of origin	*shahādat mansha'*	شهادة منشأ
certificate of posting	*shahādat irsāl bi'l-barīd*	شهادة ارسال بالبريد
chain store	*matjar fī silsilat matājir*	متجر فى سلسلة متاجر
chairman of the board	*ra'īs majlis al-idāra*	رئيس مجلس الادارة
chamber of commerce	*ghurfat at-tijāra*	غرفة تجارة
Chamber of Commerce	*ghurfat at-tijāra*	غرفة التجارة
chambers (of a barrister)	*maktab muḥāmī*	مكتب محام
character recognition	*ta^carruf ^cala 'l-ḥurūf*	تعرّف على الحروف
chargeable expenses	*maṣrūfāt taḥmīliyya*	مصروفات تحميلية
charge account	*ḥisāb ^camīl*	حساب عميل
charter	*yu'ajjir*	يؤجّر
chartered accountant	*muḥāsib qānūnī*	محاسب قانونى
charter party	*^caqd ījār safīna*	عقد ايجار سفينة
chemicals	*muntajāt kīmyā'iyya*	منتجات كيميائية
chemical works	*maṣna^c muntajāt kīmyā'iyya*	مصنع منتجات كيميائية
chemist	*ṣaydalī, kīmyā'ī*	صيدلى • كيميائى
cheque	*shīk, ṣakk*	شيك • صكّ
chequebook	*daftar shīkāt*	دفتر شيكات

cheque, dishonoured	*shīk marfūḍ*	شيك مرفوض
cheque, open	*shīk ᶜādī*	شيك عادى
cheques payable	*shīkāt mustaḥiqqat ad-dafᶜ*	شيكات مستحقّة الدفع
chief executive	*kabīr al-idāriyyīn*	كبير الاداريين
choice brand	*ᶜalāmat ikhtiyār*	علامة اختيار
chronological order	*tartīb zamanī*	ترتيب زمنى
circumstantial evidence	*adilla ᶜaraḍiyya*	أدلّة عرضية
citizen	*muwāṭin*	مواطن
citizenship	*jinsiyya, muwāṭana*	جنسية • مواطنة
civil action	*daᶜwā madaniyya*	دعوى مدنية
civil administration	*idāra madaniyya*	ادارة مدنية
civil court	*maḥkama madaniyya*	محكمة مدنية
civil law	*qānūn madanī*	قانون مدنى
civil liability	*mas'ūliyya madaniyya*	مسؤولية مدنية
civil rights	*ḥuqūq madaniyya*	حقوق مدنية
civil servant	*muwaẓẓaf ḥukūmī*	موظّف حكومى
claim	*iddiᶜā', ṭalab*	ادّعاء • طلب
claimant	*al-muddaᶜī, al-muṭālib*	المدّعى • المطالب
claim for damage	*mutālaba bi-taᶜwīḍ al-aḍrār*	مطالبة بتعويض الاضرار
claims department	*qism at-taᶜwīḍāt*	قسم التعويضات
claim settlement	*taswiyat muṭālabāt al-ḥawādith*	تسوية مطالبات الحوادث

claim, statement of	*bayān muṭālaba*	بيان مطالبة
class of insurance	*nawᶜ at-ta'mīn/aḍ-ḍamān*	نوع التأمين/الضمان
clean bill of exchange	*kambiyāla bilā taḥaffuẓāt*	كمبيالة بلا تحفّظات
clean bill of lading	*būlīṣat shaḥn naẓīfa*	بوليصة شحن نظيفة
clearance sale	*bayᶜ at-taṣfiya*	بيع التصفية
clearing bank	*ghurfat muqāṣṣa*	غرفة مقاصّة
clearing house	*ghurfat muqāṣṣa*	غرفة مقاصّة
clear majority	*al-aktharīyya 'l-muṭlaqa*	الاكثرية المطلقة
clear profit	*ribḥ ṣāfī*	ربح صاف
clerk	*kātib*	كاتب
client	*ᶜamīl, muwakkil*	عميل ٠ موكّل
clock card	*biṭāqat waqt al-ḥuḍūr*	بطاقة وقت الحضور
closed shop	*mu'assasa muqfala*	مؤسّسة مقفلة
closing date	*tārīkh al-iqfāl*	تاريخ الاقفال
closing price	*siᶜr al-iqfāl*	سعر الاقفال
coastal navigation	*milāḥa sāḥiliyya*	ملاحة ساحلية
coastal trade	*tijāra sāḥiliyya*	تجارة ساحلية
code of ethics	*qānūn al-akhlāq*	قانون الاخلاق
codicil	*mulḥaq waṣiyya*	ملحق وصية
co-insurer	*ḍāmin mushtarak*	ضامن مشترك
cold store	*mustawdaᶜ tabrīd*	مستودع تبريد

cold war	*al-ḥarb al-bārida*	الحرب الباردة
collateral security	*ḍamān iḍāfī*	ضمان اضافى
colleague	*zamīl*	زميل
collecting agency	*wikālat taḥṣīl*	وكالة تحصيل
collecting charges	*maṣārīf at-taḥsīl*	مصاريف التحصيل
collection charge	*rasm taḥṣīl*	رسم تحصيل
collection of taxes	*jibāyat aḍ-ḍarā'ib*	جباية الضرائب
collective agreement	*ittifāqiyya jamāᶜiyya*	اتّفاقية جماعية
collective bargaining	*musāwama jamāᶜiyya*	مساومة جماعية
collective insurance	*ta'mīn/ḍamān jamāᶜī*	تأمين/ضمان جماعى
collective ownership	*milkiyya mushtaraka*	ملكية مشتركة
collective responsibility	*mas'ūliyya jamāᶜiyya*	مسؤولية جماعية
collision insurance	*taᶜmīn ḍidd at-taṣādum*	تأمين ضدّ التصادم
collision risk	*khaṭar at-taṣādum*	خطر التصادم
commence	*yabda', yashraᶜ*	يبدأ ، يشرع
commencement of legal proceedings	*bad' al-ijrā'āt al-qānūniyya*	بدء الاجراءات القانونية
commerce	*tijāra*	تجارة
commercial	*tijārī*	تجارى
commercial agent	*wakīl tijārī*	وكيل تجارى
commercial agreement	*ittifāqiyya tijāriyya*	اتّفاقية تجارية
commercial bank	*maṣrif tijārī*	مصرف تجارى

commercial court	*al-maḥkama 't-tijāriyya*	المحكمة التجارية
commercial custom	*al-ᶜurf at-tijārī*	العرف التجارى
commercial director	*mudīr tijārī*	مدير تجارى
commercial discount	*khaṣm tijārī*	خصم تجارى
commercial law	*qānūn tijārī*	قانون تجارى
commercial operations	*ᶜamaliyyāt tijāriyya*	عمليات تجارية
commission	*ᶜumūla*	عمولة
commission agent	*wakīl bi'l-ᶜumūla*	وكيل بالعمولة
commitment	*taᶜahhud, iltizām*	تعهّد ، التزام
committee	*lajna*	لجنة
committee of arbitration	*lajnat at-taḥkīm*	لجنة التحكيم
committee of experts	*lajnat al-khubarā'*	لجنة الخبراء
committee of inquiry	*lajnat at-taḥqīq*	لجنة التحقيق
commodity	*biḍāᶜa, silᶜa*	بضاعة ، سلعة
common law	*qānūn ᶜāmm*	قانون عامّ
common market	*sūq mushtaraka*	سوق مشتركة
Common Market, The	*as-sūq al-mushtaraka*	السوق المشتركة
communications satellite	*qamar muwāṣalāt*	قمر مواصلات
communist	*shuyūᶜī*	شيوعى
communist party	*ḥizb shuyūᶜī*	حزب شيوعى
community property	*milk ᶜumūmī*	ملك عمومى

company	*sharika*	شركة
company director	*mudīr ash-sharika*	مدير الشركة
company law	*qānūn ash-sharikāt*	قانون الشركات
company secretary	*sikirtair sharika*	سكرتير شركة
compensation	*taʿwīḍ*	تعويض
compensation for loss	*taʿwīḍ ʿan al-khasāra*	تعويض عن الخسارة
compensatory damages	*aḍrār taʿwīḍiyya*	أضرار تعويضية
competent witness	*shāhid dhū ahliyya*	شاهد ذو أهلية
compete with	*yunāfis*	ينافس
competition	*munāfasa*	منافسة
competitive bid	*ʿaṭā' tanāfusī*	عطاء تنافسي
competitive economy	*iqtiṣād munāfis*	اقتصاد منافس
competitive prices	*asʿār lā taqbal al-munāfasa*	أسعار لا تقبل المنافسة
competitor	*munāfis*	منافس
complaint	*shakwā*	شكوى
composite rate of depreciation	*muʿaddal al-istihlāk al-murakkab*	معدّل الاستهلاك المركّب
compound interest	*fā'ida murākkaba*	فائدة مركّبة
comprehensive insurance	*ta'mīn shāmil*	تأمين شامل
comprehensive policy	*ta'mīn/ḍamān shāmil*	تأمين/ضمان شامل
compromise	*tarāḍī*	تراض
comptroller	*murāqib al-ḥisābāt*	مراقب الحسابات

compulsory insurance	*ta'mīn/ḍamān ilzāmī*	تأمين/ضمان الزامى
compulsory purchase	*shirā' ijbārī*	شراء اجبارى
compulsory settlement	*taswiya ijbāriyya*	تسوية اجبارية
computer	*kumbyūtar,* ^{c}*aql iliktirūnī*	كومبيوتر. عقل اليكترونى
computer input	*al-mu*^{c}*ṭayāt al-mulaqqana li'l-kumbyūtar*	المعطيات الملقّنة للكمبيوتر
computer instruction code	*ramz ta*^{c}*līmāt al-kumbyūtar*	رمز تعليمات الكمبيوتر
computerise	*yast*^{c}*mil niẓām al-kumbyūtar*	يستعمل نظام الكمبيوتر
computer output	*ḥasīlat al-kumbyūtar*	حصيلة الكمبيوتر
concession	*imtiyāz*	امتياز
concession rights	*ḥuqūq al-imtiyāz*	حقوق الامتياز
conciliation	*tawfīq*	توفيق
conciliation board	*majlis al-muṣālaḥa*	مجلس المصالحة
conclusive	*ḥāsim*	حاسم
conclusive evidence	*adilla qāṭi*^{c}*a*	أدلّة قاطعة
conditional acceptance	*qubūl mashrūṭ*	قبول مشروط
conditional contract	^{c}*aqd mashrūṭ*	عقد مشروط
conditional sale	*bay*^{c} *mashrūṭ*	بيع مشروط
conditions of agreement	*shurūṭ al-ittifāqiyya*	شروط الاتّفاقية
conditions of payment	*shurūṭ ad-daf*^{c}	شروط الدفع
conditions of sale	*shurūṭ al-bay*^{c}	شروط البيع
conference	*mu'tamar*	مؤتمر

confidence (in)	*thiqa*	ثقة
confidential	*sirrī, khāṣṣ*	سرّى/خاصّ
confidential documents	*wathā'iq sirriyya/khāṣṣa*	وثائق سرّية/خاصّة
confidential reports	*taqārīr sirriyya*	تقارير سرّية
confirmation note	*mudhakkirat ta'kīd*	مذكرة تأكيد
confiscation of property	*muṣādarat al-mumtalakāt*	مصادرة الممتلكات
conflicting claims	*taḍārub al-iddiᶜā'āt*	تضارب الادّعاءات
conflict of laws	*tanāzuᶜ al-qawānīn*	تنازع القوانين
consequential	*nātij ᶜan*	ناتج عن
consequential damages	*aḍrār/taᶜwīḍāt tābiᶜa*	أضرار/تعويضات تابعة
consequential effects	*āthār tābiᶜa*	آثار تابعة
conservative estimate	*taqdīr mutaḥaffiẓ*	تقدير متحفّظ
consideration	*ᶜiwaḍ*	عوض
consignee	*mursal ilayh*	مرسل اليه
consignment	*irsāliyya*	ارسالية
consignment note	*waraqat shaḥn*	ورقة الشحن
consignor	*mursil*	مرسل
consolidated account	*ḥisāb muwaḥḥad*	حساب موحّد
consolidated balance sheet	*al-mīzāniyya 'l-ᶜumūmiyya 'l-muwaḥḥada*	الميزانية العمومية الموحّدة
consolidation	*tawḥīd, idmāj*	توحيد، ادماج
consortium	*kunsurtyūm*	كونسورتيوم

constitutional law	*al-qānūn ad-dustūrī*	القانون الدستورى
constitutional rights	*ḥuqūq dustūriyya*	حقوق دستورية
construction	*binā', inshā', tarkīb*	بناء، انشاء، تركيب
constructive criticism	*naqd bannā'*	نقد بنّاء
consul	*qunṣul*	قنصل
consular immunities	*al-ḥaṣānāt al-qunṣuliyya*	الحصانات القنصلية
consular services	*al-khadamāt al-qunṣuliyya*	الخدمات القنصلية
consultant	*mustashār*	مستشار
consumer	*mustahlik*	مستهلك
consumer advertising	*iᶜlān li'l-mustahlikīn*	اعلان للمستهلكين
consumer credit	*taslīf al-mustahlik*	تسليف المستهلك
consumer durable	*silᶜa 'stihlākiyya matīna*	سلعة استهلاكية متينة
consumer goods	*silaᶜ istihlākiyya*	سلع استهلاكية
consumer industries	*ṣināᶜāt istihlākiyya*	صناعات استهلاكية
consumer price index	*mu'ashshir asᶜār al-mustahlikīn*	مؤشّر اسعار المستهلكين
consumers' co-operative	*jamᶜiyyat taᶜāwuniyyat al-mustahlikīn*	جمعية تعاونية المستهلكين
consumption	*istihlāk*	استهلاك
container trade	*ḥāwiya, wiᶜā'*	حاوية، وعاء
contempt of court	*ihānat al-maḥkama*	اهانة المحكمة
contents	*muḥtawayāt*	محتويات
contingency fund	*iḥtiyāṭi 'ṭ-ṭawāri'*	احتياطى الطوارئ

contingency reserve	*iḥtiyāṭī ṭawāri'*	احتياطى طوارئ
contingent liability	*mas'ūliyya ᶜaraḍiyya, iltizām iḥtimālī*	مسؤولية عرضية • التزام احتمالى
continuation clause	*sharṭ istimrār at-ta'mīn*	شرط استمرار التأمين
continuous flow production	*intāj bi't-tasalsul al-mustamirr*	انتاج بالتسلسل المستمرّ
continuous process	*ᶜamaliyya mustamirra*	عملية مستمرّة
continuous stocktaking	*jard al-makhzūnāt al-mustamirr*	جرد المخزونات المستمرّ
contraband	*baḍā'iᶜ maḥẓūra*	بضائع محظورة
contract	*ᶜaqd*	عقد
contracting parties	*al-mutaᶜāqidūn, al-aṭrāf al-mutaᶜāqida*	المتعاقدون • الأطراف المتعاقدة
contract note	*mudhakkirat al-ᶜaqd*	مذكرة العقد
contract of employment	*ᶜaqd al-ᶜamal/at-taᶜyīn*	عقد العمل/التعيين
contract of insurance	*ᶜaqd at-ta'mīn*	عقد التأمين
contract of sale	*ᶜaqd al-bayᶜ*	عقد البيع
contractor	*muqāwil, mutaᶜahhid*	مقاول • متعهّد
contractual obligation	*iltizām taᶜāqudī*	التزام تعاقدى
contribution	*tabarruᶜ, musāᶜada*	تبرّع • مساعدة
contributory infringement	*taᶜaddī musānid*	تعدّ مساند
contributory insurance scheme	*ta'mīnāt ijtimāᶜiyya*	تأمينات اجتماعية
contributory negligence	*ihmāl musāᶜid*	اهمال مساعد
controlled economy	*iqtiṣād muwajjah*	اقتصاد موجّه
controller	*murāqib*	مراقب

controlling company	*sharika mālika li-ukhrā*	شركة مالكة لاخرى
control point	*nuqṭat al-murāqaba*	نقطة المراقبة
control tower	*burj al-murāqaba*	برج المراقبة
conversion cost	*taklifat at-taḥwīl*	تكلفة التحويل
cooling off period	*fatrat tahdi'a*	فترة تهدئة
co-operation	*taᶜāwun*	تعاون
co-operative agreement	*ittifāqiyya taᶜāwuniyya*	اتّفاقية تعاونية
co-operative bank	*maṣrif taᶜāwunī*	مصرف تعاونى
co-owner	*sharīk*	شريك
co-ownership	*milkiyya mushtaraka*	ملكية مشتركة
co-partner	*sharīk mutaḍāmin*	شريك متضامن
co-partnership	*mushāraka*	مشاركة
copy	*nuskha, ṣūra*	نسخة • صورة
copyright	*ḥaqq at-ta'līf wa'n-nashr*	حقّ التأليف والنشر
corporate body	*hay'a ᶜāmma*	هيئة عامّة
corporate bond	*sanad sharika*	سند شركة
corporate planning	*at-takhṭīṭ fi'sh-sharika*	التخطيط فى الشركة
corporate tax	*ḍarībat ash-sharikāt*	ضريبة الشركات
corporation	*jam'iyya, sharika, hay'a*	جمعية • شركة • هيئة
cost	*kulfa, siᶜr*	كلفة • سعر
cost accountant	*muḥāsib at-takālīf*	محاسب تكاليف

cost accounting	*muḥāsabat at-takālīf*	محاسبة التكاليف
cost analysis	*taḥlīl at-takālīf*	تحليل التكاليف
cost-benefit analysis	*taḥlīl at-takālīf wa'l-ᶜā'idāt*	تحليل التكاليف والعائدات
cost centre	*markaz at-takālīf*	مركز التكاليف
cost effectiveness	*jadwa 't-takālīf*	جدوى التكاليف
cost elements	*ᶜanāṣir at-takālīf*	عناصر التكاليف
cost, insurance, freight	*thaman al-biḍāᶜa maᶜ at-ta'mīn wa'sh-shaḥn*	ثمن البضاعة مع التأمين والشحن
cost of living	*takālīf al-maᶜīsha*	تكاليف المعيشة
cost-of-living adjustment	*taᶜdīl al-ujūr li-ghalā' al-maᶜīsha*	تعديل الاجور لغلاء المعيشة
cost-of-living allowance	*ᶜilāwat ghalā' al-maᶜīsha*	علاوة غلاء المعيشة
cost-of-living bonus	*ᶜalāwat ghalā' al-maᶜīsha*	علاوة علاء المعيشة
cost-of-living index	*dalīl takālīf al-maᶜīsha*	دليل تكاليف المعيشة
cost of production	*takālīf al-intāj*	تكاليف الانتاج
cost of sales	*kulfat al-mabīᶜāt*	كلفة المبيعات
'cost plus' principle	*siᶜr at-taklifa zā'id nisba*	سعر التكلفة زائدا نسبة
cost price	*siᶜr at-taklifa*	سعر التكلفة
cost variance	*tafāwut at-takālīf*	تفاوت التكاليف
counsel	*mustashār qānūnī*	مستشار قانونى
counterclaim	*daᶜwā muḍādda*	دعوى مضادّة
counterfeit	*muzawwar, muzayyaf*	مزوّر، مزيّف
counter-proposal	*iqtirāḥ/ᶜarḍ muḍādd*	اقتراح/عرض مضادّ

countersign	*yuwaqqiᶜ maᶜ al-ghayr*	يوقّع مع الغير
court	*maḥkama*	محكمة
court costs	*maṣārīf al-maḥkama*	مصاريف المحكمة
court of arbitration	*majlis taḥkīmī*	مجلس تحكيمى
court of cassation	*maḥkamat an-naqḍ/at-tamyīz*	محكمة النقض/التمييز
court of inquiry	*maḥkamat taḥqīq ᶜaskarī*	محكمة تحقيق عسكرى
court of law	*maḥkama qānūniyya*	محكمة قانونية
courtroom	*qāᶜat al-maḥkama*	قاعة المحكمة
covenant	*taᶜahhud, mīthāq*	تعهّد • ميثاق
covering letter	*khiṭāb maᶜ murfaqāt*	خطاب مع مرفقات
cover note	*taghṭiya muᶜaqqata*	تغطية موقّتة
crash	*yaṣṭadim, yuḥaṭṭim*	يصطدم • يحطّم
creative thinking	*tafkīr khallāq*	تفكير خلّاق
credentials	*awrāq iᶜtimād as-safīr*	أوراق اعتماد السفير
credit	*iᶜtimād, taslīf*	اعتماد • تسليف
credit account	*ḥisāb iᶜtimād*	حساب اعتماد
credit agency	*wakālat i'timān*	وكالة ائتمان
credit balance	*raṣīd dā'in*	رصيد دائن
credit control	*murāqabat at-taslīf*	مراقبة التسليف
credit manager	*mudīr at-taslīf*	مدير التسليف
credit note	*ishᶜār dā'in*	اشعار دائن

credit operation	*ᶜamal li-ajal, ṣafqa li-ajal*	عمل لاجل. صفقة لاجل
creditor	*dā'in*	دائن
credit rating	*darajat al-malā'a*	درجة الملاءة
credit squeeze	*taḍyīq al-iᶜtimād*	تضييق الاعتماد
credit system	*niẓām al-'i'timān*	نظام الائتمان
credit transaction	*ᶜamaliyya ājila*	عملية آجلة
creditworthiness	*malā'a*	ملاءة
crew	*baḥḥāra, mallāḥūn*	بحّارة . ملاّحون
crime	*jarīma*	جريمة
criminal action	*daᶜwā jinā'iyya*	دعوى جنائية
criminal law	*qānūn al-jināyāt*	قانون الجنايات
criminal negligence	*ihmāl jinā'ī*	اهمال جنائى
crisis	*azma*	أزمة
critical condition	*ḥāla khaṭīra*	حالة خطيرة
critical path method	*uslūb al-aᶜmāl al-ḥarija*	أسلوب الاعمال الحرجة
critical period	*fatra ḥarija*	فترة حرجة
crops insurance	*ta'mīn ᶜala 'l-maḥāṣīl*	تأمين على المحاصيل
crossed cheque	*shīk musaṭṭar*	شيك مسطّر
cross-examination	*istijwāb ash-shuhūd*	استجواب الشهود
cross-reference	*al-iḥāla*	الاحالة
crude oil	*nafṭ khām*	نفط خام

cumulative damages	*taᶜwīḍāt mutarākima*	تعويضات متراكمة
cumulative dividend	*arbāḥ ashum mutarākima*	أرباح أسهم متراكمة
currency	*ᶜumla*	عملة
currency dealings	*tadāwul al-qaṭᶜ al-ajnabī*	تداول القطع الأجنبى
currency exchange	*maḥall ṣirāfat al-ᶜumlāt*	محلّ صرافة العملات
currency reserve	*iḥtiyāṭi 'n-naqd*	احتياطى النقد
current account	*ḥisāb jārī*	حساب جار
current asset	*al-aṣl al-hālī*	الاصل الحالى
current expense	*maṣrūfāt jāriya*	مصروفات جارية
current insurance	*ta'mīn/ḍamān sārī*	تأمين/ضمان سارى
current liability	*iltizām ḥālī*	التزام حالى
current value	*al-qīma 'l-ḥāliyya*	القيمة الحالية
customer	*ᶜamīl, zubūn*	عميل، زبون
customs	*jumruk, rusūm jumrukiyya*	جمرك ، رسوم جمركية
customs clearance	*ifrāj jumrukī*	افراج جمركى
customs duties	*rusūm jumrukiyya*	رسوم جمركية
customs entry	*al-bayānāt al-muqaddama li'l-jumruk*	البيانات المقدّمة للجمرك
customs formalities	*ijrā'āt jumrukiyya*	اجراءات جمركية
customs house	*markaz jumrukī*	مركز جمركى
customs regulations	*lawā'iḥ/anẓima jumrukiyya*	لوائح/أنظمة جمركية
customs tariff	*at-taᶜrīfa 'l-jumrukiyya*	التعريفة الجمركية

cut back	*yunqiṣ*	ينقص
cut price	*si^c^r mukhaffaḍ*	سعر مخفّض
cut-throat competition	*munāfasa fattāka*	منافسة فتّاكة

D

daily average production	*muᶜaddal al-intāj al-yawmī*	معدّل الانتاج اليومى
daily capacity	*aṭ-ṭāqa 'l-yawmiyya*	الطاقة اليومية
daily output	*al-intāj al-yawmī*	الانتاج اليومى
dairy products	*muntajāt al-albān*	منتجات الالبان
daily wage	*al-ujra 'l-yawmiyya*	الاجرة اليومية
damage	*ḍarar, taᶜwīḍ*	ضرر. تعويض
damages	*aḍrār, taᶜwīḍāt*	أضرار. تعويضات
dangerous goods	*baḍā'iᶜ khaṭra*	بضائع خطرة
data	*bayānāt, muᶜṭayāt*	بيانات. معطيات
data processing	*iᶜdād al-bayānāt*	اعداد البيانات
date of acquisition	*tārīkh al-iqtinā'*	تاريخ الاقتناء
date of effect	*tārīkh as-sarayān*	تاريخ السريان
date of maturity	*tārīkh istiḥqāq ad-dafᶜ*	تاريخ استحقاق الدفع
daybook	*daftar al-yawmiyya*	دفتر اليومية

day shift	*nawba nahāriyya*	نوبة نهارية
days of grace	*muhla*	مهلة
deadline	*ākhir mawᶜid*	آخر موعد
deadlock	*fashal al-mufāwaḍāt*	فشل المفاوضات
deadweight	*ḥumūla sākina*	حمولة ساكنة
deal	*ṣafqa*	صفقة
deal, to	*yataᶜāmal*	يتعامل
death certificate	*shahādat wafāh*	شهادة وفاة
debenture bond	*sanad qarḍ*	سند قرض
debenture holder	*ḥāmil as-sanad*	حامل السند
debt	*dayn*	دين
debtor	*madīn*	مدين
debts, outstanding	*duyūn mustaḥaqqa*	ديون مستحقّة
debt, to write off a bad	*yatakhallā ᶜan dayn mayyit*	يتخلّى عن دين ميّت
decentralization	*al-lāmarkaziyya*	اللامركزية
decision-making	*ittikhādh al-qarārāt*	اتّخاذ القرارات
decision tree	*shajarat al-qarārāt*	شجرة القرارات
declaration of bankruptcy	*ishhār iflās*	اشهار افلاس
declared dividend	*arbāḥ ashum muᶜlana*	ارباح اسهم معلنة
decrease in value	*naqṣ al-qīma*	نقص القيمة
decreasing productivity	*tanāquṣ al-intājiyya*	تناقص الانتاجية

decree	*marsūm*	مرسوم
deed of association	^{c}*aqd sharika*	عقد شركة
deed of partnership	^{c}*aqd shirāka*	عقد شراكة
defamation	*qadhf, tashhīr*	قذف، تشهير
defective	*ma*^{c}*īb*	معيب
Defense Ministry	*wizārat ad-difā*^{c}	وزارة الدفاع
deferred annuity	*duf*^{c}*a sanawiyya mu'ajjala*	دفعة سنوية مؤجّلة
deferred dividend	*ribḥ sahm mu*^{c}*ajjal*	ربح سهم مؤجّل
deferred payments	*duf*^{c}*āt mu*^{c}*ajjala*	دفعات مؤجّلة
deflationary measures	*ijrā*^{c}*āt inkimāshiyya*	اجراءات انكماشية
del credere agent	*wakīl ḍamān al-wafā'*	وكيل ضمان الوفاء
delegate	*mandūb*	مندوب
delegation of authority	*takhwīl sulṭa*	تخويل سلطة
delivery note	*ish*^{c}*ār taslīm*	اشعار تسليم
delivery, terms of	*shurūṭ at-taslīm*	شروط التسليم
demand note	*kambiyāla* ^{c}*ind aṭ-ṭalab*	كمبيالة عند الطلب
demarcation line	*al-ḥadd al-fāṣil*	الحدّ الفاصل
demonstration	*bayān* ^{c}*amalī*	بيان عملي
demurrage	*rasm arḍiyya/khazn*	رسم ارضية/خزن
department	*idāra, qism*	ادارة ، قسم
department of external affairs	*wizārat al-khārijiyya*	وزارة الخارجية

dependent contract	*ᶜaqd muᶜallaq ᶜalā sharṭ*	عقد معلّق على شرط
depreciation allowance	*badal istihlāk*	بدل استهلاك
depreciation method	*ṭarīqat al-istihlāk*	طريقة الاستهلاك
depreciation rate	*muᶜaddal al-istihlāk*	معدّل الاستهلاك
depressed market	*sūq rākida*	سوق راكدة
depression	*rukūd/kasād iqtiṣādī*	ركود/ كساد اقتصادى
deputy chairman	*nā'ib ar-ra'īs*	نائب الرئيس
deputy director	*nā'ib al-mudīr*	نائب المدير
deputy minister	*nā'ib al-wazīr*	نائب الوزير
desalination	*taḥliyat miyāh al-baḥr*	تحلية مياه البحر
design	*taṣmīm*	تصميم
design capacity	*al-qudra 'l-muṣammama*	القدرة المصمّمة
designer	*muṣammim*	مصمّم
design fault	*khaṭa' fi't-taṣmīm*	خطأ فى التصميم
design principles	*mabādi' at-taṣmīm*	مبادئ التصميم
despatch note	*ishᶜār irsāl*	اشعار ارسال
detailed report	*taqrīr mufaṣṣal*	تقرير مفصّل
detergent additives	*iḍāfāt muzīla li'l-awsākh*	اضافات مزيلة للاوساخ
devaluation of currency	*takhfīḍ al-ᶜumla*	تخفيض العملة
development bond	*sanad tanmiya*	سند تنمية
development cost	*takālīf at-taṭwīr*	تكاليف التطوير

development programme	*birnāmaj tanmiya*	برنامج تنمية
diesel engine	*muḥarrik dīzil*	محرّك ديزل
diesel fuel	*waqūd ad-dīzil*	وقود الديزل
differential treatment	*mu^{c}āmala tafḍīliyya*	معاملة تفضيلية
diminishing returns, law of	*qānūn tanāquṣ al-ghalla*	قانون تناقص الغلّة
diplomat	*diblūmāsī*	دبلوماسى
diplomatic channels	*aṭ-ṭuruq ad-diblūmāsiyya*	الطرق الدبلوماسية
diplomatic immunities	*ḥaṣāna diblūmāsiyya*	حصانة دبلوماسية
diplomatic status	*markaz diblūmāsī*	مركز دبلوماسى
direct costs	*takālīf mubāshira*	تكاليف مباشرة
direction of labour	*tawjīh al-^{c}amal*	توجيه العمل
director general	*mudīr ^{c}āmm*	مدير عامّ
direct selling	*bay^c mubāshir*	بيع مباشر
direct taxation	*ḍarība mubāshira*	ضريبة مباشرة
dirty bill of lading	*wathīqat shaḥn ma^c taḥaffuẓ*	وثيقة شحن مع تحفّظ
disability clause	*sharṭ al-^{c}ajz*	شرط العجز
disablement benefit	*i^{c}ānat al-^{c}ajz ^{c}an al-^{c}amal*	اعانة العجز عن العمل
disagreement	*khilāf*	خلاف
disciplinary measures	*ijrā'āt ta'dībiyya*	اجراءات تأديبية
disclaimer	*tanaṣṣul*	تنصّل
discount	*takhfīḍ, ḥasm*	تخفيض، حسم

discrimination	*tamyīz*	تمييز
discriminatory	*tamyīzī*	تمييزى
dishonour	*yarfuḍ*	يرفض
disinflationary measures	*ijrā'āt muḍādda li't-taḍakhkhum*	اجراءات مضادّة للتضخّم
dismissal	*faṣl, ᶜazl*	فصل • عزل
dismissal compensation	*taᶜwīḍ faṣl min al-khidma*	تعويض فصل من الخدمة
dispatching charge	*maṣārīf irsāl*	مصاريف ارسال
disposable income	*dakhl mutāḥ*	دخل متاح
dispute, industrial	*munāzaᶜāt ṣināᶜiyya*	منازعات صناعية
dispute, labour	*munāzaᶜāt ᶜummāliyya*	منازعات عمّالية
dissenting opinion	*ra'y mukhālif*	رأى مخالف
dissolution	*ḥall*	حلّ
dissolve a company	*yafuḍḍ sharika*	يفضّ شركة
distant future	*al-mustaqbal al-baᶜīd*	المستقبل البعيد
distinguishing mark	*ᶜalāma mumayyiza*	علامة مميّزة
distortion of facts	*tashwīh al-ḥaqā'iq*	تشويه الحقائق
distributable profit	*ribḥ qābil li't-tawzīᶜ*	ربح قابل للتوزيع
distribution	*tawzīᶜ*	توزيع
distribution agency	*wakālat tawzīᶜ*	وكالة توزيع
distribution expenses	*taklifat at-tawzīᶜ*	تكلفة التوزيع
distribution facilities	*tashīlāt at-tawzīᶜ*	تسهيلات التوزيع

distribution network	*shabakat tawzīᶜ*	شبكة توزيع
distribution of profits	*tawzīᶜ al-arbāḥ*	توزيع الارباح
distributor	*muwazziᶜ*	موزّع
district attorney	*muddaᶜī ᶜāmm al-manṭiqa*	مدّعى عامّ المنطقة
district council	*majlis al-manṭiqa*	مجلس المنطقة
district courts	*maḥākim al-manṭiqa*	محاكم المنطقة
diversification	*tanwīᶜ*	تنويع
diversify	*yunawwiᶜ*	ينوّع
dividend	*ḥiṣṣat arbāḥ as-sahm*	حصّة ارباح السهم
dividend payable	*arbāh ashum ghayr madfūᶜa*	ارباح اسهم غير مدفوعة
dock labour board	*majlis ᶜummāl aḥwāḍ*	مجلس عمّال احواض
dock warrant	*tafwīḍ istilām raṣīfī*	تفويض استلام رصيفى
doctor	*ṭabīb, duktūr*	طبيب ، دكتور
document	*wathīqa, mustanad*	وثيقة ، مستند
documentary bill of exchange	*kambiyāla mustanadiyya*	كمبيالة مستندية
documentary evidence	*adillat mustanadāt*	أدلّة مستندات
documents	*mustanadāt*	مستندات
doing business as ...	*yaᶜmal ka ...*	يعمل ك ...
dollar block	*kutlat ad-dūlār*	كتلة الدولار
dollar deficit	*al-ᶜajz fi'd-dūlār*	العجز فى الدولار
dollar exchange	*taḥwīl bi'd-dūlār*	تحويل بالدولار

dollar gap	*fajwa dūlāriyya*	فجوة دولارية
dollar premium	*ᶜilāwat ad-dūlār*	علاوة الدولار
domestic consumption	*istihlāk dākhilī*	استهلاك داخلى
domestic demand	*aṭ-ṭalab al-maḥallī*	الطلب المحلّى
domestic exports	*ṣādirāt dākhiliyya*	صادرات داخلية
domestic heating	*tadfi'a manziliyya*	تدفئة منزلية
domicile	*mawṭin, maḥall iqāma*	موطن ، محلّ اقامة
double-entry book-keeping	*mask ad-dafātir bi'l-qayd al-muzdawaj*	مسك الدفاتر بالقيد المزدوج
double taxation	*izdiwāj ḍarībī*	ازدواج ضريبى
down-market	*maḥall mustawā shaᶜbī*	محلّ مستوى شعبى
down payment	*dufᶜa mabda'iyya*	دفعة مبدئية
downward trend	*ittijāh nuzūlī*	اتّجاه نزولى
draft agenda	*mashrūᶜ jadwal al-aᶜmāl*	مشروع جدول الاعمال
draft agreement	*mashrūᶜ ittifāq*	مشروع اتّفاق
draw a bill	*yasḥab kambiyāla*	يسحب كمبيالة
drawee	*masḥūb ᶜalayh*	مسحوب عليه
drawer	*sāḥib*	ساحب
drilling contractor	*muqāwil aᶜmāl ḥafr*	مقاول أعمال حفر
drilling equipment	*muᶜiddāt al-ḥafr*	معدّات الحفر
dry dock	*ḥawḍ jāff*	حوض جافّ
dry hole	*bi'r jāffa*	بئر جافّة

dry well	*bi'r jāffa*	بئر جافّة
due date	*tārīkh al-istiḥqāq*	تاريخ الاستحقاق
dumping	*ighrāq as-sūq, bay^{c} bakhs*	اغراق السوق • بيع بخس
duplicate document	*ṣūra ṭibq al-aṣl*	صورة طبق الاصل
durable goods	*sila^{c} matīna*	سلع متينة
duration	*mudda*	مدّة
duress	*ikrāh*	اكراه
duty-free	*mu^{c}fā min ar-rusūm al-jumrukiyya*	معفى من الرسوم الجمركية
dynamic management	*idāra fa^{cc}āla*	ادارة فعّالة

E

earned income	*dakhl muktasab*	دخل مكتسب
economic	*iqtiṣādī*	اقتصادى
economic activity	*an-nashāṭ al-iqtiṣādī*	النشاط الاقتصادى
economic adviser	*mustashār iqtiṣādī*	مستشار اقتصادى
economic boycott	*muqāṭaᶜa iqtiṣādiyya*	مقاطعة اقتصادية
economic crisis	*azma iqtiṣādiyya*	ازمة اقتصادية
economic growth	*numuww iqtiṣādī*	نموّ اقتصادى
economic policy	*siyāsa iqtiṣādiyya*	سياسة اقتصادية
economic pressures	*ḍughūṭ iqtiṣādiyya*	ضغوط اقتصادية
economic stability	*istiqrār iqtiṣādī*	استقرار اقتصادى
economist	*ᶜālim iqtiṣādī*	عالم اقتصادى
economy	*iqtiṣād*	اقتصاد
effective date	*tārīkh sarayān al-mafᶜūl*	تاريخ سريان المفعول
efficiency expert	*khabīr fi'l-kifāya*	خبير فى الكفاية

electricity	*kahrabā'*	كهرباء
elevator certificate	*shahādat al-miṣ^{c}ad*	شهادة المصعد
embargo	*ḥaẓr*	حظر
embassy	*sifāra*	سفارة
embezzlement	*ikhtilās*	اختلاس
emergency	*ḥāla ṭāri'a*	حالة طارئة
emergency meeting	*ijtimā^c ^{c}ājil*	اجتماع عاجل
emergency regulations	*anẓimat ḥālat aṭ-ṭawāri'*	انظمة حالة الطوارئ
emigration office	*maktab al-hijra, dā'irat al-hijra*	مكتب الهجرة ، دائرة الهجرة
employee	*muwaẓẓaf*	موظّف
employer	*mustakhdim, ṣāḥib al-^{c}amal*	مستخدم ، صاحب العمل
employer's liability insurance	*ta'mīn al-mustakhdim ḍidd ḥawādith al-^{c}amal*	تأمين المستخدم ضدّ حوادث العمل
employment agency	*wikālat istikhdām*	وكالة استخدام
employment, contract of	*^{c}aqd ^{c}amal*	عقد عمل
endorse	*yuẓahhir shīk aw yuḥawwiluh*	يظهّر شيكا أو يحوّله
endowment assurance	*būlīṣa tudfa^c qīmatuhā fī sinn mu^{c}ayyan aw ^{c}inda 'l-wafāh*	بوليصة تدفع قيمتها فى سنّ معين أو عند الوفاة
end product	*an-nātij an-nihā'ī*	الناتج النهائى
energy	*ṭāqa*	طاقة
enforcement of law	*tanfīdh al-qānūn*	تنفيذ القانون
engineering	*handasa*	هندسة

enquiry	*taḥqīq*	تحقيق
enquiry office	*maktab al-istiᶜlāmāt*	مكتب الاستعلامات
enterprise	*mashrūᶜ*	مشروع
entertainment expenses	*maṣārif ḍiyāfa*	مصاريف ضيافة
entertainment tax	*ḍarībat al-malāhī*	ضريبة الملاهى
entrepreneur	*mutaᶜahhid*	متعهّد
entry visa	*taṣrīḥ dukhūl*	تصريح دخول
environment	*bī'a*	بيئة
equal	*musāwī*	مساوى
equilibrium price	*siᶜr at-tawāzun*	سعر التوازن
equitable interest	*ribḥ ᶜādil*	ربح عادل
equitable mortgage	*rahn inṣāfī*	رهن انصافى
equity	*ᶜadāla muṭlaqa, inṣāf*	عدالة مطلقة ، انصاف
erosion	*taᶜriya, taḥātt*	تعرية ، تحاتّ
error	*khaṭa'*	خطأ
errors and omissions excepted	*māᶜada al-khaṭa' wa's-sahw*	ماعدا الخطأ والسهو
escalation clause	*sharṭ az-ziyāda*	شرط الزيادة (فى الاسعار)
escape clause	*sharṭ al-insiḥāb wa't-tamalluṣ*	شرط الانسحاب والتملّص
escheat	*iyālat mīrāth ila 'd-dawla*	ايالة ميراث الى الدولة
escrow	*sanad muᶜallaq at-taslīm*	سند معلق التسليم
espionage	*tajassus*	تجسّس

essential	*asāsī, jawharī*	اساسى. جوهرى
establish	*yu'assis*	يؤسّس
established international practice	*at-taᶜāmul ad-dawlī al-muttabaᶜ*	التعامل الدولى المتّبع
establishment	*munsha'a, muᶜassasa*	منشأة . مؤسّسة
estimate	*taqdīr*	تقدير
estimated cost	*taklifa muqaddara*	تكلفة مقدّرة
estimated profits	*arbāḥ taqdīriyya*	ارباح تقديرية
estimated value	*al-qīma 'l-muqaddara*	القيمة المقدّرة
Eurodollar market	*sūq ad-dūlār al-'ūrubbī*	سوق الدولار الاوروبّى
evaluation	*taqdīr, taqwīm*	تقدير. تقويم
evidence	*dalīl, ḥujja*	دليل. حجّة
evidence, written	*burhān khaṭṭī*	برهان خطّى
examination	*istijwāb, faḥṣ, imtiḥān*	استجواب. فحص. امتحان
examination of proposal	*dirāsat al-ᶜarḍ*	دراسة العرض
examination report	*taqrīr faḥṣ, taqrīr imtiḥān*	تقرير فحص. تقرير امتحان
examiner	*muḥaqqiq, mumtaḥin*	محقّق. ممتحن
exceed	*yufruṭ, yazīd ᶜala'l-ḥadd*	يفرط. يزيد على الحد
exceptional circumstances	*ẓurūf istithnā'iyya*	ظروف استثنائية
excess capacity	*ṭāqa zā'ida*	طاقة زائدة
excessive price	*siᶜr fāḥish*	سعر فاحش
excess profits tax	*ḍarībat al-arbāḥ az-zā'ida*	ضريبة الأرباح الزائدة

exchange control	ar-riqāba 'ala 'n-naqd	الرقابة على النقد
exchange of views	tabādul al-ārā'	تبادل الآراء
exchange rate	siᶜr at-taḥwīl	سعر التحويل
excise tax	ḍarībat intāj	ضريبة انتاج
exclusion of risk	istithnā' al-khaṭar	استثناء الخطر
executed contract	ᶜaqd nāfidh	عقد نافذ
execution of contract	tanfīdh al-ᶜaqd	تنفيذ العقد
executive	muwaẓẓaf tanfīdhī	موظّف تنفيذى
executive committee	lajna tanfīdhiyya	لجنة تنفيدية
executive director	mudīr idāra	مدير ادارة
executor	munaffidh	منفّذ
executory contract	ᶜaqd qābil li't-tanfīdh	عقد قابل للتنفيذ
exemplary damages	taᶜwīḍāt zā'ida ittiᶜāẓiyya	تعويضات زائدة اتّعاظية
exemption from customs duties	iᶜfāᶜ min rusūm al-jumruk	اعفاءمن رسوم الجمرك
exemption from taxes	iᶜfā' min aḍ-ḍarā'ib	عفاء من الضرائب
ex gratia	majjānan	مجّانا
exhibit	mustanad muqaddam da-dalīl.shay' maᶜrūḍ	مستند مقدّم كدليل.شىء معروض
exhibition	ᶜarḍ	عرض
exit	makhraj	مخرج
ex officio	biḥukm al-waẓīfa, biḥukm al-markaz	بحكم الوظيفة . بحكم المركز
expansion	tawassuᶜ	توسّع

expansion programme	*barnāmaj tawassu*ᶜ	برنامج توسّع
expatriate	*mughtarib, ajnabī*	مغترب · اجنبى
expedite	*yusri*ᶜ*, yu*ᶜ*ajjil, yursil*	يسرع · يعجّل· يرسل
expel	*yaṭrud*	يطرد
expenditure	*infāq*	انفاق
expenditure, capital	*maṣārīf ra's al-māl*	مصاريف رأس المال
expenditure,operating	*nafaqāt at-tashghīl*	نفقات التشغيل
expense account	*ḥiṣāb al-maṣrūfāt*	حساب المصروفات
expense control	*ḍabṭ al-maṣārīf*	ضبط المصاريف
expenses, administrative	*maṣārīf idāriyya*	مصاريف ادارية
expenses, overhead	*maṣrūfāt* ᶜ*āmma*	مصروفات عامّة
expenses, manufacturing	*maṣārīf taṣnī*ᶜ	مصاريف تصنيع
expenses,travelling	*nafaqāt safar*	نفقات سفر
experience	*khibra*	خبرة
experimental	*tajrībī*	تجريبى
expert	*khabīr*	خبير
expiry date	*tārīkh intihā' aṣ-ṣalāḥiya*	تاريخ انتهاء الصلاحية
explanatory memorandum	*mudhakkira īḍāḥiyya*	مذكرة ايضاحية
exploration expenses	*nafaqāt at-tanqīb, nafaqāt al-istikshāf*	نفقات التنقيب · نفقات الاستكشاف
exploration well	*bi'r istikshāfiyya*	بئر استكشافية
exploratory period	*fatrat al-istikshāf*	فترة الاستكشاف

exploratory talks	*muḥādathāt istiṭlā^{c}iyya*	محادثات استطلاعية
export agent	*wakīl taṣdīr*	وكيل تصدير
export control	*murāqabat aṣ-ṣādirāt*	مراقبة الصادرات
export credit	*i^{c}timād li't-taṣdīr*	اعتماد للتصدير
export declaration	*bayān taṣdīr*	بيان تصدير
export department	*qism at-taṣdīr*	قسم التصدير
export duty	*rasm aṣ-ṣādir, ḍarībat aṣ-ṣādir*	رسم الصادر. ضريبة الصادر
export embargo	*ḥaẓr at-taṣdīr*	حظر التصدير
export licence	*rukhṣat taṣdīr*	رخصة تصدير
exports	*ṣādirāt*	صادرات
exports credit guarantee department	*idārat ḍamān ḥisābāt at-taṣdīr*	ادارة ضمان حسابات التصدير
export trade	*tijārat at-taṣdīr*	تجارة التصدير
express, or implied, obligation	*iltizām ṣarīh, iltizām ḍimnī*	التزام صريح. التزام ضمنى
express warranty	*ḍamān ṣarīḥ*	ضمان صريح
ex ship	*taslīm al-bākhira*	تسليم الباخرة
extended credit	*i^{c}timād mumtadd*	اعتماد ممتدّ
extent of damage	*mada 'ḍ-ḍarar*	مدى الضرر
extenuating circumstances	*ẓurūf mukhaffifa*	ظروف مخفّفة
external	*khārijī*	خارجى
external audit	*tadqīq khārijī*	تدقيق خارجى
external control	*ar-raqāba 'l-khārijiyya*	الرقابة الخارجية

external influence	*nufūdh ajnabī*	نفوذ أجنبى
external relations	*ᶜalāqāt khārijiyya*	علاقات خارجية
extinguisher	*miṭfa'a*	مطفأة
extra costs	*takālīf iḍāfiyya*	تكاليف اضافية
extract	*yastakhliṣ, yastakhrij*	يستخلص. يستخرج
extradition	*taslīm al-mujrimīn*	تسليم المجرمين
extraordinary general meeting	*ijtimāᶜ ᶜāmm fawqa 'l-ᶜāda*	اجتماع عامّ فوق العادة
extravagance	*tabdhīr*	تبذير
ex works	*taslīm al-maṣnaᶜ*	تسليم المصنع

F

fabricated materials	*mawādd muṣanna*^{c}*a*	موادّ مصنّعة
fabrication	*ṣun*^{c}*, talfīq*	صنع • تلفيق
face value	*qīma ismiyya*	قيمة اسمية
facilities	*tahīlāt*	تسهيلات
fact finding	*istiqṣā' al-ḥaqā'iq*	استقصاء الحقائق
factor	^{c}*āmil, bā*^{c}*ith*	عامل• باعث
factory	*maṣna*^{c}*, ma*^{c}*mal*	مصنع • معمل
factory acts	*qawānīn al-*^{c}*amal fi'l-maṣāni*^{c}	قوانين العمل فى المصانع
factory cost	*at-taklifa fi'l-maṣna*^{c}	التكلفة فى المصنع
factory inspector	*mufattish maṣāni*^{c}	مفتّش مصانع
factory prices	*as*^{c}*ār al-maṣna*^{c}	اسعار المصنع
factory worker	^{c}*āmil fī maṣna*^{c}	عامل فى مصنع
failure to pay	*tawaqquf/*^{c}*ajz* ^{c}*an ad-daf*^{c}	توقّف/عجز عن الدفع
fair	*munṣif*	منصف • عادل

fair comment	*intiqād ʿādil*	انتقاد عادل
fair competition	*munāfasa mashrūʿa*	منافسة مشروعة
fair play	*inṣāf, taṣarruf ḥasab al-uṣūl*	انصاف . تصرف حسب الأصول
fair prices	*asʿār ʿādila*	أسعار عادلة
fair trade	*siyāsat al-muʿāmala bi'l-mithl*	سياسة المعاملة بالمثل
fair trial	*muḥākama ʿādila*	محاكمة عادلة
fair wear and tear	*al-bila wa't-talaf bi'l-istihlāk al-ʿādī*	البلى والتلف بالاستهلاك العادي
fall due	*istaḥaqq*	استحق
falling market	*sūq hābiṭa*	سوق هابطة
falling off	*naqṣ, inkhifāḍ*	نقص. انخفاض
fall in output	*ḥubūṭ fi'l-intāj*	هبوط فى الانتاج
fall in prices	*hubūṭ al-asʿār*	هبوط الاسعار
false accusation	*tuhma bāṭila/kādhiba*	تهمة باطلة/كاذبة
false advertising	*iʿlān kādhib*	اعلان كاذب
false pretences	*iddiʿā' kādhib*	ادّعاء كاذب (للحصول على أموال الغير)
false testimony	*shahāda zūr*	شهادة زور
falsification of accounts	*talāʿub/tazwīr bil-ḥisābāt*	تلاعب /تزوير بالحسابات
farm	*mazraʿa*	مزرعة
farm out	*yu'ajjir min al-bāṭin*	يؤجّر من الباطن
far-reaching decision	*qarār baʿīd al-madā*	قرار بعيد المدى
fatal	*mumīt, qātil*	مميت. قاتل

fatal accident	*ḥādith mumīt*	حادث مميت
fatal injury	*jurḥ mumīt, īdhā' qātil*	جرح مميت . ايذاء قاتل
fats	*shuḥūm, duhūn*	شحوم . دهون
favourable balance of payments	*mizān madfūᶜāt fī ṣāliḥ al-balad*	ميزان مدفوعات فى صالح البلد
favourable rates	*asᶜār mulā'ima*	أسعار ملائمة
feasibility study	*dirāsat al-jadwā*	دراسة الجدوى
federal taxes	*ḍarā'ib ittiḥādiyya*	ضرائب اتّحاديّة
feedback	*taghdhiya murtadda*	تغذية مرتدّة
felony	*jināya, jarīma*	جناية . جريمة
fertilizer	*simād*	سماد
fiasco	*fashal dharīᶜ*	فشل ذريع
fibre	*līfa, tīlat ghazl*	ليفة . تيلة غزل
fictitious assets	*uṣūl wahmiyya*	أصول وهمية
fictitious profits	*arbāḥ ṣūriyya*	ارباح صورية
fiduciary loan	*qarḍ bi-dūn ḍamān*	قرض بدون ضمان
field staff	*muwaẓẓafūn fi'l-maydān*	موظفون فى الميدان
field study	*dirāsa maydāniyya*	دراسة ميدانية
field test	*ikhtibār maydānī*	اختبار ميدانى
file a petition	*yuqaddim ṭalab/ᶜarīḍa*	يقدم طلب/عريضة
filing clerk	*kātib al-ḥifẓ*	كاتب الحفظ
final instalment	*al-qisṭ al-akhīr*	القسط الاخير

final notice	*ikhṭār nihā'ī*	اخطار نهائى
final payment	*duf^{c}a akhīra*	دفعة اخيرة
final products	*al-muntajāt an-nihā'iyya*	المنتجات النهائية
finance	*yumawwil, al-māliyya*	يموّل. المالية
finance company	*sharikat tamwīl*	شركة تمويل
finance house	*bayt tamwīl*	بيت تمويل
financial adviser	*mustashār mālī*	مستشار ماليّ
financial crisis	*azma māliyya*	ازمة مالية
financial incentive	*ḥāfiz mālī*	حافز ماليّ
financial operation	*^{c}amaliyya māliyya*	عملية مالية
financial planning	*takhṭīṭ mālī*	تخطيط مالي
financial policy	*as-siyāsa al-māliyya*	السياسة المالية
financial responsibility	*mas'ūliyya māliyya*	مسؤولية مالية
financial statement	*bayān mālī*	بيان مالى
financial year	*sana māliyya*	سنة مالية
financier	*mumawwil*	مموّل
finished goods	*baḍā'i^{c} tāmmat aṣ-ṣun^{c}*	بضائع تامّة الصنع
finished product	*intāj tāmm aṣ-ṣun^{c}*	انتاج تامّ الصنع
fire alarm	*ālat indhār al-ḥarīq*	آلة انذار الحريق
fire damage	*aḍrār al-ḥarīq*	أضرار الحريق
fire insurance	*ta'mīn ḍidd al-ḥarīq*	تأمين ضدّ الحريق

fire prevention	*wiqāya ḍidd al-ḥarīq*	وقاية ضد الحريق
fire-proof	*ṣāmid li'n-nār*	صامد للنار
fire risk	*khaṭar al-ḥarīq*	خطر الحريق
firm	*mu'assasa, munsha'a*	مؤسسة . منشأة
firm contract	*^{c}aqd mulzim*	عقد ملزم
firm offer	*^{c}arḍ thābit*	عرض ثابت
firm price	*at-taklifa 'l-aṣliyya*	التكلفة الاصلية
first-class mail	*barīd daraja ūlā*	بريد درجة أولى
first in, first out	*al-biḍā^{c}a 'd-dākhila awwalan tuṣarraf awwalan*	البضاعة الداخلة أوّلا تصرف أوّلا
first mortgage	*rahn awwal*	رهن اوّل
fiscal agent	*wakīl mālī*	وكيل ماليّ
fiscal period	*fatra māliyya*	فترة مالية
fiscal policy	*as-siyāsa al-māliyya*	السياسة المالية
fiscal year	*as-sana al-māliyya*	السّنة المالية
fishing port	*mīnā' li-ṣayd al-asmāk*	ميناء لصيد الاسماك
fish market	*sūq as-samak*	سوق السمك
five-year plan	*khiṭṭa khamsiyya*	خطّة خمسية
fixed assets	*mawjūdāt*	موجودات
fixed capital	*ar-ra'smāl ath-thābit*	الرأسمال الثابت
fixed charges	*maṣārīf thābita*	مصاريف ثابتة
fixed cost	*at-taklifa ath-thābita*	التكلفة الثابتة

fixed income	*dakhl thābit*	دخل ثابت
fixed interest	*fā'ida thābita*	فائدة ثابتة
fixed liability	*iltizām thābit*	التزام ثابت
fixed overheads	*maṣrūfāt thābita*	مصروفات ثابتة
fixed premium	*qisṭ maḥdūd*	قسط محدود
fixed price	*siᶜr thābit*	سعر ثابت
fixed term	*ajal maḥdūd*	أجل محدود
fixtures	*tarkībāt*	تركيبات
flat rate	*siᶜr muwaḥḥad*	سعر موحّد
flexibility of prices	*marūnat al-asᶜār*	مرونة الاسعار
flight time	*waqt aṭ-ṭayarān*	وقت الطيران
floating capital	*ra'smāl ḥurr/sā'ir*	رأسمال حرّ/سائر
floating charge	*taklifa ghayr thābita*	تكلفة غير ثابتة
floating rate	*siᶜr ᶜā'im*	سعر عائم
flood	*fayaḍān, ghamr*	فيضان، غمر
flood insurance	*ta'mīn ḍidd akhṭār al-fayaḍan*	تأمين ضد اخطار الفيضان
flow chart	*rasm bayānī li-sayr al-aᶜmāl*	رسم بيانى لسير الأعمال
flow diagram	*rasm takhṭīṭī li-sayr al-a'māl*	رسم تخطيطي لسير الأعمال
fluctuation of prices	*taqallubāt al-asᶜār*	تقلبات الأسعار
follow up	*yulāḥiq, mulāḥaqa*	يلاحق، ملاحقة
food allowance	*badal ṭaᶜām*	بدل طعام

food industries	*ṣināᶜāt ghidhā'iyya*	صناعات غذائية
food products	*muntajāt ghidhā'iyya*	منتجات غذائية
food supplies	*ma'ūnāt ghidhā'iyya*	مؤونات غذائية
foot the bill	*yadfaᶜ al-ḥisāb*	يدفع الحساب
for account of	*li-ḥisāb*	لحساب
forbidden area	*al-minṭaqa al-ḥarām*	المنطقة الحرام
force, in	*sāri'l-mafᶜūl*	ساري المفعول
force majeure	*quwwa qāhira, sabab qahrī*	قوّة قاهرة ، سبب قهري
forecast	*tanabbu', takahhun*	تنبّؤ ، تكهّن
foreclose a mortgage	*aghlaq ar-rahn*	أغلق الرهن
foreign bill of exchange	*kimbiyāla ajnabiyya*	كمبيالة اجنبية
foreign corporation	*sharika ajnabiyya*	شركة اجنبية
foreign currency	*ᶜumla ajnabiyya*	عملة اجنبية
foreigner	*ajnabī*	أجنبي
foreign exchange	*taḥwīl ajnabī*	تحويل أجنبي
foreign exchange market	*sūq al-qaṭᶜ al-ajnabī*	سوق القطع الاجنبي
foreign influence	*nufūdh ajnabī*	نفوذ أجنبيّ
foreign investments	*istithmārāt ajnabiyya*	استثمارات اجنبية
foreign law	*qānūn ajnabī*	قانون اجنبي
foreign minister	*wazīr khārijiyya*	وزير خارجية
Foreign Office	*wizārat al-khārijiyya bi-injiltirā*	وزارة الخارجية (بانجلترا)

foreign trade	*tijāra khārijiyya*	تجارة خارجية
foreman	*mulāḥiẓ ᶜummāl*	ملاحظ عمّال
forfeit a patent	*yafqid ḥaqqahu fī rukhṣa*	يفقد حقّه فى رخصة
forgery	*tazwīr*	تزوير
fork-lift truck	*ᶜaraba bi-mirfāᶜ shawkī*	عربة بمرفاع شوكي
form a company, to	*yu'assis sharika*	يؤسس شركة
formal consent	*qabūl rasmī*	قبول رسمي
formal contract	*ᶜaqd rasmī*	عقد رسمي
formalities	*ijrā'āt shakliyya*	اجراءات شكلية
formality of registration	*ijrā'āt at-tasjīl*	اجراءات التسجيل
formal notice	*indhār rasmī*	انذار رسمى
formation expenses	*nafaqāt ta'sīs*	نفقات تأسيس
formation of a company	*takwīn sharika*	تكوين شركة
form of application	*istimārat taqdīm aṭ-ṭalab*	استمارة تقديم الطلب
forward accounting	*muḥāsaba tanabbu'iyya*	محاسبة تنبؤية
forwarding agent	*wakīl ash-shaḥn/an-naql*	وكيل الشحن/النقل
founders' shares	*ashum al-muᶜassisīn*	أسهم المؤسسين
franchise	*iᶜfā', imtiyāz, ḥaqq*	اعفاء. امتياز. حقّ
franchise clause	*sharṭ al-imtiyāz*	شرط الامتياز
fraud	*iḥtiyāl, naṣb*	احتيال. نصب
fraudulent	*iḥtiyālī, muzawwar*	احتيالى. مزوّر

fraudulent bankruptcy	*iflās iḥtiyālī*	افلاس احتيالى
free alongside ship (f.a.s.)	*taslīm raṣīf mīnā' ash-shaḥn*	تسليم رصيف ميناء الشحن
free competition	*munāfasa ḥurra*	منافسة حرّة
freedom of choice	*ḥurriyat al-ikhtiyār*	حرّية الاختيار
freedom of speech	*ḥurriyyat al-kalām*	حرّية الكلام
free enterprise	*iqtiṣād ḥurr*	اقتصاد حرّ
free entry	*ad-dukhūl majjānan, samāḥ bi'l-murūr*	الدخول مجّانا . سماح بالمرور
free goods	*baḍā'iᶜ ḥurra*	بضائع حرّة
freehold	*milk ḥurr*	ملك حرّ
freelance	*mustaqill, ḥurr*	مستقلّ . حرّ
free market	*sūq ḥurra*	سوق حرة
free of income tax	*muᶜfā min ḍarībat ad-dakhl*	معفى من ضريبة الدخل
free of premium	*muᶜfā min al-aqsāṭ*	معفى من الاقساط
free on board (f.o.b.)	*at-taslīm ᶜala 'l-bākhira*	التسليم على الباخرة (فوب)
free port	*mīnā' ḥurr*	ميناء حرّ
free trade	*tijāra ḥurra*	تجارة حرّة
free trade zone	*manṭaqat tijāra ḥurra*	منطقة تجارة حرّة
freeze	*yujammid*	يجمّد
freight	*ujrat shaḥn*	اجرة شحن
freight car	*ᶜarabat shaḥn biḍāᶜa*	عربة شحن بضاعة
freighter	*mu'ajjir as-safīna*	مؤجّر السفينة

freight insurance	*at-ta'mīn ᶜala 'sh-shaḥn*	التأمين على الشحن
freight rates	*fi'āt ujūr ash-shaḥn*	فئات اجور الشحن
freight release	*ta'shīra bidafᶜ ujrat ash-shaḥn*	تأشيرة بدفع أجرة الشحن
frequency distribution	*tawzīᶜ at-tawātur*	توزيع التواتر
fringe benefit	*manāfiᶜ iḍāfiyya*	منافع اضافية
fuel	*waqūd*	وقود
fulfil a contract	*yunaffidh ᶜaqdan*	ينفّذ عقدا
full capacity	*ṭāqa quṣwā*	طاقة قصوى
full member	*ᶜuḍw ᶜāmil*	عضو عامل
full name	*al-ism bil-kāmil*	الاسم بالكامل
full partner	*sharīk kāmil*	شريك كامل
full-value insurance	*ta'mīn kāmil al-qīma*	تأمين كامل القيمة
fully subscribed capital	*ra'smāl muktatab bihi bi'l-kāmil*	رأسمال مكتتب به بالكامل
functional responsibilities	*al-mas'ūliyyāt al-waẓīfiyya*	المسؤوليّات الوظيفية
fundamental problem	*mushkila asāsiyya*	مشكلة أساسية
funded reserve	*iḥtiyāṭī mustathmar*	احتياطي مستثمر
funding loans	*qurūḍ at-tamwīl*	قروض التمويل
further information	*maᶜlūmāt iḍāfiyya*	معلومات اضافية
future delivery	*taslīm ājil*	تسليم آجل
future prospects	*iḥtimālāt al-mustaqbal*	احتمالات المستقبل

G

gain	*yarbaḥ, yaksab, yastafīd*	يربح · يكسب · يستفيد
gamble	*qimār, muqāmara*	قمار · مقامرة
gasoline	*banzīn*	بنزين
gas reserves	*iḥtiyāti 'l-ghāz*	احتياطي الغاز
general agreement	*ittifāq ^{c}āmm*	اتّفاق عامّ
general assembly	*al-jam^{c}iyya 'l-^{c}umūmiyya/'l-^{c}āmma*	الجمعية العمومية/العامّة
general audit	*murāja^{c}a ^{c}āmma, tadqīq 'āmm*	مراجعة عامّة · تدقيق عامّ
general circulation	*tawzī^{c} ^{c}āmm*	توزيع عامّ
general expenses	*maṣrūfāt ^{c}āmma*	مصروفات عامّة
general intelligence test	*ikhtibār adh-dhakā' al-^{c}āmm*	اختبار الذكاء العام
general manager	*mudīr ^{c}āmm*	مدير عامّ
general meeting	*ijtimā^{c} ^{c}āmm, jam^{c}iyya ^{c}umūmiyya*	اجتماع عامّ · جمعية عمومية
general policy	*siyāsa ^{c}āmma*	سياسة عامّة
general strike	*iḍrāb ^{c}āmm*	اضراب عامّ

generate growth	*yuwallid an-numuww*	يولّد النموّ
generator	*muwallid kahrabā'ī, dinamū*	مولّد كهربائي، دينامو
gentleman's agreement	*ittifāq jintilmān/sharaf*	اتّفاق جنتلمان/شرف
geological survey	*masḥ jiyulūjī*	مسح جيولوجي
geophysical survey	*misāḥa jiyūphīzīqiyya*	مساحة جيوفيزيقية
get in touch with	*yattaṣil bi*	يتّصل ب
giant corporations	*sharikāt ḍakhma*	شركات ضخمة
gilt-edge	*mudhahhab al-aṭrāf, mumtāz*	مذهّب الاطراف، ممتاز
gilt-edged securities	*awrāq māliyy darja ūlā*	أوراق مالية درجة اولى
giro	*niẓām naql al-i'timān*	نظام نقل الائتمان
give an opinion	*yudlī bi-ra'y*	يدلي برأي
give-away price	*siᶜr zahīd*	سعر زهيد
give effect to	*yunaffidh*	ينفّذ
give evidence	*yudli bishahāda*	يدلى بشهادة
go ahead	*yataqaddam/yamḍī quduman*	يتقدّم/يمضي قدما
going concern	*mu'assasa nājiḥa*	مؤسّسة ناجحة
going price	*as-siᶜr al-jārī*	السعر الجاري
going rate	*al-muᶜaddal as-sārī*	المعدّل السارى
gold	*dhahab*	ذهب
gold bullion standard	*niẓām sabā'ik adh-dhahab*	نظام سبائك الذهب
gold currency	*ᶜumla dhahabiyya*	عملة ذهبية

gold market	*sūq adh-dhahab*	سوق الذهب
gold reserve	*iḥtiyāṭi 'dh-dhahab*	احتياطى الذهب
gold standard	*niẓām adh-dhahab*	نظام الذهب
gold stock	*ar-raṣīd adh-dhahabī*	الرصيد الذهبى
good faith	*ḥusn an-niyya*	حسن النيّة
goods	*baḍā'i*^{c}*, sila*^{c}	بضائع • سلع
goods in stock	*baḍā'i*^{c} *fi 'l-mustawda*^{c}	بضائع فى المستودع
goods in transit	*biḍā*^{c}*a fi 'ṭ-ṭarīq*	بضاعة فى الطريق
goods on sale	*biḍā*^{c}*a li'l-bay*^{c}	بضاعة للبيع
good title	*ḥaqq milkiyya ṣaḥīḥ*	حقّ ملكية صحيح
goodwill	*shuhrat al-maḥall, huṣn an-niyya*	شهرة المحلّ • حسن النية
go-slow	*mutabāṭi'*	متباطئ
government	*ḥukūma*	حكومة
government authorities	*sultāt ḥukūmiyya*	سلطات حكومية
government contracts	^{c}*uqūd ḥukūmiyya*	عقود حكومية
government corporation	*sharika ḥukūmiyya*	شركة حكومية
government department	*maṣlaḥa ḥukūmiyya*	مصلحة حكومية
government grant	*minḥa ḥukūmiyya*	منحة حكومية
government intervention	*tadakhkhul ḥukūmī*	تدخّل حكومي
government loan	*qarḍ min 'd-dawla/li'd-dawla*	قرض من الدولة /للدولة
government official	*muwaẓẓaf ḥukūmī*	موظّف حكومي

government subsidy	*iᶜāna ḥukūmiyya*	اعانة حكومية
grace period	*fatrat samāḥ, muhla*	فترة سماح، مهلة
grain market	*sūq al-ḥubūb/al-ghilāl*	سوق الحبوب/الغلال
grant a request	*yulabbī ṭalaban*	يلبّى طلبا
grant a visa	*yamnaḥ ta'shīra*	يمنح تأشيرة
grant immunity	*yamnaḥ ḥaṣāna*	يمنح حصانة
granting authority	*as-sulṭa 'l-māniḥa*	السلطة المانحة
graphic representation	*tamthīl takhṭīṭī*	تمثيل تخطيطي
grass roots	*judhūr, uṣūl*	جذور، أصول
gratuity	*minḥa, mukāfa'a*	منحة ، مكافأة
grave situation	*mawqif ḥarij/khaṭīr*	موقف حرج/خطير
grievance	*maẓlama, shakwā*	مظلمة ، شكوى
gross earnings	*makāsib ijmāliyya*	مكاسب اجمالية
gross income	*dakhl ijmālī*	دخل اجمالى
gross interest	*ijmāli 'l-fā'ida*	اجمالي الفائدة
gross negligence	*ihmāl jasīm*	اهمال جسيم
gross premium	*qisṭ ijmālī*	قسط اجمالي
gross profit	*ijmāli 'r-ribḥ*	اجمالى الربح
gross profit margin	*ḥadd ar-ribḥ al-ijmālī*	حدّ الربح الاجمالي
gross sales	*mabīᶜāt ijmāliyya*	مبيعات اجمالية
gross weight	*al-wazn al-ijmālī*	الوزن الاجمالى

gross yield	*ijmāli 'l-^{c}ā'id*	اجمالي العائد
ground rent	*ījār al-arḍ*	ايجار الأرض
group health	*ta'mīn jamā^{c}ī ḍidd al-maraḍ*	تأمين جماعي ضد المرض
group incentives	*tashjī^{c}āt jamā^{c}īyya*	تشجيعات جماعية
group insurance	*ta'mīn jamā^{c}ī*	تأمين جماعى
group life assurance	*ta'mīn jamā^{c}ī ^{c}alā 'l-ḥayāh*	تأمين جماعي على الحياة
group of companies	*majmū^{c}at sharikāt*	مجموعة شركات
group trading	*tijāra jamā^{c}iyya*	تجارة جماعية
group training	*tadrīb jamā^{c}ī*	تدريت جماعي
growth	*numuww*	نموّ
growth industry	*ṣinā^{c}a nāmiya*	صناعة نامية
growth rate	*mu^{c}addal an-numuww*	معدل النموّ
guarantee	*ḍamān*	ضمان
guaranteed prices	*as^{c}ār maḍmūna*	اسعار مضمونة
guarantor	*ḍāmin*	ضامن
guide-line	*khaṭṭ irshād*	خط ارشاد
guiding principles	*mabādi' tawjīhiyya*	مبادئ توجيهية

H

habitable	*ṣāliḥ li's-suknā*	صالح للسكني
haggle	*yusāwim, yumāḥik*	يساوم • يماحك
half-and-half	*munāṣafatan*	مناصفة
half-measures	*anṣāf ḥulūl*	انصاف حلول
half-pay	*niṣf ajr*	نصف اجر
half-price	*bi niṣf as-si^cr*	بنصف السعر
half-time	*niṣf dawām, niṣf al-waqt*	نصف دوام • نصف الوقت
hall-mark	*damghat al-maṣūghāt.ᶜalāmat al-jawda*	دمغة المصوغات.علامة الجودة
handbill	*iᶜlān yuwazzaᶜ bi' l-yad*	اعلان يوزّع باليد
handbook	*dalīl, kutayyib al-maᶜlūmāt*	دليل• كتيّب المعلومات
hand-to-mouth	*ᶜaysh kafāf*	عيش كفاف
harbour	*mīnā', marfa'*	ميناء• مرفأ
harbour authorities	*sulṭāt al-mīnā'*	سلطات الميناء
harbour dues	*rusūm al-mīnā'*	رسوم الميناء

hard bargain	*musāwama qāsiya*	مساومة قاسية
hard cash	*naqd ṣaᶜb*	نقد صعب
hard currency	*ᶜumla ṣaᶜba*	عملة صعبة
hard measures	*ijrā'āt shadīda*	اجراءات شديدة
hard selling	*bayᶜ ṣaᶜb*	بيع صعب
hardship	*mashaqqa, ḍīq*	مشقّة • ضيق
hardware	*adawāt maᶜdiniyya*	ادوات معدنية
harvest	*maḥṣūl, ḥaṣād*	محصول• حصاد
haulage	*saḥb, ujrat an-naql*	سحب • اجرة النقل
hazard	*khaṭar, maṣdar khaṭar*	خطر • مصدر خطر
hazardous	*maḥfūf bi'l-khaṭar*	محفوف بالخطر
head cashier	*amīn ṣundūq ra'īsī*	امين صندوق رئيسى
headline	*ᶜunwān bi-ḥurūf kabīra fī awwal ṣafḥa*	عنوان بحروف كبيرة فى اول صفحة
head of a delegation	*ra'īs wafd*	رئيس وفد
head of department	*ra'īs qism, ra'īs maṣlaḥa*	رئيس قسم • رئيس مصلحة
head office	*markaz ra'īsī*	مركز رئيسى
health certificate	*shahāda ṣiḥḥiyya*	شهادة صحية
health examination	*faḥṣ ṭibbī*	فحص طبّى
health insurance	*ta'mīn ṣiḥḥī*	تأمين صحّى
health statistics	*iḥṣā'āt ṣiḥḥiyya*	احصاءات صحّية
hearing	*jalsa, samāᶜ daᶜwā*	جلسة • سماع دعوى

hearsay	*shahādat samā*^{c} *min al-ghayr*	شهادة سماع من الغير
hearsay evidence	*shahāda mustanida* ^{c}*alá samā*^{c} *min al-ghayr*	شهادة مستندة على سماع من الغير
heating	*taskhīn, tadfi'a*	تسخين. تدفئة
heating installations	*tarkībāt li't-tadfi'a*	تركيبات للتدفئة
heavy expenditure	*nafaqāt bāhiẓa*	نفقات باهظة
heavy freight	*baḍā'i*^{c} *thaqīla*	بضائع ثقيلة
heavy industry	*ṣinā*^{c}*a thaqīla*	صناعة ثقيلة
heavy losses	*khasārāt jasīma*	خسارات جسيمة
heavy sales	*mabī*^{c}*āt ḍakhma*	مبيعات ضخمة
hedging operation	^{c}*amaliyyat murāwagha*	عملية مراوغة
hedging transactions	^{c}*amaliyyāt taghṭiya*	عمليات تغطية (فى البورصة)
heir	*wārith*	وارث
heredity	*al-wirātha*	الوراثة
hidden asset	*aṣl makhfī*	اصل مخفى
hidden reserve	*iḥtiyāṭī makhfī*	احتياطى مخفى
highest bidder	*ṣāḥib a*^{c}*lā* ^{c}*aṭā'*	صاحب أعلي عطاء
high finance	*māliyya* ^{c}*ulyā*	مالية عليا
high grade	*min ṣanf mumtāz*	من صنف ممتاز
high-grade products	*muntajāt min daraja* ^{c}*āliya*	منتجات من درجة عالية
high interest rate	*si*^{c}*r fā'ida murtafi*^{c}	سعر فائدة مرتفع
high level	*mustawā* ^{c}*ālī*	مستوى عالى

highly developed economy	*iqtiṣād ^{c}alā daraja ^{c}āliya min at-taqaddum*	اقتصاد على درجة عالية من التقدّم
highly-paid labourers	*^{c}ummāl dhawū ujūr ^{c}āliya*	عمّال ذوو أجور عالية
high pressure	*ḍaghṭ ^{c}ālī*	ضغط عالى
high-priced goods	*sila^c ^{c}āliyat al-thaman*	سلع عالية الثمن
high seas	*biḥār khārij al-miyāh al-iqlīmiyya*	بحار خارج المياه الاقليمية
highway	*ṭarīq ^{c}umūmī, ṭarīq ṭawwālī*	طريق عمومى. طريق طوّالى
high-yielding	*wafīr al-ghalla*	وفير الغلّة
hijacker	*mukhtaṭif*	مختطف
hindsight	*idrāk ba^{c}d al-awān*	ادراك بعد الأوان
hire, for	*li'l-'ujra*	للاجرة
hire purchase	*shīrā' bi't-taqsīṭ*	شراء بالتقسيط
hire-purchase agreement	*ittifāqiyyat shirā' baḍā'i^c bi't-taqsīṭ*	اتّفاقية شراء بضائع بالتّقسيط
hire-purchase company	*sharikat bay^c bi't-taqsīṭ*	شركة بيع بالتقسيط
hire-purchase control	*riqāba ^{c}ala'l-mabī^{c}āt bi't-taqsīṭ*	رقابة على المبيعات بالتقسيط
hire-purchase credit	*i^{c}timād al-bay^c bi't-taqsīṭ*	اعتماد البيع بالتقسيط
hire-purchase restrictions	*quyūd al-bay^c bi't-taqsīṭ*	قيود البيع بالتقسيط
hold as security	*yaḥjiz shay' bi-ṣifat rahn*	يحجز شيئا بصفة رهن
holding company	*sharika qābiḍa*	شركة قابضة
holiday	*^{c}uṭla ^{c}āmma*	عطلة عامّة
holiday with pay	*ijāza bi-ajr*	اجازة بأجر
home consumption	*istihlāk maḥallī*	استهلاك محلّي

home-made	*muntaj maḥalliyyan*	منتجّ محليا
home markets	*al-aswāq ad-dākhiliyya*	الاسواق الداخلية
homework	*ᶜamal yunjaz fi'l-bayt*	عمل ينجز فى البيت
honorary member	*ᶜuḍw sharaf, ᶜuḍw fakhrī*	عضو شرف. عضو فخري
honour a bill of exchange	*yaqbal kambiyāla*	يقبل كمبيالة
horizontal integration	*takāmul ufuqī*	تكامل افقى
horsepower	*quwwat ḥiṣān*	قوّة حصان
horticultural products	*muntajāt basātīn*	منتجات بساتين
horticulture	*filāḥat al-basātīn*	فلاحة البساتين
hostage	*rahīna*	رهينة
host country	*al-balad al-muḍīf*	البلد المضيف
hostile activity	*nashāṭ ᶜidā'ī*	نشاط عدائى
hostile witness	*shāhid ᶜidā'ī*	شاهد عدائى
hourly	*fi's-sāᶜa*	فى الساعة
hourly costs	*at-takālīf fi's-sāᶜa*	التكاليف فى الساعة
hourly-paid worker	*ᶜāmil yudfaᶜ lahu 'l-ajr bi's-sāᶜa*	عامل يدفع له الاجر بالساعة
hourly rate	*al-muᶜaddal fi's-sāᶜa*	المعدّل فى الساعة
hour, output per	*al-mardūd bi's-sāᶜa*	المردود بالساعة
household goods	*amtiᶜa manziliyya*	امتعة منزلية
house-to-house selling	*bayᶜ bi'ṭ-ṭawāf 'ala 'l-buyūt*	بيع بالطواف على البيوت
housing allowance	*ᶜilāwat sakan*	علاوة سكن

housing shortage	*naqṣ bi'l-masākin, azmat masākin*	قص بالمساكن • ازمة مساكن
hue and cry	*ṣayḥat muṭāradat mujrim*	يحة مطاردة مجرم
human relations	*al-ᶜalāqāt al-insāniyya*	علاقات الانسانية
humiliation	*idhlāl, ihāna*	اذلال • اهانة
hunger strike	*iḍrāb ᶜan aṭ-ṭaᶜām*	اضراب عن الطعام
hush money	*rashwat iskāt*	رشوة اسكات
hydraulic power	*kahrabā' mā'iyya*	كهرباء مائية
hyperinflation	*taḍakhkhum mālī mufriṭ*	تضخّم مالى مفرط

I

idle period	*fatrat qillat al-^{c}amal*	فترة قلّة العمل
illegal	*ghayr shar^{c}ī, ghayr qānūnī*	غير شرعى، غير قانونى
illegal contract	*^{c}aqd ghayr qānūnī*	عقد غير قانونى
illegal entry	*dukhūl ghayr mashrū^{c}*	دخول غير مشروع
illegal practices	*a^{c}māl ghayr qānūniyya*	اعمال غير قانونية
illegal sale	*bay^{c} ghayr qānūnī*	بيع غير قانونى
illness	*maraḍ, dā'*	مرض، داء
illustration	*īḍāḥ, mithāl tawḍīḥī*	ايضاح، مثال توضيحى
immediate delivery	*taslīm fawrī*	تسليم فورى
immediate investigation	*taḥqīq fawrī*	تحقيق فورى
immigration	*hijra (ilā balad)*	هجرة (الى بلد)
immigration laws	*qawānīn al-hijra*	قوانين الهجرة
implementation	*tanfīdh, injāz*	تنفيذ، انجاز
implied condition	*sharṭ ḍimnī*	شرط ضمنى

implied contract	*ʿaqd ḍimnī*	عقد ضمنى
implied warranty	*kafāla ḍimniyya*	كفالة ضمنية
importation	*istīrād*	استيراد
import ban	*ḥaẓr al-istīrād*	حظر الاستيراد
import credit	*iʿtimād al-istīrād*	اعتماد الاستيراد
import duty	*ḍarībat/rasm istīrād*	ضريبة /رسم استيراد
importer	*mustawrid*	مستورد
import licence	*tarkhīṣ istīrād*	ترخيص استيراد
import quota	*ḥiṣṣat al-mawādd al-mustawrada*	حصّة المواد المستوردة
imports	*wāridāt*	واردات
imports and exports	*al-wāridāt wa'ṣ-ṣādirāt*	الواردات والصادرات
import surplus	*fā'iḍ al-mustawradāt*	فائض المستوردات
impose duties	*yafriḍ rusūm jumrukiyya*	يفرض رسوما جمركية
impossible contract	*ʿaqd mustaḥīl*	عقد مستحيل
impound	*yaḥjiz, yaḥtabis*	يحجز، يحتبس
imprisonment	*ḥabs, sajn*	حبس، سجن
improved methods of production	*yuḥassin asālīb al-intāj*	يحسّن اساليب الانتاج
impurities	*shawā'ib*	شوائب
imputed negligence	*ihmāl muftaraḍ, ihmāl sababī*	اهمال مفترض، اهمال سببى
inaccessible	*lā yūṣal ilayhi*	لا يوصل اليه
inaccurate	*ghayr daqīq, ghayr ṣaḥīḥ*	غير دقيق، غير صحيح

nactive market	*sūq khāmila*	سوق خاملة
n bulk	*bi'l-jumla*	بالجملة
ncapacity	*^{c}ajz, ^{c}adam kifā'a*	عجز، عدم كفاءة
ncapacity to work	*^{c}ajz ^{c}an al-^{c}amal*	عجز عن العمل
ncentive	*ḥāfiz, tashjī^{c}ī*	حافز، تشجيعى
incentive bonus	*^{c}ilāwa tashjī^{c}iyya*	علاوة تشجيعية
incentive scheme	*khiṭṭa tashjī^{c}iyya*	خطّة تشجيعية
income	*dakhl, īrād*	دخل، ايراد
income, annual	*dakhl sanawī*	دخل سنوى
incomes policy	*siyāsat ad-dukhūl*	سياسة الدخول
income statement	*bayān al-dakhl*	بيان الدخل
income tax	*ḍarībat ad-dakhl*	ضريبة الدخل
incompetent	*^{c}ājiz, ghayr kuf'*	عاجز، غير كفء
inconclusive	*ghayr ḥāsim*	غير حاسم
ncorporate	*yudmij/yu'assis sharika*	يدمج، يؤسّس شركة
incorporated company	*sharika musāhama*	شركة مساهمة
incorporation certificate	*shahādat ta'sīs sharika*	شهادة تأسيس شركة
ncorrect	*ghayr ṣaḥīḥ, khaṭa'*	غير صحيح، خطأ
increase	*ziyāda, irtifā^{c}*	زيادة، ارتفاع
increase	*yazīd, yartafi^{c}*	يزيد، يرتفع
increased cost of living	*ziyādat takālīf al-ma^{c}īsha*	زيادة تكاليف المعيشة

increase in value	*ziyād fi'l-qīma*	زيادة فى القيمة
increase taxes	*yazīd aḍ-ḍarā'ib*	يزيد الضرائب
increment	*ziyāda*	زيادة (فى المقدار أو القيمة)
indebted	*madīn*	مدين
in demand	*maṭlūb*	مطلوب
indemnify	*yu^{c}awwiḍ, yu'ammin ḍidd khasāra aw ḍarar*	يعوّض. يؤمّن ضدّ خسارة أو ضرر
indemnity contract	*^{c}aqd ta^{c}wīḍ*	عقد تعويض
indemnity bonds	*sanadāt ta^{c}wīḍ*	سندات تعويض
indemnity period	*muddat at-ta^{c}wīḍ*	مدّة التعويض
independent contractor	*muqāwil mustaqill*	مقاول مستقل
independent witness	*shāhid mustaqill*	شاهد مستقلّ
index, cost of living	*ar-raqm al-qiyāsī li-takālīf al-ma^{c}īsha*	الرقم القياسى لتكاليف المعيشة
index of retail prices	*ar-raqm al-qiyāsī li-as^{c}ār at-tajzi'a*	الرقم القياسى لاسعار التجزئة
indicator	*mu'ashshir, dalīl*	مؤشّر. دليل
indirect	*maṣārīf ghayr mubāshira*	مصاريف غير مباشرة
indirect cost	*taklifa ghayr mubāshira*	تكلفة غير مباشرة
indirect selling	*bay^{c} ghayr mubāshir*	بيع غير مباشر
indirect tax	*ḍarība ghayr mubāshira*	ضريبة غير مباشرة
individual ownership	*milkiyya fardiyya*	ملكية فردية
inducement	*bā^{c}ith, ḥāfiz, mughrī*	باعث. حافز. مغرى
in due course	*fi'l-waqt al-munāb, ba^{c}d mudda munāsiba*	فىالوقت المناسب. بعد مدّة مناسبة

industrial accidents	*ḥawādith aṣ-ṣināᶜa*	حوادث الصناعة
industrial court	*maḥkama ṣināᶜiyya*	محكمة صناعية
industrial disease	*maraḍ ṣināᶜī*	مرض صناعى
industrial dispute	*nizāᶜ ṣināᶜī/fi'l-ᶜamal*	نزاع صناعى/فى العمل
industrial expansion	*tawassuᶜ ṣināᶜī*	توسّع صناعى
industrial injury	*iṣābat ᶜamal*	اصابة عمل
industrial insurance	*ta'mīn ṣināᶜī*	تأمين صناعى
industrialization	*taṣnīᶜ*	تصنيع
industrial production	*intāj ṣināᶜī*	انتاج صناعى
industrial relations	*ᶜalāqāt ṣināᶜiyya*	علاقات صناعية
industrial risk	*khaṭar ṣināᶜī*	خطر صناعى
industry	*ṣināᶜa*	صناعة
inexpensive	*rakhīṣ, qalīl at-taklifa*	رخيص. قليل التكلفة
inflated price	*siᶜr mutaḍakhkhim*	سعر متضخّم
inflation	*taḍakhkhum mālī*	تضخّم مالى
inflationary spiral	*ḥalazūn at-taḍakhkhum*	حلزون التضخّم
in force	*sāri 'l-maf'ūl*	سارى المفعول
informal	*ghayr rasmī*	غير رسمى
informal contract	*ᶜaqd ghayr rasmī*	عقد غير رسمى
informal meeting	*ijtimāᶜ ghayr rasmī*	اجتماع غير رسمى
information centre	*markaz al-iᶜlām*	مركز الاعلام

infringe	*yukhālif, yakhriq, yantahik ḥuramat*	يخالف، يخرق، ينتهك حرمة
infringe a copyright	*yataʿaddā ʿalā ḥaqq ta'līf*	يتعدّى على حقّ تأليف
infringement	*intihāk, mukhālafa, kharq*	انتهاك ، مخالفة ، خرق
initial costs	*takālīf/nafaqāt awwaliyya*	تكاليف/نفقات اوّلية
initial investigation	*taḥqīq awwalī*	تحقيق أولى
initial premium	*qisṭ asāsī*	قسط أساسى
initial proceedings	*ijrā'āt awwaliyya*	اجراءات أوّلية
injunction	*amr qaḍā'ī māniʿ*	امرقضائى مانع
injury	*iṣāba, ḍarar*	اصابة ، ضرر
injury rate	*muʿaddal al-iṣāba*	معدّل الاصابة
inland revenue	*ʿā'id aḍ-ḍarā'ib ad-dākhiliyya*	عائد الضرائب الداخلية
input	*al-ṭāqa/al-maʿlūmāt al-latī tuzawwad*	الطاقة/المعلومات التى تزوّد
inquiry agency	*wikālat istiʿlāmāt*	وكالة استعلامات
inquiry office	*maktab al-istiʿlāmāt*	مكتب الاستعلامات
insert a clause in a contract	*yudrij sharṭ bi-ʿaqd*	يدرج شرطا بعقد
insolvent	*muʿsir, ʿājiz ʿan al-wafā'*	معسر، عاجز عن الوفاء
inspection	*taftīsh, muʿāyana*	تفتيش، معاينة
inspection certificate	*shahādat faḥṣ, shahādat muʿāyana*	شهادة فحص، شهادة معاينة
inspection fee	*rasm taftīsh*	رسم تفتيش
inspection register	*sijill at-taftīsh*	سجلّ التفتيش
inspector of taxes	*murāqib aḍ-ḍarā'ib, ma'mūr aḍ-ḍarā'ib*	مراقب الضرائب ، مأمور الضرائب

instability	*^{c}adam al-istiqrār, iḍṭirāb*	عدم الاستقرار، اضطراب
instability of demand	*^{c}adam istiqrār aṭ-ṭalab*	عدم استقرار الطلب
installation	*tarkīb, munsha'a*	تركيب، منشأة
instalment	*qisṭ, duf^{c}a*	قسط، دفعة
instalment, by	*bi't-taqsīṭ*	بالتقسيط
instalment loan	*qarḍ yusaddad bi't-taqsīṭ*	قرض يسدّد بالتقسيط
instalment premium	*qisṭ muqassaṭ*	قسط مقسّط
institute	*yu'assis, yunshi'*	يؤسّس، ينشئ
instructions	*ta^{c}līmāt, awāmir*	تعليمات، أوامر
insufficient funds	*amwāl ghayr kāfiya*	اموال غير كافية
insurable interest	*fā'ida yu'amman 'alayhā*	فائدة يؤمّن عليها
insurable value	*al-qīma 'l-mu'ammana*	القيمة المؤمّنة
insurance against loss or damage	*ta'mīn ḍidd al-aḍrār wa'l-khasā'ir*	تأمين ضدّ الاضرار والخسائر
insurance agent	*wakīl ta'mīn*	وكيل تأمين
insurance broker	*simsār ta'mīn*	سمسار تأمين
insurance certificate	*shahādat ta'mīn*	شهادة تأمين
insurance company	*sharikat ta'mīn*	شركة تأمين
insurance, fire	*ta'mīn ḍidd al-ḥarīq*	تأمين ضدّ الحريق
insurance inspector	*mufattish ta'mīn*	مفتّش تأمين
insurance policy	*^{c}aqd ta'mīn, būlīṣat ta'mīn*	عقد تأمين، بوليصة تأمين
insurance premium	*qisṭ ta'mīn*	قسط تأمين

insured	*al-mu'amman ᶜalayhi*	المؤمّن عليه
insured risk	*khaṭar mu'amman ḍiddih*	خطر مؤمّن ضدّه
insured value	*al-qīma 'l-muᶜamman ᶜalayhā*	القيمة المؤمّن عليها
insurer	*al-mu'ammin*	المؤمّن
integrated data processing	*muᶜālajat al-muᶜṭayāt al-mutakāmila*	معالجة المعطيات المتكاملة
integration	*tawḥīd,damj*	توحيد · دمج
inter-bank transfer	*taḥwīlat bayn al-maṣārif*	تحويلات بين المصارف
interchangeable parts	*qiṭaᶜ badīla*	قطع بديلة
inter-company transactions	*ᶜamaliyyāt tijāriyya bayn sharika wa ukhra*	عمليات تجارية بين شركة وأخرى
interest, accrued	*fā'ida mutarākima*	فائدة متراكمة
interest on capital	*fā'idat ra's al-māl*	فائدة رأس المال
interest rate	*siᶜr al-fā'ida*	سعر الفائدة
interim audit	*murājaᶜa marḥaliyya, tadqīq marḥalī*	مراجعة مرحلية · تدقيق مرحلى
interim budget	*mīzāniyya mu'aqqata*	ميزانية مؤقّتة
interim dividend	*ribḥ mu'aqqat*	ربح موقّت
interim measures	*ijrā'āt mu'aqqata*	اجراءات موقّتة
interim period	*fatrat intiqāl*	فترة انتقال
internal audit	*murājaᶜa dākhiliyya li'l-hisābāt, tadqīq dākhilī li'l-ḥisābāt*	مراجعة داخلية للحسابات · تدقيق داخلى للحسابات
internal auditor	*murājiᶜ dākhilī, mudaqqiq dākhilī*	مراجع داخلى· مدقّق داخلى
internal control	*raqāba dākhiliyya*	رقابة داخلية

international agreements	*ittifāqiyyāt dawliyya*	اتّفاقيات دولية
international dispute	*nizā*ᶜ *dawlī*	نزاع دولى
international money order	*ḥawāla māliyya dawliyya*	حوالة مالية دولية
international trade	*tijāra dawliyya*	تجارة دولية
interpretation clause	*band tafsīrī*	بند تفسيرى
interpreter	*mutarjim, mufassir*	مترجم ٠ مفسّر
interview	*muqābala shakhṣiyya*	مقابلة شخصية
in transit	ᶜ*ābir, fī ḥālat murūr*	عابر ٠ فى حالة مرور
intrinsic value	*qīma dhātiyya*	قيمة ذاتية
introduction	*muqaddima, taqdīm, idkhāl*	مقدّمة ٠ تقديم ٠ ادخال
invalid	*bāṭil, lāghin*	باطل ٠ لاغ
invalidate the contract	*yulghi 'l-*ᶜ*aqd*	يلغى العقد
inventory	*qā'imat jard*	قائمة جرد
inventory control	*murāqabat al-jard*	مراقبة الجرد
inventory of raw materials	*qā'imat jard al-mawādd al-khāmm*	قائمة جرد المواد الخامّ
invest	*yastathmir, yuqallid manṣiban*	يستثمر ٠ يقلّد منصبا
investigate	*yabḥath, yataḥarrā*	يبحث ٠ يتحرّى
investigation	*faḥṣ, taḥqīq*	فحص ٠ تحقيق
investment	*istithmār*	استثمار
investment adviser	*khabīr istithmār*	خبير استثمار
investment company	*sharikat istithmār*	شركة استثمار

investment incentive	*ḥāfiz al-istithmār*	حافز الاستثمار
investment income	*dakhl al-istithmār*	دخل الاستثمار
investment portfolio	*maḥfaẓat mustanadāt al-istithmār*	محفظة مستندات الاستثمار
invisible trade	*tijāra ghayr manẓūra*	تجارة غير منظورة
invitation to tender	*daᶜwa li-taqdīm ᶜaṭā'*	دعوة لتقديم عطاء
invoice	*fātūra*	فاتورة
invoice, final	*fātūra nihā'iyya*	فاتورة نهائية
invoice value	*qīmat al-biḍāᶜa ḥasab al-fātūra*	قيمة البضاعة حسب الفاتورة
irrevocable credit	*iᶜtimād ghayr qābil li'n-naqḍ*	اعتماد غير قابل للنقض
irrecoverable debt	*dayn lā yustaradd*	دين لا يستردّ
issue at par	*iṣdār bi-siᶜr at-taᶜādul*	اصدار بسعر التعادل
issued capital	*ra's al-māl al-muṣdar*	رأس المال المصدر
itemized balance sheet	*mīzāniyya mufaṣṣala bi'l-bunūd*	ميزانية مفصّلة بالبنود
items of expenditure	*bunūd al-infāq*	بنود الانفاق
items on the agenda	*mawḍūᶜāt jadwal al-aᶜmāl*	موضوعات جدول الاعمال
itinerary	*bayān khaṭṭ sayr ar-riḥla,dalīl al-musāfirīn*	بيان خطّ سيرالرحلة، دليل المسافرين

J

jail	*sijn, ḥabs*	سجن. حبس
jail, to	*yasjin, yaḥbis*	يسجن. يحبس
jeopardy, in	*fī khaṭar*	فى خطر
jet engine	*muḥarrik naffāth*	محرّك نفّاث
jet fuel	*waqūd aṭ-ṭā'irāt an-naffātha*	وقود الطائرات النفّاثة
job analysis	*taḥlīl al-waẓīfa, dirāsat al-waẓīfa*	تحليل الوظيفة . دراسة الوظيفة
job breakdown	*tafṣīl al-ᶜamal*	تفصيل العمل
job classification	*taṣnīf al-waẓā'if*	تصنيف الوظائف
job description	*waṣf al-waẓīfa*	وصف الوظيفة
job discrimination	*tafriqa fi'l-ᶜimāla, tamyīz fi'l-ᶜamal*	تفرقة فى العمالة . تمييز فى العمل
job evaluation	*taqyīm al-waẓā'if, taqyīm al-ᶜamal*	تقييم الوظائف. تقييم العمل
job grading	*tadrīj al-waẓā'if*	تدريج الوظائف
jobless	*bidūn ᶜamal, ᶜāṭil*	بدون عمل. عاطل
job-lot	*mawādd mukhtalifa tubāᶜ bi 'l-jumla*	موادّ مختلفة تباع بالجملة

job simplification	*tabsīṭ al-ᶜamal*	تبسيط العمل
job specification	*muwāṣafat al-waẓīfa*	مواصفات الوظيفة
joint account	*hisāb mushtarak*	حساب مشترك
joint action	*daᶜwā mushtaraka, ijrā' mushtarak*	دعوى مشتركة اجراء مشترك
joint agreement	*iltifāqiyya mushtaraka*	اتّفاقيّة مشتركة
joint and several contract	*ᶜaqd taḍāmunī takāfulī*	عقد تضامنى تكافلى
joint and several liability	*iltizām mushtarak bi't-taḍāmun*	التزام مشترك بالتضامن
joint appeal	*nidā' mushtarak*	نداء مشترك
joint authority	*sulṭa mushtaraka*	سلطة مشتركة
joint committee	*lajna mushtaraka*	لجنة مشتركة
joint consultation	*tashāwur mushtarak*	تشاور مشترك
joint costs	*takālīf mushtaraka*	تكاليف مشتركة
joint liability	*iltizām mushtarak*	التزام مشترك
joint life assurance	*ta'mīn mushtarak ᶜala 'l-ḥayāh*	تأمين مشترك على الحياة
joint ownership	*milkiyya mushtaraka*	ملكية مشتركة
joint resolution	*qarār mushtarak*	قرار مشترك
joint responsibility	*mas'ūliyya mushtaraka*	مسؤلية مشتركة
joint statement	*bayān mushtarak*	بيان مشترك
joint stock company	*sharika musāhama*	شركة مساهمة
joint tenancy	*ijāra mushtaraka*	اجارة مشتركة
joint undertaking	*mashrūᶜ mushtarak*	مشروع مشترك

joint venture	*mashrūʿ mushtarak*	مشروع مشترك
journal	*daftar al-yawmiyya*	دفتر اليومية
journal entry	*qayd fī daftar al-yawmiyya*	قيد فى دفتراليومية
judge	*qāḍī, ḥākim*	قاضى. حاكم
judgement	*ḥukm, qaḍā'*	حكم . قضاء
judgement creditor	*dā'in maḥkūm lahu*	دائن محكوم له
judgement debtor	*madīn maḥkūm ʿalayh*	مدين محكوم عليه
judicial adviser	*mustashār qānūnī*	مستشار قانونى
judicial committee	*lajna qaḍā'iyya*	لجنة قضائية
judicial council	*majlis qaḍā'ī*	مجلس قضائى
judicial decision	*qarār/ḥukm qaḍā'ī*	قرار/حكم قضائى
judicial inquiry	*taḥqīq qaḍā'ī*	تحقيق قضائى
judicial notice	*ikṭār qaḍā'ī*	اخطار قضائى
judicial proceedings	*ijrā'āt qaḍā'iyya*	اجراءات قضائية
judicial settlement	*taswiya qaḍā'iyya*	تسوية قضائية
junior partner	*sharīk aṣghar*	شريك اصغر
jurisdiction	*ikhtiṣāṣ, dāʿirat ikhtiṣāṣ*	اختصاص. دائرة اختصاص
jurisdiction of the court	*dā'ira ikhtiṣāṣ al-maḥkama*	دائرة اختصاص المحكمة
jury	*al-muḥallifūn, hay'at al-muḥallifīn*	المحلّفون. هيئة المحلّفين
just compensation	*taʿwīḍ ʿādil*	تعويض عادل
just price	*as-siʿr al-ʿadl*	السعر العدل

JUST WAGE

just wage	*al-ajr al-ᶜadl*	الأجر العدل

K

keen competition	*munāfasa shadīda*	منافسة شديدة
keen prices	*asᶜār tanāfusiyya*	اسعار تنافسية
keep out	*ibtaᶜid*	ابتعد
kerosene	*kīrūsīn, zayt al-barāfīn*	كيروسين، زيت البرافين
key industry	*ṣināᶜa asāsiyya*	صناعة اساسية
key position	*manṣib ra'īsī*	منصب رئيسى
key punch machine	*ālat tathqīb*	آلة تثقيب
kilo	*kilū, alf*	كيلو، الف
knockdown prices	*asᶜār mukhaffaḍa li adnā ḥadd*	اسعار مخفّضة لأدنى حدّ
know-how	*maᶜrifa fanniyya*	معرفة فنّية

L

label	*biṭāqa*	بطاقة
labour	*^{c}amal, al-aydi 'l-^{c}āmila*	عمل • الايدى العاملة
labour contract	*^{c}aqd al-^{c}amal*	عقد العمل
labour cost	*taklifat al-yad al-^{c}āmila*	تكلفة اليد العاملة
labour dispute	*nizā^{c} ummāl*	نزاع عمّال
labour, division of	*taqsīm al-^{c}amal*	تقسيم العمل
labour force	*al-quwa 'l-^{c}āmila*	القوى العاملة
labour-intensive	*kathīf al-^{c}amal*	كثيف العمل
labour-intensive process	*yaḥtāj li-^{c}amal kathīf*	يحتاج لعمل كثيف
labour laws	*qawānīn al-^{c}amal*	قوانين العمل
labour legislation	*tashrī^{c}āt al-^{c}amal*	تشريعات العمل
labour market	*sūq al-^{c}amal*	سوق العمل
labour organization	*munaẓẓama ^{c}ummāliyya*	منظّمة عمّالية
labour permit	*tarkhīṣ bi'l-^{c}amal*	ترخيص بالعمل

labour relations	*ᶜalāqāt al-ᶜamal*	علاقات العمل
labour-saving (a)	*yuwaffir fi'l-ᶜamal*	يوفّر فى العمل
labour-saving device	*wasīla tuwaffir al-ᶜamal*	وسيلة توفّر العمل
labour shortage	*naqṣ al-ᶜamal*	نقص العمل
labour, the saving of	*tawfīr bi'l-aydi 'l-ᶜāmila*	توفير بالايدى العاملة
labour troubles	*mashākil al-ᶜamal*	مشاكل العمل
lading	*shaḥn*	شحن
lading, bill of	*būlīṣat shaḥn*	بوليصة شحن
land agent	*simsār/wakīl ᶜaqārāt*	سمسار/وكيل عقارات
land bank	*maṣrif zirāᶜī*	مصرف زراعى
land improvement	*taḥsīn al-arāḍī*	تحسين الاراضى
landing certificate	*shahādat tafrīgh/nuẓūl*	شهادة تفريغ /نزول
landing charges	*nafaqāt tafrīgh*	نفقات تفريغ
landing permit	*rukhṣat tafrīgh/nuzūl*	رخصة تفريغ /نزول
landlord	*mālik al-ᶜaqār*	مالك العقار
landowner	*mālik al-arḍ*	مالك الارض
land register	*sijill al-misāḥa/al-arāḍī*	سجلّ المساحة / الاراضى
land tax	*ḍarībat al-arāḍī*	ضريبة الاراضى
land transport	*an-naql al-barrī*	النقل البرّى
language	*lugha*	لغة
lapsed	*munqaḍī*	منقض

lapse of time	*fawāt al-waqt*	فوات الوقت
larceny	*sariqa*	سرقة
large order	*ṭalabiyya kabīra*	طلبية كبيرة
large-scale	*wāsiᶜ an-niṭāq, kabīr*	واسع النطاق، كبير
large-scale production	*intāj bi-kammiyyāt kabīra*	انتاج بكميات كبيرة
last in, first out	*al-wārid akhīran yuṣraf awwalan*	الوارد أخيرا يصرف أوّلا
last resort	*al-marjiᶜ al-akhīr*	المرجع الاخير
last will and testament	*ākhir waṣiyya*	آخر وصية
late delivery	*taslīm muta'akhkhir*	تسليم متأخّر
late fee	*rasm iḍāfī*	رسم اضافى
latent ambiguity	*ghumūḍ mustatir*	غموض مستتر
latent defect	*ᶜayb kāmin*	عيب كامن
latent methods of production	*aḥdath wasā'il al-intāj*	احدث وسائل الانتاج
lateral integration	*takāmul jānibī*	تكامل جانبى
latest date	*ākhir mawᶜid*	آخر موعد
launch	*yaṭraḥ fi's-sūq, yuṭliq*	يطرح فى السوق، يطلق
launch a new project	*yabda' mashrūᶜ jadīd*	يبدأ مشروعا جديدا
law	*qānūn*	قانون
law courts	*maḥākim*	محاكم
law expenses	*nafaqāt qaḍā'iyya*	نفقات قضائية
lawful	*qānūnī, sharᶜī*	قانونى، شرعى

lawful entry	*dukhūl sharᶜī*	دخول شرعى
lawful trade	*tijāra mashrūᶜa*	تجارة مشروعة
law merchant	*al-qānūn at-tijārī*	القانون التجارى
law of averages	*qānūn al-mutawassiṭāt*	قانون المتوسطات
law of contracts	*qānūn al-ᶜuqūd*	قانون العقود
law of diminishing returns	*qānūn tanāquṣ al-ghalla*	قانون تناقص الغلّة
law of probabilities	*qānūn al-iḥtimālāt*	قانون الاحتمالات
law of supply and demand	*qānūn al-ᶜarḍ wa'ṭ-ṭalab*	قانون العرض والطلب
lawsuit	*daᶜwā qaḍā'iyya*	دعوى قضائية
lawyer	*muḥāmin*	محام
lay a complaint	*yuqaddim shakwā*	يقدّم شكوى
lay off	*yaṣrif/yusarriḥ al-ᶜummāl*	يصرف/يسرح العمّال
lead	*raṣāṣ*	رصاص
leadership	*qiyāda, zaᶜāma*	قيادة • زعامة
leading article	*maqāl ra'īsī, iftitāḥiyya*	مقال رئيسى • افتتاحية
leading question	*su'āl, yūḥī bi'l-ijāba*	سؤال يوحى بالاجابة
lead time	*waqt muᶜtariḍ, muhla*	وقت معترض • مهلة
leakage	*tasarrub, sayalān*	تسرّب • سيلان
lease	*ᶜaqd ījār*	عقد ايجار
leasehold	*ᶜaqār musta'jar*	عقار مستأجر
leasehold improvements	*iṣlāḥat al-arḍ al-mu'ajjara*	اصلاحات الارض المؤجّرة

leasehold property	*^{c}aqār muḥtakar*	قار محتكر
lease or buy	*ista'jir aw ishtari*	ستأجر أو استر
leasing	*isti'jār*	ستئجار
leasing company	*sharikat ta^{c}jīr ^{c}aqārāt*	ركة تأجير عقارات
leather	*jild*	لد
leave (n)	*ijāza, rukhṣa*	جازة • رخصة
leave of absence	*idhn ghiyāb*	ذن غياب
leave out	*yatruk, yansā*	ترك• ينسى
leave with pay	*ijāza bi-murattab*	جازة بمرتّب
leaving certificate	*shahādat ikhlā' ṭaraf*	هادة اخلاء طرف
lecture	*muḥāḍara*	حاضرة
lecture, to	*yuḥāḍir*	حاضر
ledger	*daftar al-ustādh*	فتر الاستاذ
ledger account	*ḥisāb ustādhī*	ساب استاذى
ledger control	*raqīb ustādhī*	قيب استاذى
ledgerless accounting	*muḥāsaba bidūn dafātir*	حاسبة بدون دفاتر
legal	*qanūnī*	انونى
legal advice	*mashūra qānūniyya*	شورة قانونية
legal adviser	*mustashār qānūnī*	ستشار قانونى
legal capacity	*ahliyya qānūniyya*	هلية قانونية
legal charges	*nafaqāt qaḍā'iyya*	فقات قضائية

legal consideration	*ᶜiwaḍ qānūnī*	عوض قانونى
legal contract	*ᶜaqd qānūnī*	عقد قانونى
legal department	*qism al-qaḍāya 'l-qānūniyya*	قسم القضايا القانونية
legal document	*wathīqa qānūniyya*	وثيقة قانونية
legal expert	*khabīr qānūnī*	خبير قانونى
legalization	*tawthīq, taqnīn*	توثيق • تقنين
legalize	*yuwaththiq, yuqannin*	يوثّق • يقنّن
legal liability	*mas'ūliyya qānūniyya*	مسؤولية قانونية
legal opinion	*fatwā qānūniyya*	فتوى قانونية
legal position	*markaz qānūnī*	مركز قانونى
legal procedure	*al-ijrā'āt al-qānūniyya*	الاجراءات القانونية
legal system	*an-niẓām al-qānūnī*	النظام القانونى
legal tender	*ᶜumla qānūniyya*	عملة قانونية
legal title	*ḥaqq milkiyya qānūnī*	حقّ ملكية قانونى
legation	*mufawwaḍiyya*	مفوّضية
legislation	*tashrīᶜ*	تشريع
legislative assembly	*al-jamᶜiyya 't-tashrīᶜiyya*	الجمعية التشريعية
legislative power	*as-sulṭa 't-tashrīᶜiyya*	السلطة التشريعية
leisure industries	*ṣināᶜāt at-tarfīh*	صناعات الترفيه
leisure time	*waqt al-farāgh*	وقت الفراغ
lend	*yuqriḍ, yusallif, yuᶜīr*	يقرض • يسلّف • يعير

lender	*al-muqriḍ*	المقرض
lending agency	*wikālat taslīf*	وكالة تسليف
lend money on mortgage	*yuqriḍ māl bi-rahn*	يقرض مالا برهن
lend money on security	*yuqriḍ māl bi-kafāla*	يقرض مالا بكفالة
lessee	*musta'jir*	مستأجر
lessor	*mu'ajjir*	مؤجّر
let, to	*yu'ajjir*	يؤجّر
letter	*risāla, khiṭāb*	رسالة . خطاب
letter of acceptance	*kitāb qabūl*	كتاب قبول
letter of acknowledgement	*kitāb iqrār*	كتاب اقرار
letter of administration	*kitāb takhwīl idārat tarika*	كتاب تخويل ادارة تركة
letter of advice	*kitāb ishʿār*	كتاب اشعار
letter of application	*ṭalab istikhdām*	طلب استخدام
letter of appointment	*khiṭāb taʿyīn*	خطاب تعيين
letter of confirmation	*kitāb ta'kīd*	كتاب تأكيد
letter of credit	*kitāb iʿtimād*	كتاب اعتماد
letter of guarantee	*khiṭāb ḍamān*	خطاب ضمان
letter of introduction	*risālat taʿrīf*	رسالة تعريف
letter of licence	*kitāb imhāl*	كتاب امهال
letter of resignation	*khiṭāb istiqāla*	خطاب استقالة
letter rate	*taʿrifat ar-rasā'il al-barīdiyya*	تعرفة الرسائل البريدية

letters patent	*barā'at tamlīk*	براءة تمليك
level of demand	*mustawa 'ṭ-ṭalab*	مستوى الطلب
level of water	*mustawa 'l-mā'*	مستوى الماء
levy	*ḍarība*	ضريبة
levy, to	*yafriḍ ḍarība*	يفرض ضريبة
liabilities	*iltizāmāt, khuṣūm*	التزامات ، خصوم
liabilities, fixed	*maṭlūbāt thābita*	مطلوبات ثابتة
liabilities, long term	*duyūn ṭawīlat al-ajal*	ديون طويلة الاجل
liabilities of a bank	*khuṣūm bank*	خصوم بنك
liabilities of a company	*khuṣūm sharika*	خصوم شركة
liability	*mas'ūliyya, dayn, khaṣm*	مسؤولية ، دين، خصم
liability insurance	*ta'mīn min al-mas'ūliyya*	تأمين من المسؤولية
liable for tax	*khāḍiᶜ li'ḍ-ḍarība*	خاضع للضريبة
liable to duties	*khāḍiᶜ li'r-rusūm al-jumrukiyya*	خاضع للرسوم الجمركية
libel	*tashhīr*	تشهير
licence	*rukhṣa, ijāza, taṣrīḥ*	رخصة ، اجازة ، تصريح
licence, export	*tarkhīṣ taṣdīr*	ترخيص تصدير
licence, import	*tarkhīṣ istīrād*	ترخيص استيراد
licence, manufacturing	*rukhṣat taṣnīᶜ*	رخصة تصنيع
licence, under	*bi-mūjib rukhṣa*	بموجب رخصة
licensed dealer	*bā'iᶜ murakhkhaṣ lahu*	بائع مرخّص له

licensed imports	*wāridāt murakhkhaṣ bihā*	واردات مرخّص بها
licensee	*al-murakhkhaṣ lahu*	المرخّص له
licensing authority	*as-sulṭa 'l-murakhkhiṣa*	السلطة المرخّصة
licensing procedures	*ijrā'āt at-tarkhīṣ*	اجراءات الترخيص
licensor	*al-murakhkhiṣ*	المرخّص
lien	*imtiyāz, ḥaqq ḥajz*	امتياز. حقّ حجز
life annuity	*maᶜāsh sanawī ᶜumrī*	معاش سنوى عمرى
life assurance/insurance	*ta'mīn/ḍamān ᶜala 'l-ḥayāh*	تأمين/ضمان على الحياة
life tenant	*ḥā'iz mada 'l-ḥayāh*	حائز مدى الحياة
lift (n)	*miṣᶜad*	مصعد
light industry	*aṣ-ṣināᶜa 'l-khafīfa*	الصناعة الخفيفة
limitation of liability	*taḥdīd al-mas'ūliyya*	تحديد المسؤولية
limited company	*sharika maḥdūda*	شركة محدودة
limited liability	*mas'ūliyya maḥdūda*	مسؤولية محدودة
limited liability company	*sharika dhāt mas'ūliyya maḥdūda*	شركة ذات مسؤولية محدودة
limited market	*sūq maḥdūda/ḍayyiqa*	سوق محدودة/ضيّقة
limited partner	*ash-sharīk al-muwaṣṣī*	الشريك الموصّى
limited partnership	*sharikat tawṣiya basīṭa*	شركة توصية بسيطة
limited private company	*sharika khāṣṣa dhāt mas'ūliyya maḥdūda*	شركة خاصّة ذات مسؤولية محدودة
limited responsibility	*mas'ūliyya maḥdūda*	مسؤولية محدودة
limit of indemnity	*ḥadd at-taᶜwīḍ*	حدّ التعويض

limit of size	*ḥadd al-ḥajm*	حدّ الحجم
limit of weight	*ḥadd al-wazn*	حدّ الوزن
linear programming	*waḍᶜ al-barāmij al-khaṭṭī*	وضع البرامج الخطّى
line management	*idāra tanfīdhiyya*	الادارة التنفيذية
line production	*al-intāj al-khaṭṭī*	الانتاج الخطّى
liner rate	*ujrat ash-shaḥn fi'l-bākhira*	اجرة الشحن فى الباخرة
liquid asset	*aṣl sā'il*	أصل سائل
liquidate a company	*yuṣaffī sharika*	يصفّى شركة
liquidated damages	*aḍrār maqtūᶜa*	أضرار مقطوعة
liquidation	*taṣfiya*	تصفية
liquidation, compulsory	*taṣfiya ijbāriyya*	تصفية اجبارية
liquidation, go into	*yujrī 't-taṣfiya*	يجرى التصفية
liquidation of a business	*taṣfiyat mashrūᶜ*	تصفية مشروع
liquidation, voluntary	*taṣfiya ikhtiyāriyya*	تصفية اختيارية
liquidator	*ma'mūr taṣfiya*	مأمور تصفية
liquidity	*as-suyūla*	السيولة
liquid resources	*mawārid jāhiza*	موارد جاهزة
listed security	*sahm musajjal fi'l-burṣa*	سهم مسجّل فى البورصة
list of applicants	*qā'imat al-mutaqaddimīn bi-ṭalabāt*	قائمة المتقدّمين بطلبات
list of investments	*qā'imat al-istithmārāt*	قائمة الاستثمارات
list of subscribers	*qā'imat al-mushtarikīn*	قائمة المشتركين

list price	*as-siʿr ḥasb qā'imat al-asʿār*	لسعر حسب قائمة الاسعار
litigant	*khaṣm*	خصم
litigation	*muqāḍāh*	مقاضاة
livestock	*māshiya*	ماشية
live weight	*al-wazn al-ḥayy*	لوزن الحى
Lloyd's agent	*wakīl sharikat Lloyd*	وكيل شركة لويد
Lloyd's List	*qā'imat/nashrat Lloyd*	قائمة/نشرة لويد
Lloyds Register of Shipping	*sijillāt Lloyds li's-sufun*	سجلّات لويد للسفن
load (n)	*ḥumūla*	حمولة
load, to	*yashḥan, yuḥammil*	يشحن ٠ يحمّل
loading	*taḥmīl*	تحميل
loading charges	*ujūr at-taḥmīl*	اجور التحميل
loading port	*marfa' at-taḥmīl*	مرفأ التحميل
loan	*qarḍ*	قرض
loan account	*ḥisāb al-qurūḍ*	حساب القروض
loan ceiling	*al-ḥadd al-aʿlā li'l-qarḍ*	الحدّ الاعلى للقرض
loan certificate	*sanad qarḍ*	سند قرض
loan department	*qism al-qurūḍ*	قسم القروض
loan on overdraft	*qarḍ makshūf*	قرض مكشوف
loan value	*qīmat al-qarḍ*	قيمة القرض
local	*maḥallī, mawḍiʿī*	محلّى. موضعى

local advertising	*iᶜlān maḥallī*	اعلان محلّى
local authority	*sulṭa maḥalliyya*	سلطة محلّية
local company	*sharika maḥalliyya*	شركة محلّية
local court	*maḥkama maḥalliyya*	محكمة محلّية
local currency	*ᶜumla maḥalliyya*	عملة محلّية
local custom	*ᶜurf maḥallī*	عرف محلّى
local freight	*shaḥn maḥallī*	شحن محلّى
local government	*ḥukūma maḥalliyya*	حكومة محلّية
local taxation	*farḍ ḍarā'ib maḥalliyya*	فرض ضرائب محلّية
location	*mawqiᶜ*	موقع
lockout	*īqāf al-ᶜamal li'ḍ-ḍaghṭ ᶜala 'l-ᶜummāl*	ايقاف العمل للضغط على العمّال
log-book	*daftar yawmiyyat al-milāḥa*	دفتر يومية الملاحة
long-distance transport	*an-naql ilā masāfāt baᶜīda*	النقل الى مسافات البعيدة
long lease	*ḥikr ṭawīl al-ajal*	حكر طويل الاجل
long-range objectives	*ahdāf baᶜīdat al-madā*	اهداف بعيدة المدى
long-term	*ṭawīl al-ajal*	طويل الاجل
long-term contract	*ᶜaqd ṭawīl al-ajal*	عقد طويل الاجل
long-term insurance	*ta'mīn/ḍamān ṭawīl al-ajal*	تأمين/ضمان طويل الاجل
long-term investment	*istithmārāt ṭawīlat al-ajal*	استثمارات طويلة الاجل
long-term lease	*ījār li mudda ṭawīla*	ايجار لمدّة طويلة
long-term liability	*maṭlūbāt ṭawīlat al-ajal*	مطلوبات طويلة الاجل

long-term loans	*qurūḍ ṭawīlat al-ajal*	قروض طويلة الاجل
long-term planning	*takhṭīṭ ṭawīl al-madā*	تخطيط طويل المدى
long-term policy	*siyāsa ṭawīlat al-madā*	سياسة طويلة المدى
look into	*yafḥaṣ, yadrus*	يفحص، يدرس
loophole	*thaghra*	ثغرة
loss	*khasāra*	خسارة
loss assessment	*taqdīr aḍ-ḍarar*	تقدير الضرر
loss in weight	*fuqdān fi'l-wazn*	فقدان فى الوزن
loss leader	*as-silᶜa 'l-mujtadhiba*	السلعة المجتذبة
loss ratio	*nisbat al-khasāra*	نسبة الخسارة
lost time	*waqt fāqid*	وقت فاقد
low cost fuel	*waqūd qalīl at-taklifa*	وقود قليل التكلفة
lowest price	*adnā siᶜr*	ادنى سعر
low grade	*daraja munkhafiḍa*	درجة منخفضة
low income group	*jamāᶜa dhāt dakhl maḥdūd*	جماعة ذات دخل محدود
lucrative	*murbiḥ*	مربح
luggage in advance	*amtiᶜa mursala salafan*	امتعة مرسلة سلفا
lump sum	*mablagh ijmālī*	مبلغ اجمالى
lump sum purchase	*shirā' ijmālī*	شراء اجمالى
lump-sum settlement	*taswiya bimablagh ijmālī*	تسوية بمبلغ اجمالى
luxury articles	*silaᶜ kamāliyya*	سلع كمالية

luxury trade	*tijārat al-kamāliyyāt*	تجارة الكماليات

M

machine	*āla, yuṣanni^c bi'l-āla*	آلة • يصنّع بالالة
machinery	*mākīnāt, ālāt*	ماكينات • آلات
machinery breakdown insurance	*ta'mīn/ḍamān kasr al-ālāt*	تأمين/ضمان كسر الآلات
machine tool	*āla makaniyya*	آلة مكنية
magistrate	*qāḍī jazā'/ṣulḥ*	قاضي جزاء/صلح
magnetic ink	*ḥibr maghunāṭīsī*	حبر مغناطيسي
magnetic store	*al-makhzan al-mighnāṭīsī*	المخزن المغناطيسي
magnetic tape	*sharīṭ mighnāṭīsī*	شريط مغناطيسي
mail	*barīd*	بريد
mailing list	*qā'imat al-ᶜanāwin al-barīdiyya*	قائمة العناوين البريدية
mail order	*ṭalab barīdī*	طلب بريدى
mail-order advertising	*iᶜlān li-tashjīᶜ ṭalab baḍā'iᶜ bi'l-barīd*	اعلان لتشجيع طلب بضائع بالبريد
mail order business	*tijārat aṭ-ṭalabāt al-barīdiyya*	تجارة الطلبات البريدية
mail-order catalogue	*katalūj aṭ-ṭalab bi'l-barīd*	كتالوج الطلب بالبريد

mail order house	*maḥall aṭ-ṭalab bi'l-barīd*	محل الطلب بالبريد
main article	*maqāl ra^{c}īsī, iftitāḥiyya*	مقال رئيسى، افتتاحية
main committee	*al-lajna 'r-ra'īsiyya*	اللجنة الرئيسية
main line	*khaṭṭ ra'īsī*	خطّ رئيسى
main objective	*al-hadaf ar-ra'īsī*	الهدف الرئيسى
main office	*al-maktab ar-ra'īsī*	المكتب الرئيسى
main point	*an-nuqṭa 'r-ra'īsiyya*	النقطة الرئيسية
maintain	*yaṣūn, ya^{c}ūl*	يصون، يعول
maintenance	*ṣiyāna, i^{c}āla*	صيانة ، اعالة
maintenance allowance	*ta^{c}wīḍ ṣiyāna*	تعويض صيانة
maintenance cost	*taklifat ṣiyāna*	تكلفة صيانة
maintenance department	*qism aṣ-ṣiyāna*	قسم الصيانة
maintenance fee	*nafaqāt ṣiyāna/idāra*	نفقات صيانة/ادارة
maintenance of order	*al-muḥāfaẓa ^{c}ala 'n-niẓām*	المحافظة على النظام
major	*ra'īsī, kabīr, hāmm*	رئيسى، كبير، هامّ
major alterations	*ta^{c}dīlāt jawhariyya*	تعديلات جوهرية
majority	*aktharīyya, sinn ar-rushd*	أكثرية ، سنّ الرشد
majority, absolute	*aghlabiyya muṭlaqa*	أغلبية مطلقة
majority holding	*musāhamat al-aktharīyya*	مساهمة الاكثرية
majority-owned subsidiary	*far^{c} sharika tamlikuh aktharīyya*	فرع تملكه أكثرية
majority votes	*aghlabiyyat al-aṣwāt*	أعلبية الأصوات

make	*yasna*ᶜ*, ya*ᶜ*mal*	يصنع • يعمل
make a decision	*yattakhidh qarār*	يتّخذ قرارا
make amends	*yu*ᶜ*awwiḍ*	يعوّض
make a settlement	*yujrī taswiya*	يجرى تسوية
make clear	*yuwaḍḍiḥ*	يوضّح
make good	*yunjiz, yafī*	ينجز• يفى
maker	*ṣāni*ᶜ*, wāḍi*ᶜ	صانع • واضع
make to order	*ya*ᶜ*mal ḥasab aṭ-ṭalab*	يعمل حسب الطلب
malice	*ḥiqd, ta*ᶜ*ammud al-adhā*	حقد • تعمّد الاذى
malice aforethought	*taṣarruf bisū' niyya*	تصرّف بسوء نيّة
malicious intent	*qaṣd sayyi'*	قصد سيّىء
malicious prosecution	*ijrā' khabīth al-maqṣid*	اجراء خبيث المقصد
malinger	*yatamāraḍ*	يتمارض
malpractice	*sū' taṣarruf*	سوء تصرّف
manage	*yudīr*	يدير
management	*idāra*	ادارة
management accounting	*muḥāsabat al-idāra*	محاسبة الادارة
management analysis	*taḥlīl al-idāra*	تحليل الادارة
management appraisal	*taqyīm al-idāra*	تقييم الادارة
management audit	*tadqīq/murāja*ᶜ*at al-idāra*	تدقيق/مراجعة الادارة
management consultant	*mustashār idāra*	مستشار ادارة

management development	*taṭwīr al-idāra*	تطوير الادارة
management expenses	*maṣārīf al-idāra*	مصاريف الادارة
management investment company	*sharikat idārat istithmār*	شركة ادارة استثمار
Management Operating System	*niẓām al-tashghīl al-idārī*	نظام التشغيل الادارىّ
management services	*khadamāt al-idāra*	خدمات الادارة
manager	*mudīr*	مدير
managerial expenses	*nafaqāt idāriyya*	نفقات ادارية
managerial staff	*muwaẓẓafūn idāriyyūn*	موظّفون اداريون
managing director	*mudīr muntadab*	مدير منتدب
man days	*ayyām ᶜamal rajul*	أيام عمل رجل
man hours	*sāᶜāt ᶜamal rajul*	ساعات عمل رجل
manifesto	*bayān shaḥn, manifestū*	بيان شحن ، مانيفستو
manpower	*al-quwa 'l-ᶜāmila*	القوى العاملة
manpower planning	*takhṭīṭ al-quwa 'l-ᶜāmila*	تخطيط القوى العاملة
manslaughter	*qatl khaṭa'*	قتل خطأ
manual	*yadawī*	يدوى
manual, a	*dalīl*	دليل
manual of accounting	*dalīl al-muḥāsaba*	دليل المحاسبة
manual of procedures	*dalīl al-ijrā'āt*	دليل الاجراءات
manufacture	*yaṣnaᶜ*	يصنع
manufactured goods	*silaᶜ maṣnūᶜa*	سلع مصنوعة

manufacturer	*muṣanniᶜ*	مصنّع
manufacturer's agent	*wakīl ṣāḥib al-maṣnaᶜ*	وكيل صاحب المصنع
manufacturer's brand	*ᶜalāmat al-maṣnaᶜ*	علامة المصنع
manufacturer's price	*as-siᶜr fi'l-maṣnaᶜ*	السعر فى المصنع
manufacturer's representative	*mumaththil aṣ-ṣāniᶜ*	ممثّل الصانع
manufacturing	*ṣunᶜ, taṣnīᶜ*	صنع • تصنيع
manufacturing account	*ḥisāb at-taṣnīᶜ*	حساب التصنيع
manufacturing cost	*kulfat ṣunᶜ as-silᶜa*	كلفة صنع السلعة
manufacturing enterprise	*mashrūᶜ ṣināᶜī*	مشروع صناعى
manufacturing expense	*masrūfāt aṣ-ṣunᶜ*	مصروفات الصنع
manufacturing licence	*rukhṣat tasnīᶜ*	رخصة تصنيع
manufacturing overheads	*nafaqāt taṣnīᶜ*	نفقات تصنيع
manufacturing process	*ṭuruq at-taṣnīᶜ*	طرق التصنيع
manuscript	*makhṭūṭa*	مخطوطة
man-weeks	*asābīᶜ ᶜamal rajul*	أسابيع عمل رجل
margin	*ḥadd*	حدّ
marginal analysis	*at-taḥlīl al-ḥaddī*	التحليل الحدّى
marginal benefit	*fā'ida ḥaddiyya*	فائدة حدّية
marginal cost	*taklifa ḥaddiyya*	تكلفة حدّية
marginal productivity	*al-intājiyya 'l-ḥaddiyya*	الانتاجية الحدّية
marginal profits	*al-arbāḥ al-ḥaddiyya*	الارباح الحدّية

marginal return	*al-ghalla 'l-ḥaddiyya*	الغلّة الحدّية
margin of profit	*hāmish ar-ribḥ*	هامش الربح
margin of safety	*ḥadd al-amān*	حدّ الامان
marine contract	*ᶜaqd baḥrī*	عقد بحرى
marine disaster	*kāritha baḥriyya*	كارثة بحرية
marine insurance	*ta'mīn baḥrī*	تأمين بحرى
marine surveyor	*mudaqqiq ta'mīn baḥrī*	مدقّق تأمين بحرى
marine transport	*naql baḥrī*	نقل بحرى
marital domicile	*mawṭin az-zawjiyya*	موطن الزوجية
maritime bill of lading	*būlīṣat shaḥn baḥrī*	بوليصة شحن بحرى
mark	*ᶜalāma, marka*	علامة ، ماركة
markdown	*takhfīḍ*	تخفيض
marked improvement	*taḥassun malḥūẓ*	تحسّن ملحوظ
market	*sūq*	سوق
marketability	*rawāj, ṭalab*	رواج ، طلب
marketable	*qābil li't-taswīq*	قابل للتسويق
market behaviour	*sulūk as-sūq*	سلوك السوق
market day	*yawm as-sūq*	يوم السوق
market facilities	*tashīlāt as-sūq*	تسهيلات السوق
market forecast	*tanabbu' ᶜan al-aswāq*	تنبّؤ عن الاسواق
marketing	*taswīq*	تسويق

marketing allowance	*masmūḥ at-taswīq*	مسموح التسويق
marketing arrangements	*tartībāt at-taswīq*	ترتيبات التسويق
marketing company	*sharikat taswīq*	شركة تسويق
marketing co-operative	*jam^{c}iyyat ta^{c}āwun at-taswīq*	جمعية تعاون التسويق
marketing cost	*taklifat at-taswīq*	تكلفة التسويق
marketing organization	*munaẓẓamat taswīq*	منظمة تسويق
marketing plan	*khuṭṭat at-taswīq*	خطة التسويق
marketing policy	*siyāsat at-taswīq*	سياسة التسويق
marketing research	*abḥath at-taswīq*	أبحاث التسويق
market penetration	*ikhtirāq as-sūq*	اختراق السوق
market place	*sāḥat as-sūq*	ساحة السوق
market planning	*takhṭīṭ at-taswīq*	تخطيط التسويق
market potential	*imkāniyyat as-sūq*	امكانية السوق
market price	*si^{c}r as-sūq*	سعر السوق
market rate	*si^{c}r/nisbat al-ḥasm*	سعر/نسبة الحسم
markets, foreign	*aswāq ajnabiyya*	أسواق أجنبية
market, steady	*sūq thābita*	سوق ثابتة
market town	*al-madīna allatī yu^{c}qad biha 's-sūq*	المدينة التى يعقد بها السوق
market value	*si^{c}r as-sūq*	سعر السوق
mark up	*yarfa^{c} as-si^{c}r*	يرفع السعر
marriage contract	*^{c}aqd zawāj*	عقد زواج

mass media	*wasā'il al-ittiṣāl bi'l-jamāhīr*	وسائل الاتّصال بالجماهير
mass meeting	*ijtimāᶜ shaᶜbī*	اجتماع شعبى
mass movement	*ḥaraka shaᶜbiyya*	حركة شعبية
mass production	*intāj bi'l-jumla*	انتاج بالجملة
mass unemployment	*biṭāla ᶜalā niṭāq wāsiᶜ*	بطالة على نطاق واسع
master policy	*būlīṣa ra'īsiyya*	بوليصة رئيسية
master-servant relationship	*ᶜalāqat al-ājir bi'l-ajīr*	علاقة الآجر بالأحير
material damage	*ḍarar māddī*	ضرر مادّى
materials	*mawādd*	موادّ
materials and services	*mawādd wa khadamāt*	موادّ وخدمات
materials control	*murāqabat al-mawādd*	مراقبة الموادّ
materials cost	*taklifat al-mawādd*	تكلفة الموادّ
materials handling	*munāwalat al-mawādd*	مناولة الموادّ
maternity insurance	*ta'mīn al-wilāda*	تأمين الولادة
mathematical programming	*al-barmaja 'r-riyāḍiyya*	البرمجة الرياضية
matter of course	*mas'ala ᶜādiyya*	مسألة عادية
matter of fact	*amr haqīqī*	أمر حقيقى
matter of law	*qaḍiyya qānūniyya*	قضية قانونية
matter of opinion	*mas'alat ra'y*	مسألة رأى
matters, procedural	*masā'il ijrā'iyya*	مسائل اجرائية
mature bond	*sanad mustaḥiqq*	سند مستحقّ

matured debt	*dayn mustaḥiqq ad-daf^c*	دين مستحقّ الدفع
matured mortgage	*rahn mustaḥiqq*	رهن مستحقّ
maturity date	*tārīkh al-istiḥqāq*	تاريخ الاستحقاق
maximise profits	*yazīd al-arbāḥ li-aqṣā ḥadd*	يزيد الارباح لاقصى حدّ
maximise resources	*yazīd al-mawārid li-aqṣā ḥadd*	يزيد الموارد لأقصى حد
maximum	*al-ḥadd al-a^clā*	الحدّ الاعلى
maximum capacity	*ṭāqa quṣwā*	طاقة قصوى
maximum load	*aqṣā ḥiml*	أقصى حمل
maximum loss	*aqṣā ḥadd li'l-khasāra*	أقصى حدّ للخسارة
maximum output	*aqṣā intāj*	اقصى انتاج
maximum penalty	*^cuqūba quṣwā*	عقوبة قصوى
mean difference	*mutawassiṭ al-furūq*	متوسّط الفروق
means of communication	*wasā'il al-muwāṣalāt*	وسائل المواصلات
means of payment	*wasīlat ad-daf^c*	وسيلة الدفع
means of production	*wasīlat intāj*	وسيلة انتاج
mean value	*mutawassiṭ al-qīma*	متوسّط القيمة
measure	*ijrā', miqyās*	اجراء، مقياس
measurement	*qiyās*	قياس
measure of damages	*miqyās al-aḍrār*	مقياس الاضرار
measure of value	*mi^cyār al-qīma*	معيار القيمة
measures, disciplinary	*tadābir ta'dībiyya*	تدابير تأديبية

measures, protective	*tadābīr wāqiya*	تدابير واقية
measures, to take	*yattakhidh tadābīr*	يتخذ تدابير
mechanic	*mīkānīkī*	ميكانيكى
mechanical accounting	*al-muḥāsaba 'l-āliyya*	المحاسبة الالية
mechanical engineer	*muhandis mikānīkī*	مهندس ميكانيكى
mechanical industry	*ṣināᶜa āliyya*	صناعة آلية
mechanisation	*maykana*	ميكنة
media advertising	*iᶜlān biwasā'il an-nashr*	اعلان بوسائل النشر
mediation	*tawassuṭ*	توسّط
medical certificate	*shahāda ṭibbiyya*	شهادة طبّية
medical examination	*faḥṣ ṭibbī*	فحص طبّى
medical expenses insurance	*ḍamān maṣārīf ṭibbiyya*	ضمان مصاريف طبّية
medical treatment	*ᶜilāj ṭibbī*	علاج طبّى
medium	*wasīla, wāsiṭa, wasaṭ*	وسيلة • واسطة • وسط
medium of exchange	*wasīlat ṣarf*	وسيلة صرف
medium-term loan	*qarḍ mutawassiṭ al-ajal*	قرض متوسط الاجل
meet demand, to	*yuwājih aṭ-ṭalab*	يواجه الطلب
meeting	*ijtimāᶜ, jalsa*	اجتماع • جلسة
meeting, executive	*jalsa tanfīdhīya*	جلسة تنفيذية
meeting, general	*ijtimāᶜ ᶜāmm*	اجتماع عامّ
meeting is closed	*intaha 'l-ijtimāᶜ*	انتهى الاجتماع

meeting is open	*iftutiḥa 'l-ijtimāʿ*	افتتح الاجتماع
meeting of creditors	*ijtimāʿ ad-dā'inīn*	اجتماع الدائنين
meeting, ordinary	*ijtimāʿ ʿādī*	اجتماع عادى
meet one's commitments, to	*yafī bi'ltizāmātih*	يفى بالتزاماته
member	*ʿuḍw*	عضو
member of a committee	*ʿuḍw lajna*	عضو لجنة
member of the board	*ʿuḍw majlis al-idāra*	عضو مجلس الادارة
membership	*ʿuḍwiyya*	عضوية
members of the council	*aʿḍā' al-majlis*	أعضاء المجلس
memorandum	*mudhakkira*	مذكرة
Memorandum of Association	*ʿaqd at-ta'sīs*	عقد التأسيس
mental capacity	*ahliyya ʿaqliyya*	أهلية عقلية
mental hospital	*mustashfa 'l-amrāḍ al-ʿaqliyya*	مستشفى الامراض العقلية
mercantile agency	*wikāla tijāriyya*	وكالة تجارية
mercantile credit	*iʿtimād tijārī*	اعتماد تجارى
mercantile law	*qānūn tijārī*	قانون تجارى
merchandise	*baḍā'iʿ*	بضائع
merchandise marks	*ʿalāmāt as-silaʿ at-tijāriyya*	علامات السلع التجارية
merchandising	*tarwīj al-biḍāʿa*	ترويج البضاعة
merchandising manager	*mudīr tijārī*	مدير تجارى
merchant	*tājir, tijārī*	تاجر، تجارى

merchantable	*ṣāliḥ li's-sūq*	صالح للسوق
merchant bank	*maṣrif tijārī*	مصرف تجاری
merchant seaman	*baḥḥār tijārī*	بحّار تجاری
merchant shipping	*milāḥa tijāriyya*	ملاحة تجارية
merger	*indimāj, inḍimām*	اندماج ، انضمام
merit increase	*ziyādat jadāra*	زيادة جدارة
merit rating	*taqdīr al-jadāra*	تقدير الجدارة
metal products	*muntajāt maᶜdiniyya*	منتجات معدنية
meter	*mitr*	متر
method	*uslūb, ṭarīqa*	أسلوب ، طريقة
method of operation	*ṭarīqat at-tashghīl*	طريقة التشغيل
method of payment	*ṭarīqat ad-dafᶜ*	طريقة الدفع
method of voting	*ṭarīqat at-taṣwīt*	طريقة التصويت
method study	*dirāsat al-asālīb*	دراسة الاساليب
metric system	*an-niẓām al-mitrī*	النظام المترى
middleman	*wasīṭ*	وسيط
middle management	*al-idāra 'l-wusṭā*	الادارة الوسطى
migration of labour	*hijrat al-ᶜummāl*	هجرة العمّال
mileage	*aṭ-ṭūl bi'l-amyāl*	الطول بالاميال
mineral lease	*ᶜaqd ījār istithmār maᶜādin*	عقد ايجار استثمار معادن
minimise	*yakhaffiḍ li-adnā ḥadd*	يخفّض لادنى حدّ

minimise the risk	*takhfiḍ al-khaṭar li-adnā ḥadd*	تخفيض الخطر لادنى حدّ
minimum charge	*adnā ḥadd li'r-rusūm*	أدنى حدّ للرسوم
minimum lending rate	*siʿr al-iqrāḍ al-adnā*	سعر الاقراض الادنى
minimum premium	*qisṭ adnā*	قسط ادنى
minimum rate	*adnā fi'a/siʿr*	أدنى فئة/سعر
minimum value	*al-qīma 'd-dunyā*	القيمة الدنيا
minimum wage	*al-ḥadd al-adnā li'l-ajr*	الحد الادنى للاجر
ministry of agriculture	*wizārat az-zirāʿa*	وزارة الزراعة
ministry of commerce	*wizārat at-tijāra*	وزارة التجارة
ministry of external trade	*wizārat at-tijāra 'l-khārijiyya*	وزارة التجارة الخارجية
ministry of finance	*wizārat al-māliyya*	وزارة المالية
ministry of industry	*wizārat aṣ-ṣināʿa*	وزارة الصناعة
ministry of internal affairs	*wizārat ash-shu'ūn ad-dākhiliyya*	وزارة الشؤون الداخلية
ministry of justice	*wizārat al-ʿadl*	وزارة العدل
ministry of labour	*wizārat al-ʿamal*	وزارة العمل
ministry of petroleum	*wizārat an-nafṭ*	وزارة النفط
ministry of production	*wizārat al-intāj*	وزارة الانتاج
ministry of supply	*wizārat at-tamwīn*	وزارة التموين
ministry of the interior	*wizārat ad-dākhiliyya*	وزارة الداخلية
ministry of transport	*wizārat an-naql*	وزارة النقل
minority	*aqalliyya, ḥadātha*	أقلّية . حداثة

minority interest	*musāhamat al-aqalliyya*	مساهمة الاقلّية
minority report	*taqrīr al-aqalliyya*	تقرير الاقلية
minority representation	*tamthīl al-aqalliyya*	تمثيل الاقلية
minutes	*maḥḍar ijtimāʿ*	محضر اجتماع
misapplication	*isāʿat istiʿmāl/taṭbīq*	اساءة استعمال/تطبيق
misappropriation	*ikhtilās, isā'at istiʿmāl*	اختلاس، اساءة استعمال
misbehaviour	*sū' sulūk/taṣarruf*	سوء سلوك/تصرّف
miscalculate	*yukhṭi' at-taqdīr*	يخطئ التقدير
miscarriage of justice	*isā'at taṭbīq aḥkām al-ʿadāla*	اساءة تطبيق احكام العدالة
miscellaneous expenses	*maṣārīf mutanawwiʿa*	مصاريف متنوّعة
miscellaneous income	*īrād mutanawwiʿ*	ايراد متنوّع
misconception	*sū' al-fahm*	سوء الفهم
misconduct	*sū' sulūk/taṣarruf*	سوء سلوك/تصرّف
misconstrue	*yusī' al-fahm*	يسيء الفهم
misinterpret	*yusī' tafsīr*	يسيء تفسير
misleading	*muḍallil*	مضلّل
misrepresentation	*taḥrīf, isā'at tamthīl*	تحريف، اساءة تمثيل
misunderstanding	*sū' fahm/tafāhum*	سوء فهم/تفاهم
misuse of power	*sū' istiʿmāl as-sulṭa*	سوء استعمال السلطة
mitigating circumstances	*ẓurūf mukhaffifa*	ظروف مخفّفة
mitigation of damages	*takhfīḍ at-taʿwīḍāt*	تخفيض التعويضات

mixed currency	*ᶜumla mukhtalaṭa*	عملة مختلطة
mixed economy	*iqtiṣād mukhtalaṭ*	اقتصاد مختلط
model	*namūdhaj*	نموذج
moderate income	*dakhl muᶜtadil*	دخل معتدل
moderate price	*thaman muᶜtadil*	ثمن معتدل
modernization	*tajdīd*	تجديد
modification	*taᶜdīl, taḥwīr*	تعديل، تحوير
monetary fund	*ṣundūq an-naqd*	صندوق النقد
monetary income	*dakhl naqdī*	دخل نقدى
monetary measures	*tadābīr naqdiyya*	تدابير نقدية
monetary policy	*siyāsa naqdiyya*	سياسة نقدية
monetary reform	*iṣlāḥ an-naqd*	اصلاح النقد
monetary stability	*istiqrār an-naqd*	استقرار النقد
monetary standard	*qāᶜidat an-naqd*	قاعدة النقد
monetary system	*niẓām naqdī*	نظام نقدى
monetary transactions	*ṣafaqāt naqdiyya*	صفقات نقدية
monetary unit	*waḥda naqdīyya*	وحدة نقدية
monetary value	*qīma naqdiyya*	قيمة نقدية
money	*nuqūd, ᶜumla, māl*	نقود، عملة، مال
money changer	*ṣarrāf*	صرّاف
money in circulation	*al-ᶜumla 'l-mutadāwala*	العملة المتداولة

money in hand	*naqd ḥāḍir*	نقد حاضر
money lender	*muqriḍ amwāl*	مقرض أموال
money market	*sūq al-ᶜumla*	سوق العملة
money order	*ḥawāla barīdiyya*	حوالة بريدية
money supply	*mawārid al-māl*	موارد المال
money's worth	*al-muᶜādil an-naqdī*	المعادل النقدى
monopoly	*iḥtikār*	احتكار
monthly account	*ḥisāb shahrī*	حساب شهرى
monthly payment	*dufᶜa shahriyya*	دفعة شهرية
monthly report	*taqrīr shahrī*	تقرير شهرى
monthly salary	*murattab shahrī*	مرتّب شهرى
monthly statement	*bayān shahrī, kashf ḥisāb shahrī*	بيان شهرى. كشف حساب شهرى
moonlighting	*al-jamᶜ bayn waẓīfatayn*	الجمع بين وظيفتين
morale	*ar-rūḥ al-maᶜnawiyya*	الروح المعنوية
moral incentive	*ḥāfiz akhlāqī*	حافز اخلاقى
mortality rate	*muᶜaddal al-wafayāt*	معدّل الوفيات
mortality risk	*khaṭar al-mawt*	خطر الموت
mortality statistics	*iḥṣāᶜiyyāt al-wafayāt*	احصائيات الوفيات
mortgage	*rahn*	رهن
mortgage bond	*sanad rahn*	سند رهن
mortgage charges	*maṣārīf rahn*	مصاريف رهن

mortgage debt	*dayn rahn*	دين رهن
mortgage deed	^{c}*aqd/sanad rahn*	عقد/سند رهن
mortgagee	*murtahin, dā'in*	مرتهن . دائن
mortgage, foreclose a	*yughliq ar-rahn*	يغلق الرهن
mortgage insurance	*ta'mīn rahn*	تأمين رهن
mortgage loan	*qarḍ liqā' rahn*	قرض لقاء رهن
mortgage, redemption of	*fakk ar-rahn*	فكّ الرهن
mortgagor	*rāhin, madīn*	راهن . مدين
most-favoured-nation clause	*sharṭ awla 'd-duwal bi'l-murā*^{c}*āh*	شرط أولى الدول بالمراعاة
motion of censure	*iqtirāḥ bi-tawjīh al-lawm*	اقتراح بتوجيه اللوم
motion, to adopt a	*yatabanna iqtirāḥ*	يتبنّى اقتراحا
motion, to amend a	*yu*^{c}*addil iqtirāḥ*	يعدّل اقتراحا
motion, to table a	*ya*^{c}*riḍ iqtirāḥ li'l-baḥth*	يعرض اقتراحا للبحث
motivate	*yaḥfiz, yadfa*^{c}	يحفز. يدفع
motivating conditions	*ẓurūf dāfi*^{c}*a*	ظروف دافعة
motivation	*ḥafz, ithārat ḥawāfiz*	حفز. اثارة حوافز
motor-car industry	*ṣinā*^{c}*at as-sayyārāt*	صناعة السيارات
motor car insurance	*ta'mīn as-sayyārāt*	تأمين سيارات
motor transport	*naql bi's-sayyārāt*	نقل بالسيارات
moveable property	*amwāl manqūla*	أموال منقولة
moveables	*manqūlāt, amti*^{c}*a*	منقولات. امتعة

movement	*ḥaraka*	حركة
movement of capital	*ḥarakat ar-ra'salmāl*	حركة الرأس مال
movement of goods	*naql as-silaᶜ*	نقل السلع
movement of labour	*intiqāl al-yad al-ᶜāmila*	انتقال اليد العاملة
multilateral	*mutaᶜaddid al-jawānib*	متعدّد الجوانب
multilateral agreement	*ittifāqiyya mutaᶜaddidat al-jawānib*	اتّفاقية متعدّدة الجوانب
multinational company	*sharika tamlikhā duwal wa taᶜmal fī duwal*	شركة تملكها دول وتعمل فى دول
multiple representation	*tamthīl mutaᶜaddid*	تمثيل متعدّد
multiple taxation	*ḍarā'ib mutaᶜaddida*	ضرائب متعدّدة
municipal bond	*sanad baladī*	سند بلدى
municipal law	*qānūn baladiyya*	قانون بلدية
municipal loans	*qurūḍ baladiyya*	قروض بلدية
municipal taxes	*ḍarā'ib al-baladiyyāt*	ضرائب البلديات
mutual agreement	*ittifāq mutabādal*	اتّفاق متبادل
mutual assistance	*musāᶜada mutabādala*	مساعدة متبادلة
mutual benefits	*manāfiᶜ mutabādala*	منافع متبادلة
mutual confidence	*thiqa mutabādala*	ثقة متبادلة
mutual consent	*riḍā' mutabādal*	رضاء متبادل
mutual consideration	*ᶜiwaḍ mutabādal*	عوض متبادل
mutual co-operation	*taᶜāwun*	تعاون
mutual debts	*duyūn mutabādala*	ديون متبادلة

mutual guarantee	*ḍamān mutabādal*	ضمان متبادل
mutual help	*musāᶜada mutabādala*	مساعدة متبادلة
mutual interests	*maṣāliḥ mushtaraka*	مصالح مشتركة
mutual promises	*wuᶜūd mutabādala*	وعود متبادلة
mutual respect	*iḥtirām mutabādal*	احترام متبادل
mutual understanding	*tafāhum mutabādal*	تفاهم متبادل

N

naked facts	*ḥaqā'iq wāḍiḥa*	حقائق واضحة
name and address	*al-ism wa'l-ᶜunwān*	الاسم والعنوان
name a price	*yuᶜayyin siᶜr*	يعيّن سعر
named insured	*ash-shakhṣ al-mu'amman ᶜalayh*	الشخص المؤمّن عليه
nameless	*ghayr musammā*	غير مسمّى
name of the company	*ism ash-sharika*	اسم الشركة
narrow market	*sūq māliyya ḍayyiqa*	سوق مالية ضيّقة
national advertising	*iᶜlān ᶜāmm*	اعلان عامّ
national bank	*al-maṣrif al-waṭanī/ḥukūmī*	المصرف الوطنى/الحكومى
national debt	*ad-dayn al-ᶜāmm*	الدين العام
national economy	*iqtiṣād qawmī*	اقتصاد قومى
national income	*dakhl qawmī*	دخل قومى
national insurance	*ta'mīn qawmī*	تأمين قومى
national interest	*maṣlaḥa qawmiyya*	مصلحة قومية

nationality	*al-jinsiyya*	الجنسية
nationalization	*ta'mīm*	تأميم
nationalization	*ta'mīm*	تأميم
nationalization of foreign investments	*ta'mīm al-istithmārāt al-ajnabiyya*	تأميم الاستثمارات الاجنبية
nationalize	*yu'ammim*	يؤمّم
nationalized industry	*ṣināʿa mu'ammama*	صناعة مؤممة
national requirement	*maṭlab qawmī*	مطلب قومى
native labour	*ʿummāl min ahl al-balad*	عمّال من اهل البلد
natural environment	*al-bī'a 'ṭ-ṭabīʿiyya*	البيئة الطبيعية
natural growth	*numuww ṭabīʿī*	نموّ طبيعى
natural increase	*ziyāda ṭabīʿiyya*	زيادة طبيعية
natural outlets for exports	*manāfidh ṭabīʿiyya li'ṣ-ṣādirāt*	منافذ طبيعية للصادرات
natural resources	*mawārid ṭabīʿiyya*	موارد طبيعية
natural wastage	*fuqdān ṭabīʿī*	فقدان طبيعى
nature of business	*ṭabīʿat al-ʿamal*	طبيعة العمل
nautical mile	*mīl baḥrī*	ميل بحرى
navigable waters	*miyāh ṣāliḥa li'l-milāḥa*	مياه صالحة للملاحة
navigation dues	*rusūm milāḥa*	رسوم ملاحة
navigation laws	*al-qawānīn al-baḥriyya*	القوانين البحرية
navigation permit	*rukhṣat milāḥa*	رخصة ملاحة
nearest port	*aqrab mīnā'*	اقرب ميناء

necessity, in case of	*ᶜind aḍ-ḍarūra*	عند الضرورة
negative attitude	*mawqif salbī*	موقف سلبى
negligence	*ihmāl*	اهمال
negligence clause	*band al-ihmāl*	بند الاهمال
negligible amount	*mablagh tāfih*	مبلغ تافه
negligible error	*khata' yumkin ihmāluh*	خطأ يمكن اهماله
negligible quantity	*kammiyya lā tastaḥiqq adh-dhikr*	كمّية لا تستحقّ الدكر
negotiable	*qābil li't-tadāwul*	قابل للتداول
negotiable bill of exchange	*kambiyāla qābila li't-tadāwul*	كمبيالة قابلة للتداول
negotiable bill of lading	*būlīṣat shaḥn qābila li't-tadāwul*	بوليصة شحن قابلة للتداول
negotiable bond	*sanad qābil li't-tadāwul*	سند قابل للتداول
negotiable documents	*wathā'iq qābila li't-tadāwul*	وثائق قابلة للتداول
negotiable instrument	*waraqa qābila li't-tadāwul*	ورقة قابلة للتداول
negotiable note	*kambiyāla qābila li't-tadāwul*	كمبيالة قابلة للتداول
negotiable title	*sanad qābil li't-taḥwīl*	سند قابل للتحويل
negotiability of a bill	*qābiliyyat as-sanad li't-taḥwīl*	قابلية السند للتحويل
negotiate	*yufāwiḍ*	يفاوض
negotiate a bargain	*yufāwiḍ ᶜalā ṣafqa*	يفاوض على صفقة
negotiate a loan	*yatafāwaḍ ᶜalā qarḍ*	يتفاوض على قرض
negotiation	*tafāwuḍ, taḥwīl*	تفاوض. تحويل
negotiations are in progress	*al-mufāwaḍāt jāriya*	المفاوضات جارية

negotiations are proceeding	*al-mufāwaḍāt jāriya*	المفاوضات جارية
negotiations, preliminary	*mufāwaḍāt tamhīdiyya*	مفاوضات تمهيدية
negotiations, recent	*al-mufāwaḍāt al-ḥadītha/al-akhīra*	المفاوضات الحديثة / الاخيرة
negotiations, to enter into	*yubāshir al-mufāwaḍāt*	يباشر المفاوضات
negotiation, under	*qayd al-mufawāḍa*	قيد المفاوضة
negotiator	*mufāwiḍ*	مفاوض
net	*ṣāfī*	صاف
net assets	*aṣl ṣāfī*	أصل صاف
net costs	*takālīf ṣāfiya*	تكاليف صافية
net earnings	*maksab ṣāfī*	مكسب صافى
net income	*dakhl/īrād ṣāfī*	دخل/ايراد صاف
net income after tax	*dakhl ṣāfī baᶜd aḍ-ḍarība*	دخل صافى بعد الضريبة
net interest	*ṣāfi 'l-fā'ida*	صافى الفائدة
net investment	*ṣāfi 'l-istithmār*	صافى الاستثمار
net loss	*ṣāfi 'l-khasāra*	صافى الخسارة
net outlay	*ṣāfi 't-takālīf al-mabda'iyya*	صافى التكاليف المبدئية
net output	*intāj ṣāfī*	انتاج صافى
net premium	*qisṭ ṣāfī*	قسط صاف
net price	*as-siᶜr aṣ-ṣāfī*	السعر الصافى
net proceeds	*ṣāfi 'l-ᶜā'id*	صافى العائد
net profit	*ribḥ ṣāfī*	ربح صاف

net profit on sales	*ṣāfī ribḥ al-mabīᶜāt*	صافى ربح المبيعات
net revenue	*ṣāfi 'l-īrād*	صافى الايراد
net sales	*ṣāfi 'l-mabīᶜāt*	صافى المبيعات
net tonnage	*ṣāfi 'l-aṭnān*	صافى الاطنان
net weight	*al-wazn al-ṣāfī*	الوزن الصافى
network	*shabaka*	شبكة
net working capital	*ṣāfi ra's al-māl al-ᶜāmil*	صافى رأس المال العامل
network of roads	*shabakat aṭ-ṭuruq*	شبكة الطرق
net yield	*an-nātij aṣ-ṣāfī*	الناتج الصافى
neutral port	*mīnā' muḥāyid*	ميناء محايد
new business	*ᶜamal jadīd*	عمل جديد
new assignment	*takhṣīṣ jadīd*	تخصيص جديد
new device	*ikhtirāᶜ jadīd*	اختراع جديد
new issue	*iṣdār jadīd*	اصدار جديد
new issue of shares	*iṣdār jadīd li'l-ashum*	اصدار جديد للاسهم
newly-employed labour	*ᶜamal mustakhdam ḥadīthan*	عمل مستخدم حديثا
new resources	*mawārid jadīda*	موارد جديدة
news agency	*wikālat anbā'*	وكالة أنباء
news bulletin	*nashrat akhbār*	نشرة أخبار
newspaper	*ṣaḥīfa, jarīda*	صحيفة ٠ جريدة
newspaper advertisement	*iᶜlān fī ṣaḥīfa*	اعلان فى صحيفة

newspaper cutting	*quṣāṣat jarīda*	قصاصة جريدة
newsprint	*waraq aṣ-ṣuḥuf*	ورق الصحف
newsreel	*anbā' as-sinama*	أنباء السينما
next month	*ash-shahr al-qādim*	الشهر القادم
next of kin	*adna 'l-aqārib*	أدنى الاقارب
night safe	*khizāna layliyya*	خزانة ليلية
night shift	*nawba layliyya*	نوبة ليلية
night watchman	*ḥāris/murāqib laylī*	حارس ليلى، مراقب ليلى
nil balance	*ar-raṣīd ṣifr*	الرصيد صفر
no admittance	*mamnū^c al-dukhūl*	ممنوع الدخول
no bid	*ghayr maṭlūb*	غير مطلوب
no change	*dūna taghyīr*	دون تغيير
noisy meeting	*ijtimā^c ṣākhib*	اجتماع صاخب
nominal	*ismī*	اسمى
nominal account	*ḥisāb ismī*	حساب اسمى
nominal capital	*ra'smāl ismī*	رأسمال اسمى
nominal damages	*aḍrār/ta^cwīḍāt ismiyya*	أضرار/تعويضات اسمية
nominal fine	*gharāma tāfiha*	غرامة تافهة
nominal interest	*fā'ida ismiyya*	فائدة اسمية
nominal output	*intāj ismī*	انتاج اسمى
nominal partner	*sharīk ismī*	شريك اسمى

nominal price	*si^cr ismī*	سعر اسمى
nominal share	*sahm ismī*	سهم اسمى
nominal value	*qīma ismiyya*	قيمة اسمية
nominal wages	*'ujūr ismiyya*	أجور اسمية
non-acceptable	*ghayr maqbūl*	غير مقبول
non-acceptance	*ᶜadam qabūl*	عدم قبول
non-access to markets	*ᶜadam al-wuṣūl ila'l-aswāq*	عدم الوصول الى الأسواق
non-aggression	*ᶜadam al-iᶜtidā'*	عدم الاعتداء
non-appearance	*ᶜadam al-ḥuḍūr*	عدم الحضور
non-assessible	*ghayr mukallaf bi'ḍ-ḍarība*	غير مكلّف بالضريبة
non-available	*ghayr mutawaffir*	غير متوفّر
non-committal	*ᶜadam iltizām*	عدم التزام
non-compliance	*ᶜadam al-imtithāl*	عدم الامتثال
non-conditional acceptance	*qubūl bilā qayd aw sharṭ*	قبول بلا قيد أو شرط
non-convertible currency	*ᶜumla ghayr qābila li't-taḥwīl*	عملة غير قابلة للتحويل
non-co-operative	*ghayr mutaᶜāwin*	غير متعاون
non-cumulative bonds	*sanadāt ghayr mujammaᶜat al-arbāḥ*	سندات غير مجمعّة الارباح
non-deductible	*ghayr qābil li'l-ḥasm*	غير قابل للحسم
non-delivery of goods	*ᶜadam taslīm a-baḍā'iᶜ*	عدم تسليم البضائع
non-disclosure	*kitmān, ᶜadam iẓhār*	كتمان، عدم اظهار
non-discriminatory	*bilā tafriqa/tamyīz*	بلا تفرقة/تمييز

non-discriminatory practices	*asālīb lā tahdif ila 't-tafriqa*	اساليب لا تهدف الى التفرقة
non-disposal of goods	*ᶜadam taṣrīf as-silaᶜ*	عدم تصريف السلع
non-durable	*tālif, hālik*	تالف . هالك
non-durable goods	*baḍā'iᶜ ghayr matīna*	بضائع غير متينة
non-effective	*ᶜadīm al-athar*	عديم الاثر
non-essentials	*mawādd ghayr asāsiyya*	موادّ غير اساسية
non-existence	*ᶜadam al-wujūd*	عدم الوجود
non-fulfilment	*ᶜadam al-injāz*	عدم الانجاز
non-interest-bearing account	*ḥisāb bilā fawā'id*	حساب بلا فوائد
non-interference	*ᶜadam at-tadakhkhul*	عدم التدخّل
non-intervention	*ᶜadam at-tadakhkhul*	عدم التدخّل
non-involvement	*ᶜadam at-tawarruṭ*	عدم التورّط
non-liability clause	*sharṭ ᶜadam al-mas'ūliyya*	شرط عدم المسؤولية
non-negotiable	*ghayr qābil li't-tadāwul*	غير قابل للتداول
non-operating company	*sharika ghayr ᶜāmila*	شركة غير عاملة
non-participating policy	*būlīṣa bilā mushāraka fi'l-arbāḥ*	بوليصة بلا مشاركة فى الارباح
non-payment	*ᶜadam ad-dafᶜ*	عدم الدفع
non-performance	*ᶜadam al-ᶜamal*	عدم العمل
non-productive	*ghayr muntij*	غير منتج
non-profit corporation	*mu'assasa lā tastahdif ar-ribḥ*	مؤسّسة لا تستهدف الربح
non-profit organization	*munaẓẓama lā tastahdif ar-ribḥ*	منظّمة لا تستهدف الربح

non-recurring expenses	*nafaqāt istithnā'iyya*	نفقات استثنائية
non-resident	*ghayr muqīm*	غير مقيم
non-stop	*dūna tawaqquf*	دون توقّف
non-taxable	*ghayr khāḍiᶜ li-ḍ-ḍarība*	غير خاضع للضريبة
non-tax revenue	*īrādāt laysa maṣdarha 'ḍ-ḍarā'ib*	ايرادات ليس مصدرها الضرائب
non-transferable	*ghayr qābil li't-taḥwīl*	غير قابل للتحويل
non-variable	*lā yataghayyar*	لا يتغيّر
non-voting equity	*ashum bilā ḥaqq taṣwīt*	أسهم بلا حقّ تصويت
no quotation	*ghayr muthabbat as-siᶜr bi'l-būrṣa*	غير مثبّت السعر بالبورصة
no reply	*lā jawāb*	لا جواب
norm	*miqyās, namūdhaj*	مقياس، نموذج
normal distribution	*tawzīᶜ ᶜādī/ṭabīᶜī*	توزيع عادى/طبيعى
normal price	*siᶜr ᶜādī*	سعر عادى
normal relations	*ᶜalāqāt ᶜādiyya*	علاقات عادية
normal return	*al-ᶜā'id al-ᶜādī*	العائد العادى
normal state of affairs	*al-ḥāla 'ṭ-ṭabīᶜiyya*	الحالة الطبيعية
normal value	*qīma ᶜādiyya*	قيمة عادية
normal working day	*yawm ᶜamal ᶜādī*	يوم عمل عادى
no sale	*laysa li'l-bayᶜ*	ليس للبيع
not acceptable	*ghayr maqbūl*	غير مقبول
notarial seal	*khitm tawthīqī*	ختم توثيقى

notary public	*muwaththiq ^{c}āmm, kātib al-^{c}adl*	موثّق عامّ. كاتب العدل
notary's deed	*sanad muwaththaq*	سند موثّق
notary's office	*dā'ira al-kātib al-^{c}adl*	دائرة الكاتب العدل
note, credit	*bayān bi'l-i^{c}timād*	بيان بالاعتماد
note, consignment	*mudhakkirat shaḥn/irsāl*	مذكرة شحن/ارسال
note, cover	*ish^{c}ār ta'mīn*	اشعار تأمين
note, debit	*bayān bi'd-dayn*	بيان بالدين
note payable	*kambiyālat daf^c*	كمبيالة دفع
notes in circulation	*awrāq māliyya mutadāwala*	أوراق مالية متداولة
notes issued	*awrāq māliyya muṣdara*	أوراق مالية مصدّرة
notes payable	*awrāq ad-daf^c*	أوراق الدفع
notes receivable	*awrāq al-qabḍ*	أوراق القبض
not exceeding	*lā yatajāwaz, lā yazīd ^{c}an*	لا يتجاوز. لا يزيد عن
no thoroughfare	*mamnū^c al-murūr*	ممنوع المرور
notice	*ikhṭār, ish^{c}ār, indhār*	اخطار. اشعار. انذار
notice board	*lawḥat i^{c}lānāt*	لوحة اعلانات
notice of dismissal	*kitāb tasrīḥ, khiṭāb bi'l-faṣl*	كتاب تسريح . خطاب بالفصل
notice of injury	*bayān bi-ḥādith*	بيان بحادث
notice of receipt	*ish^{c}ār istilām*	اشعار استلام
notice of termination	*ikhṭār bi'l-intihā'*	اخطار بالانتهاء
notice to pay	*indhār bi'd-daf^c*	انذار بالدفع

notice to quit	*ikhṭār musta'jir li-yukhli 'l-ᶜaqār*	اخطار مستأجر ليخلى العقار
notification of protest	*ikhṭār iḥtijāj*	اخطار احتجاج
notional income	*dakhl muftaraḍ*	دخل مفترض
not negotiable	*ghayr qābil li't-taḥwīl/li't-tādawul*	غير قابل للتحويل/للتداول
novel	*jadīd, ḥadīth*	جديد • حديث
novelty	*jidda, shay' jadīd*	جدّة • شيء جديد
now in production	*jāri 'l-intāj*	جارى الانتاج
now loading	*jāri 't-taḥmīl*	جارى التحميل
now operating	*yaᶜmal al-ān*	يعمل الآن
nuclear	*nawawī*	نووى
nuclear fuel	*waqūd nawawī*	وقود نووى
nuclear energy	*ṭāqa nawawiyya*	طاقة نووية
nuclear industry	*aṣ-ṣināᶜa 'n-nawawiyya*	الصناعة النووية
nuclear material	*mādda nawawiyya*	مادّة نووية
nuclear plant	*maṣnaᶜ nawawī*	مصنع نووى
nuclear power	*kahrabā'/quwwa nawawiyya*	كهرباء نووية
nuclear research	*abḥāth nawawiyya*	أبحاث نووية
nuclear tests	*tajārib nawawiyya*	تجارب نووية
nuclear weapon	*silāḥ nawawī*	سلاح نووى
nuisance value	*qīmat taḍarrur*	قيمة تضرّر
null	*bāṭil, lāghin*	باطل• لاغٍ

null and void	*bāṭil wa ghayr wārid*	باطل وغير وارد
nullity of contract	*buṭlān ᶜaqd*	بطلان عقد
numerical value	*qīma ᶜadadiyya*	قيمة عددية

O

objection	*iᶜtirāḍ*	اعتراض
objection overruled	*al-iᶜtirāḍ marfūḍ*	الاعتراض مرفوض
objective, ultimate	*hadaf nihā'ī*	هدف نهائى
obligation	*iltizām, ilzām*	التزام ، الزام
obligations, outstanding	*iltizāmāt muᶜallaqa*	التزامات معلقة
obligation to disclose	*iltizām bi'l-ibdā'*	التزام بالإبداء
obligatory insurance	*ta'mīn ijbārī*	تأمين اجبارى
observation	*mulāḥaẓa*	ملاحظة
obsolescence	*buṭlān istiᶜmāl, hajr*	بطلان استعمال، هجر
obtain an extension of time	*yaḥṣul ᶜalā tamdīd al-muhla*	يحصل على تمديد المهلة
occasional income	*īrād ᶜaraḍī*	ايراد عرضى
occupation	*mihna*	مهنة
occupational disease	*maraḍ mihnī*	مرض مهنى
occupational hazard	*khaṭar mihnī*	خطر مهنى

offer	*ᶜarḍ*	عرض
offer and acceptance	*ijāb wa qabūl*	ايجاب وقبول
offer, firm	*ᶜarḍ thābit*	عرض ثابت
offer for sale	*ᶜarḍ li'l-bayᶜ*	عرض للبيع
offer of services	*ᶜarḍ khadamāt*	عرض خدمات
offer, verbal	*ᶜarḍ shafahī*	عرض شفهى
office	*maktab, manṣib*	مكتب ، منصب
office, central	*al-maktab al-markazī*	المكتب المركزى
office copy	*nuskhat al-maktab*	نسخة المكتب
office equipment	*muᶜiddāt maktab*	معدّات مكتب
office expenses	*maṣārīf maktab*	مصاريف مكتب
office furniture and equipment	*athāth wa muᶜiddāt al-maktab*	اثاث ومعدات مكتب
office, head	*al-markaz ar-ra'īsī*	المركز الرئيسى
office hours	*waqt ad-dawām, waqt al-ᶜamal*	وقت الدوام ، وقت العمل
office maintenance	*ṣiyānat al-maktab*	صيانة المكتب
office management	*idārat al-maktab*	ادارة المكتب
office manager	*mudīr maktab*	مدير مكتب
office premises	*mabnā al-makātib*	مبنى المكاتب
officer	*muwaẓẓaf, ḍābiṭ*	موظّف ، ضابط
office staff	*hay'at muwaẓẓafi 'l-maktab*	هيئة موظّفى المكتب
office, to continue in	*yastamirr fi manṣibih*	يستمرّ فى منصبه

office, to extend the term of	*yumaddid muddat waẓīfa*	يمدّد مدّة وظيفة
office work	*ᶜamal maktabī*	عمل مكتبى
official announcement	*iᶜlān rasmī*	اعلان رسمى
official appointment	*mīᶜād rasmī*	ميعاد رسمى
official bond	*kafāla rasmiyya*	كفالة رسمية
official communiqué	*balāgh rasmī*	بلاغ رسمى
official confirmation	*ta'kīd rasmī*	تأكيد رسمى
official document	*wathīqa rasmiyya*	وثيقة رسمية
official estimate	*taqdīr rasmī*	تقدير رسمى
official language	*al-lugha ar-rasmiyya*	اللغة الرسمية
official notification	*ishᶜār rasmī*	اشعار رسمى
official quotation	*as-siᶜr ar-rasmī*	السعر الرسمى
official rate	*siᶜr al-khaṣm ar-rasmī*	سعر الخصم الرسمى
official rate of exchange	*siᶜr at-taḥwīl ar-rasmī*	سعر التحويل الرسمى
official receiver	*ma'mūr at-taflīsa, ḥāris qaḍā'ī*	مأمور التفليسة ، حارس قضائى
official recognition	*iᶜtirāf rasmī*	اعتراف رسمى
official secrets	*asrār rasmiyya/ḥukūmiyya*	اسرار رسمية /حكومية
official statement	*bayān rasmī*	بيان رسمى
official visit	*ziyāra rasmiyya*	زيارة رسمية
oil company	*sharikat nafṭ*	شركة نفط
oil concession	*imtiyāz nafṭ*	امتياز نفط

oil exporter	*muṣaddir li'n-nafṭ*	مصدّر للنفط
oil-field	*ḥaql nafṭ*	حقل نفط
oil importer	*mustawrid li'n-nafṭ*	مستورد للنفط
oil industry	*aṣ-ṣināᶜa an-nafṭiyya*	الصناعة النفطية
oil market	*sūq an-nafṭ*	سوق النفط
oil processing industries	*ṣināᶜāt taṣnīᶜ an-nafṭ*	صناعات تصنيع النفط
oil producers	*muntiju 'n-nafṭ*	منتجو النفط
oil resources	*mawārid nafṭiyya*	موارد نفطية
oil revenues	*īrādāt an-nafṭ*	ايرادات النفط
oil royalties	*ᶜā'idāt an-nafṭ*	عائدات النفط
oil sector	*qiṭāᶜ an-nafṭ*	قطاع النفط
oil shares	*ashum sharikāt an-nafṭ*	اسهم شركات النفط
oil supplies	*imdādāt an-nafṭ*	امدادات النفط
oil tanker	*nāqilat nafṭ*	ناقلة نفط
oil terminal	*maḥaṭṭat shaḥn nafṭ li'taṣdīr*	محطّة شحن نفط للتصدير
oil well	*bi'r nafṭ*	بئر نفط
oil wealth	*tharwa nafṭiyya*	ثروة نفطية
old papers	*awrāq qadīma*	اوراق قديمة
omission	*ighfāl, ihmāl*	اغفال. اهمال
omission to act	*imtināᶜ ᶜan fiᶜl awjabahu 'l-qānūn*	امتناع عن فعل أوجبه القانون
on account	*ᶜala'l-ḥisāb*	على الحساب

on account of	*bi-sabab*	بسبب
on application	^{c}*ind aṭ-ṭalab, bi'l-iktitāb*	عند الطلب ، بالاكتتاب
on approval	^{c}*alā sabīl at-tajriba qabl ash-shirā'*	على سبيل التجربة قبل الشراء
on credit	^{c}*ala 'l-ḥisāb, bi-dayn*	على الحساب.بدين
on delivery	^{c}*ind at-taslīm*	عند التسليم
on demand	^{c}*ind aṭ-ṭalab*	عند الطلب
onerous contract	^{c}*aqd muthqal bi'ltizām*	عقد مثقل بالتزام
on examination	*ba*^{c}*d al-mu*^{c}*āyana, ba*^{c}*d al-faḥṣ*	بعد المعاينة ، بعد الفحص
on hand	*fi'l-yad. mawjūd*	فى اليد ، موجود
on order	*taḥt aṭ-ṭalab*	تحت الطلب
on record	*mudawwan, musajjal*	مدوّن ، مسجّل
on request	^{c}*ind aṭ-ṭalab*	عند الطلب
on sale	*li'l-bay*^{c}	للبيع
on sale or return	*li'l-bay*^{c} *aw li'l-murtaja*^{c}	للبيع او للمرتجع
on-the-job training	*tadrīb athnā' al-*^{c}*amal*	تدريب أثناء العمل
open account	*ḥisāb maftūḥ*	حساب مفتوح
open-ended contract	^{c}*aqd maftūḥ*	عقد مفتوح
opening bid	*al-*^{c}*arḍ al-awwal*	العرض الاوّل
opening of tender	*fatḥ maẓārīf al-munāqaṣa*	فتح مظاريف المناقصة
opening price	*si*^{c}*r al-iftitāḥ*	سعر الافتتاح
open market	*sūq māliyya ḥurra*	سوق مالية حرّة

open meeting	*ijtimāᶜ ᶜalanī*	اجتماع علنى
open plan office	*maktab dākhiluh maftūḥ bilā ḥawājiz*	مكتب داخله مفتوح بلا حواجز
operating budget	*mizāniyyat at-tashghīl*	ميزانية التشغيل
operating capital	*ra'smāl tashghīl*	رأس مال تشغيل
operating company	*sharikat tashghīl*	شركة تشغيل
operating costs	*nafaqāt at-tashghīl*	نفقات التشغيل
operating cycle	*dawrat at-tashghīl*	دورة التشغيل
operating effectiveness	*kafā'at at-tashghīl*	كفاءة التشغيل
operating expense	*maṣrūfat at-tashghīl*	مصروفات التشغيل
operating income	*dakhl min at-tashghīl*	دخل من التشغيل
operating instructions	*taᶜlīmāt at-tashghīl*	تعليمات التشغيل
operating loss	*khasāra min at-tashghīl*	خسارة من التشغيل
operating profit	*ribḥ at-tashghīl*	ربح التشغيل
operating ratio	*nisbat at-tashghīl*	نسبة التشغيل
operating results	*natā'ij at-tashghīl*	نتائج التشغيل
operating time	*waqt al-tashghīl, waqt al-ᶜamaliyya*	وقت العملية/التشغيل
operational research	*buḥūth al-ᶜamaliyyāt*	بحوث العمليات
operations	*ᶜamaliyyāt (al-mu'assasa)*	عمليات (المؤسّسة)
operation, to come into	*yabda' al-ᶜamal*	يبدأ العمل
operator	*mushaghghil*	مشغّل
opinion of the court	*ra'y al-maḥkama*	رأى المحكمة

opinion, to request a legal	*yaṭlub ra'yan qānūniyyan*	يطلب رأيا قانونيا
optimum output	*al-intāj al-amthal*	الانتاج الامثل
option	*khiyār*	خيار
optional clause	*sharṭ/band khiyārī*	شرط/بند خيارى
optional dividend	*ḥiṣṣat arbāḥ ikhtiyāriyya*	حصّة أرباح اختيارية
option contract	*ᶜaqd ikhtiyārī*	عقد اختيارى
option price	*siᶜr sharṭī, siᶜr khiyārī*	سعر شرطى/خيارى
oral agreement	*ittifāq shafahī*	اتّفاق شفهى
oral complaint	*shakwā basīṭa*	شكوى بسيطة
oral contract	*ᶜaqd shafahī*	عقد شفهى
oral examination	*imtiḥān shafahī*	امتحان شفهى
order	*amr, ṭalab*	أمر • طلب
order book	*sijill aṭ-ṭalabāt at-tijāriyya*	سجلّ الطلبات التجارية
order department	*qism aṭ-ṭalabāt*	قسم الطلبات
order form	*istimārat aṭ-ṭalab*	استمارة الطلب
order of merit	*wisām al-istiḥqāq*	وسام الاستحقاق
order of precedence	*niẓām al-asbaqiyya*	نظام الأسبقية
ordinary	*ᶜādī*	عادى
ordinary business	*tijāra ᶜādiyya, ᶜamal ᶜādī*	تجارة عادية • عمل عادى
ordinary creditor	*dā'in ᶜādī*	دائن عادى
ordinary interest	*fā'ida ᶜādiyya*	فائدة عادية

ordinary meeting	*ijtimā^{c} ^{c}ādī*	اجتماع عادى
ordinary partnership	*sharika basīṭa ^{c}ādiyya*	شركة بسيطة عادية
ordinary shares	*ashum ^{c}ādiyya*	اسهم عادية
ordinary stock	*ashum ^{c}ādiyya*	أسهم عادية
organization	*mu'assasa, hay'a, tanẓīm*	مؤسّسة • هيئة • تنظيم
organization and methods	*at-tanẓīm wa'l-asālīb*	التنظيم والاساليب
organization chart	*rasm bayānī li't-tanẓīm*	رسم بيانى للتنظيم
organization expenses	*maṣrūfat at-tanẓīm*	مصروفات التنظيم
organization manual	*dalīl ash-sharika*	دليل الشركة
organization planning	*takhṭīṭ at-tanẓīm*	تخطيط التنظيم
organized labour	*^{c}ummāl fī tanẓīm niqābī*	عمّال فى تنظيم نقابى
organogram	*rasm at-tanẓīm*	رسم التنظيم
orientation	*tawjīh, ta^{c}rīf bi'l-^{c}amal*	توجيه • تعريف بالعمل
original bill of exchange	*kambiyāla aṣliyya*	كمبيالة أصلية
original bill of lading	*būlīṣat shaḥn aṣliyya*	بوليصة شحن أصلية
original copy	*nuskha aṣliyya*	نسخة أصلية
original entry	*al-qayd al-awwal*	القيد الاوّل
original text	*an-naṣṣ al-aṣlī*	النصّ الاصلى
other income	*īrādāt 'ukhrā*	ايرادات أخرى
outbid	*ya^{c}riḍ thaman a^{c}lā*	يعرض ثمنا أعلى
outcome	*natīja, ḥāṣil*	نتيجة • حاصل

outdated	*maḍā zamanuh, baṭal isti^cmāluh*	مضى زمنه ، بطل استعماله
outdoor staff	*muwaẓẓafūn khārijiyyūn*	موظّفون خارجيون
outgoings	*nafaqāt*	نفقات
outlay	*nafaqāt mabda'iyya*	نفقات مبدئية
outlet	*majāl li-taṣrīf as-silaᶜ*	محلّ لتصريف السلع
outlet for trade	*majāl li't-tijāra*	مجال للتجارة
outline process chart	*rasm bayānī mujmal li'l-ᶜamaliyya*	رسم بيانى مجمل للعملية
out of date	*mutaqādim, bāṭil*	متقادم ، باطل
out of hand	*khārij ᶜan as-sayṭara*	خارج عن السيطرة
out-of-pocket expenses	*maṣrūfāt nathriyya iḍāfiyya*	مصروفات نثرية اضافية
out of print	*nafadat ṭabᶜatuh*	نفدت طبعته
out of stock	*biḍāᶜa nafadat*	بضاعة نفدت
out of the question	*ghayr wārid, mustaḥīl*	غير وارد ، مستحيل
out of time	*khārij al-waqt al-muḥaddad, muta'akhkhir*	خارج الوقت المحدّد ، متأخّر
output	*maḥṣūl*	محصول
outsider	*dakhīl, gharīb*	دخيل ، غريب
outstanding	*muta'akhkhir, lam yusaddad baᶜd*	متأخّر ، لم يسدّد بعد
outstanding cheque	*shīk lam yuṣraf*	شيك لم يصرف
outstanding debt	*dayn mustaḥiqq*	دين مستحقّ
outstanding expenses	*nafaqāt mustaḥiqqat ad-dafᶜ*	نفقات مستحقّة الدفع
outstanding loans	*qurūḍ mustaḥiqqa*	قروض مستحقّة

outstanding matter	*qaḍiyya muᶜallaqa*	قضية معلّقة
outstanding payment	*dafᶜa lam tusaddad baᶜd*	دفعة لم تسدّد بعد
overall deficit	*ᶜajz ijmālī*	عجز الاجمالى
overall gain	*mujmal al-maksab*	مجمل المكسب
overall loss	*mujmal al-khasāra*	مجمل الخسارة
overall surplus	*mujmal al-fā'iḍ*	مجمل الفائض
overcapacity	*ṭāqa zā'ida*	طاقة زائدة
over-capitalize	*yufriṭ fī tamwīl*	يفرط فى تمويل
overcharge, to	*yaqtaḍī thaman fāḥish, yufriṭ fi shaḥn,*	يقتضى ثمنا فاحشا. يفرط فى شحن
overdraft	*saḥb ᶜala'l-makshūf*	سحب على المكشوف
overdraw	*yasḥab ᶜala 'l-makshūf*	يسحب على المكشوف
overdrawn account	*ḥisāb makshūf*	حساب مكشوف
overdue	*muta'akhkhir, fāt mawᶜid al-istiḥqāq*	متأخّر. فات موعد الاستحقاق
overdue payment	*dafᶜa muta'akhkhira*	دفعة متاخّرة
overestimate	*yubāligh fī taqdīr*	يبالغ فى تقدير
over-estimation	*mughālāh fi't-taqdīr*	مغالاة فى التقدير
overhaul	*yudaqqiq, yurājiᶜ*	يدقّق . يراجع
overhead	*ghayr mubāshir*	غير مباشر
overhead expenses	*maṣrūfāt thābita ghayr mubāshira*	مصروفات ثابتة غير مباشرة
overheads	*maṣrūfāt thābita ghayr mubāshira*	مصروفات ثابتة غير مباشرة
over-insurance	*ta'mīn zā'id*	تأمين زائد

over-investment	*ifrāṭ fi'l-istithmār*	افراط فى الاستثمارات
overlap	*yatarākab, yatakhaṭṭā*	يتراكب. يتخطّى
overloading of a plant	*taḥmīl maṣnaᶜ fawq ṭāqatih*	تحميل مصنع فوق طاقته
overpopulation	*fayḍ as-sukkān*	فيض السكّان
overproduction	*intāj zā'id*	انتاج زائد
override	*yuhaymin ᶜalā, yubṭil*	يهيمن على. يبطل
overseas investment	*istithmār fīmā warā' al-biḥār*	استثمار فيما وراء البحار
overseas review	*majallat mā warā' al-biḥār*	مجلّة ما وراء البحار
oversimplify	*yubāligh fī tabsīṭ*	يبالغ فى تبسيط
overspend	*yusrif fi'ṣ-ṣarf*	يسرف فى الصرف
over-staffed	*bi-ᶜāmilīn akthar min al-lāzim*	بعاملين أكثر من اللازم
overstock	*yukhazzin bi-qadr zā'id*	يخزّن بقدر زائد
oversubscribed	*muktatab fīh bi-ashum ziyāda*	مكتتب فيه بأسهم زيادة
over-tax	*yusrif fī farḍ aḍ-ḍarība*	يسرف فى فرض الضريبة
over the counter	*ṣafqa fi's-sūq ghayr ar-rasmiyya*	صفقة فى السوق غير الرسمية
overtime	*waqt iḍāfī*	وقت اضافى
overtime pay	*ajr al-waqt al-iḍāfī*	أجر الوقت الاضافى
overtime premium	*badal waqt iḍāfī*	بدل وقت اضافى
over-valued currency	*ᶜumla muqawwama bi-akthar min qīmatihā*	عملة مقوّمة بأكثر من قيمتها
overweight	*mutajāwiz al-wazn*	متجاوز الوزن
overwhelming majority	*aghlabiyya sāḥiqa*	أغلبية ساحقة

owe, to	*(huwa) madīn*	(هو) مدين
owing	*mustaḥiqq ad-daf^c*	مستحق الدفع
owing to	*bi-sabab*	بسبب
own brand	*ṣinf khāṣṣ bi'sh-sharika*	صنف خاصّ بالشركة
owner	*mālik, ṣāḥib*	مالك ، صاحب
ownership	*milkiyya*	ملكية
owner's risk	*mas'ūliyyat al-mālik*	مسؤولية المالك

P

package	*ruzma, ʿubuwwa, ṭard*	رزمة ،عبوّة ، طرد
package deal	*ṣafqa shāmila*	صفقة شاملة
packaging	*taʿbi'a*	تعبئة
packer	*muʿabbi'*	معبّئ
packing and despatch department	*qism al-ḥazm wa al-shaḥn*	قسم الحزم والشحن
packing charges	*maṣārīf al-ḥazm*	مصاريف الحزم
packing material	*mawādd taghlīf*	موادّ تغليف
paid in advance	*madfūʿ muqaddaman*	مدفوع مقدّما
paid-up capital	*ra's al-māl al-madfūʿ*	رأس المال المدفوع
paid-up policy	*būlīṣat ta'mīn madfūʿa*	بوليصة تأمين مدفوعة
pallet	*minaṣṣa naqqāla*	منصّة نقّالة
paper	*waraq*	ورق
paper money	*ʿumla waraqiyya*	عملة ورقية
par	*siʿr al-iṣdār*	سعر الاصدار

par, above	*fawq al-qīma 'l-ismiyya*	فوق القيمة الاسمية
par, at	*ḥasb al-qīma 'l-ismiyya*	حسب القيمة الاسمية
par, below	*bi-aqall min al-qīma 'l-ismiyya*	بأقلّ من القيمة الاسمية
parcel	*ṭard, qasīmat arḍ*	طرد · قسيمة أرض
parcel post	*barīd aṭ-ṭurūd*	بريد الطرود
parent company	*sharika 'umm/mālika*	شركة أمّ/مالكة
parity	*takāfu'*	تكافؤ
parity ratio	*nisbat at-takāfu'*	نسبة التكافؤ
partial acceptance	*qabūl juz'ī*	قبول جزئى
partial agreement	*ittifāq juz'ī*	اتّفاق جزئى
partial consideration	*taᶜwīḍ juz'ī*	تعويض جزئى
partial disablement	*ᶜajz juz'ī*	عجز جزئى
partial loss	*khasāra juz'īyya*	خسارة جزئية
partial payment	*sadād juz'ī*	سداد جزئى
partial shipment	*shaḥn juz'ī*	شحن جزئى
partial solution	*ḥall juz'ī*	حلّ جزئى
partial withdrawal	*insiḥāb juz'ī*	انسحاب جزئى
parties to a dispute	*aṭrāf fi-nizāᶜ*	أطراف فى نزاع
partner	*sharīk*	شريك
partnership	*sharikat taḍāmun, sharika*	شركة تضامن · شركة
partnership agreement	*ittifāqiyyat sharika basīṭa*	اتّفاقية شركة بسيطة

partnership deed	*ᶜaqd ta'sīs sharika*	عقد تأسيس شركة
part performance	*injāz juz'ī*	انجاز جزئى
part-time	*dawām juz'ī li-baᶜḍ al-waqt*	دوام جزئى لبعض الوقت
part-time agent	*wakīl ghayr dā'im*	وكيل غير دائم
part-time job	*waẓīfa li-baᶜḍ al-waqt, waẓifa bi-dawām juz'ī*	وظيفة لبعض الوقت ، وظيفة بدوام جزئى
part-time worker	*ᶜāmil li-baᶜḍ al-waqt*	عامل لبعض الوقت
par value	*al-qīma 'l-ismiyya*	القيمة الاسمية
pass, a	*taṣrīḥ murūr*	تصريح مرور
passbook	*daftar ḥisāb al-ᶜamīl*	دفتر حساب العميل
passenger	*musāfir, rākib*	مسافر ، راكب
passenger density	*kathāfat ar-rukkāb*	كثافة الركّاب
passenger insurance	*ta'mīn ar-rukkāb*	تأمين الركّاب
passenger-kilometre cost	*taklifat al-musāfir li-kull kīlūmitr*	تكلفة المسافر لكلّ كيلومتر
passenger list	*qā'imat asmā' al-musāfirīn*	قائمة أسماء المسافرين
passport	*jawāz safar*	جواز سفر
patent	*imtiyāz, barā'at ikhtirāᶜ*	امتياز ، براءة اختراع
patentee	*ṣāḥib barā'a/imtiyāz*	صاحب براءة / امتياز
patent infringement suit	*daᶜwa 'ntihāk barā'at ikhtirāᶜ*	دعوى انتهاك براءة اختراع
patentor	*māniḥ al-barā'a/al-imtiyāz*	مانح البراءة / الامتياز
patent right	*ḥaqq ikhtirāᶜ*	حقّ اختراع

patron	*zubūn, rāᶜī*	زبون • راعى
pay	*ajr*	أجر
payable	*mustaḥiqq ad-dafᶜ*	مستحقّ الدفع
payable in advance	*yudfaᶜ muqaddaman*	يدفع مقدّما
payable on demand	*yudfaᶜ ᶜind aṭ-ṭalab*	يدفع عند الطلب
P.A.Y.E. (Pay As You Earn)	*idfaᶜ aḍ-ḍarā'ib ḥīna taksab*	ادفع الضرائب حين تكسب
pay as you go	*dafᶜ an-nafaqāt waqt taḥammulhā*	دفع النفقات وقت تحمّلها
payee	*al-madfūᶜ lahu*	المدفوع له
payer	*dāfiᶜ*	دافع
pay incentive	*ḥāfiz al-ajr*	حافز الاجر
payload	*ḥumūla bi-ujra*	حمولة بأجرة
payment	*dafᶜ, dufᶜa*	دفع • دفعة
payment by results	*ad-dafᶜ ḥasb al-qadr al-muntaj*	الدفع حسب القدر المنتج
payment, ex gratia	*minḥa*	منحة
payment in advance	*dafᶜ muqaddam*	دفع مقدّم
payment in arrears	*īfā' mu'ajjal*	ايفاء مؤجّل
payment in kind	*dafᶜ nawᶜī/ᶜaynī*	دفع نوعى/عينى
payment restrictions	*quyūd ᶜala 'l-madfūᶜāt*	قيود على المدفوعات
payment terms	*shurūṭ ad-dafᶜ*	شروط الدفع
pay off	*yusaddid dayn*	يسدّد دينا
pay on delivery	*dafᶜ ᶜind at-taslīm*	دفع عند التسليم

pay on demand	*daf^c ^{c}ind aṭ-ṭalab*	دفع عند الطلب
payroll	*kashf al-'ujūr wa'r-rawātib*	كشف الأجور والرواتب
payroll tax	*aḍ-ḍarība ^{c}ala 'l-'ujūr*	الضريبة على الأجور
pay, to	*yadfa^c*	يدفع
peaceful demonstration	*muẓāhara/masīra silmiyya*	مظاهرة /مسيرة سلمية
peaceful settlement	*taswiya silmiyya*	تسوية سلمية
peak	*qimma, dhurwa*	قمّة ، ذروة
peak consumption	*a^{c}lā istihlāk*	أعلى استهلاك
peak output	*a^{c}lā 'l-intāj*	أعلى الانتاج
penalty clause	*sharṭ/band jazā'i*	شرط/بند جزائى
pending	*mu^{c}allaq li-ḥīn*	معلّق لحين
pending receipt	*li-ḥīn istilām*	لحين استلام
pension	*ma^{c}āsh at-taqā^{c}ud*	معاش التقاعد
pensioner	*mutaqā^{c}id, bi'l-ma^{c}āsh*	متقاعد ، بالمعاش
pension fund	*ṣundūq al-ma^{c}āshāt*	صندوق المعاشات
per annum	*fi's-sana*	فى السنة
per capita	*li-kull shakhṣ*	لكلّ شخص
per cent	*fi'l-mi'a*	فى المئة
percentage	*nisba mi'awiyya*	نسبة مئوية
performance	*tanfīdh, adā'*	تنفيذ ، أداء
performance appraisal	*taqyīm al-adā'*	تقييم الأداء

performance rating	*taqdīr al-adā'*	تقدير الأداء
performance sampling	*murāqabat al-adā' bi'l-mu^{c}āyana*	مراقبة الاداء بالمعاينة
period of cancellation	*muhlat al-faskh*	مهلة الفسخ
period of insurance	*muddat at-ta'mīn/aḍ-ḍamān*	مدّة التأمين/الضمان
perishable	*qābil li'l-fasād, sarī^{c} at-talaf*	قابل للفساد • سريع التلف
perjury	*tazwīr, shahāda zūr*	تزوير • شهادة زور
permanent disablement	*^{c}ajz dā'im*	عجز دائم
permit	*idhn, ijāza, taṣrīḥ*	اذن • اجازة • تصريح
permit, export	*ijārat/idhn taṣdīr*	اجازة تصدير • إذن تصدير
permit, import	*ijāzat/idhn istīrād*	اجازة/اذن استيراد
person	*shakhṣ*	شخص
personal accident insurance	*ḍamān/ta'mīn al-ḥawādith ash-shakhṣiyya*	ضمان/تأمين الحوادث الشخصية
personal capacity	*ṣifa shakhṣiyya*	صفة شخصية
personal contact	*ittiṣāl shakhṣī*	اتّصال شخصى
personal income	*dakhl shakhṣī*	دخل شخصى
personal injury	*iṣāba shakhṣiyya*	اصابة شخصية
personal insurance	*ḍamān/ta'mīn shakhṣī*	ضمان/تأمين شخصى
personal liability insurance	*ta'mīn ḍidd al-mas'ūliyya ash-shakhṣiyya*	تأمين ضدّ المسؤولية الشخصية
personal loan	*qarḍ shakhṣī*	قرض شخصى
personal property	*milk shakhṣī (manqūl)*	ملك شخصى (منقول)
personal representative	*mumaththil shakhṣī*	ممثّل شخصى

personal statement	*bayān shakhṣī*	بيان شخصى
personal tax	*ḍarība shakhṣiyya*	ضريبة شخصية
personal wealth	*tharwa shakhṣiyya*	ثروة شخصية
personnel department	*idārat shu'ūn al-afrād*	ادارة شئون الافراد
personnel director	*mudīr shu'ūn al-afrād*	مدير شئون الافراد
personnel management	*idārat shu'ūn al-muwaẓẓafīn*	ادارة شؤون الموظفين
personnel manager	*mudīr shu'ūn al-ᶜāmilīn*	مدير شؤون العاملين
personnel officer	*muwaẓẓaf shu'ūn al-ᶜāmilīn*	موظف شؤون العاملين
personnel records	*sijillāt al-muwaẓẓafīn*	سجلّات الموظفين
personnel relations	*ᶜalāqāt al-muwaẓẓafīn*	علاقات الموظفين
personnel responsibilities	*mas'ūliyyāt al-muwaẓẓafīn*	مسؤوليات الموظفين
per unit	*ḥasab al-waḥda*	حسب الوحدة
pest control	*mukāfaḥat al-āfāt*	مكافحة الآفات
pesticides	*mawādd mubīda li'l-āfāt*	موادّ مبيدة للآفات
petition	*ᶜarīḍa*	عريضة
petition in bankruptcy	*ᶜarīḍat daᶜwa 'l-iflās*	عريضة دعوى الافلاس
petitioning creditor	*dā'in mustadᶜī*	دائن مستدع
petro-chemical complex	*mujammaᶜ bitrūkīmā'ī*	مجمّع بتروكيمائى
petro-chemical industry	*ṣināᶜa bitrūkīmāwiyyāt*	صناعة البتروكيماويات
petro-chemicals	*al-bitrūkīmāwiyyāt*	البتروكيماويات
petrodollars	*dulārāt ᶜā'id an-nafṭ*	دولارات عائد النفط

petrol	*banzīn*	بنزين
petroleum	*nafṭ, bitrūl*	نفط. بترول
petroleum engineering	*handas nafṭiyya/bitrūliyya*	هندسة نفطية/بترولية
petty cash	*maṣārīf nathriyya, ḥisāb an-nathriyyāt*	مصاريف نثرية. حساب النثريات
picketing	*taḥrīḍ li-injāḥ al-iḍrāb*	تحريض لانجاح الاضراب
piece work	*^{c}amal bi'l-qiṭ^{c}a*	عمل بالقطعة
pilot project	*mashrū^{c} tajrībī*	مشروع تجريبي
pipeline	*khaṭṭ anābīb*	خط أنابيب
place of origin	*mansha^{c}, makān al-aṣl*	منشا. مكان الاصل
place of payment	*makān ad-daf^{c}*	مكان الدفع
plaintiff	*mudda^{c}ī*	مدّع
planned economy	*iqtiṣād muwajjah*	اقتصاد موجّه
planning techniques	*asālīb at-takhṭīṭ*	أساليب التخطيط
plant	*masna^{c}, ālāt*	مصنع. آلات
plant engineer	*muhandis al-maṣna^{c}*	مهندس المصنع
plant manager	*mudīr al-maṣna^{c}*	مدير المصنع
plant purchasing officer	*mudīr mushtarayāt al-maṣna^{c}*	مدير مشتريات المصنع
plant site	*mawqi^{c} al-maṣna^{c}*	موقع المصنع
plate glass insurance	*ta'mīn kasr az-zujāj*	تأمين كسر الزجاج
plea	*jawāb al-mudda^{c}ā ^{c}alayh*	جواب المدّعى عليه
pledge	*rahn*	رهن

point of sale	*nuqṭat al-bayᶜ*	نقطة البيع
point of view	*wijhat naẓar*	وجهة نظر
police	*shurṭa*	شرطة
policy	*siyāsa, būlīṣa*	سياسة • بوليصة
policy decision	*qarārāt al-khaṭṭ as-siyāsī*	قرارات الخط السياسى
policyholder	*ṣāḥib būlīṣat at-ta'mīn*	صاحب بوليصة التأمين
political risk	*khaṭar siyāsī*	خطر سياسى
poll	*iqtirāᶜ*	اقتراع
poor performance	*adā' ḍaᶜīf*	أداء ضعيف
poor quality	*nawᶜ radī'*	نوع ردىء
population explosion	*infijār sukkānī*	انفجار سكانى
population problem	*mushkilāt as-sukkān*	مشكلة السكان
port	*mīnā'*	ميناء
port authority	*sulṭat al-mīnā'*	سلطة الميناء
port dues	*rusūm al-mīnā'*	رسوم الميناء
port facilities	*at-tashīlāt al-mawjūda bi'l-mīnā'*	التسهيلات الموجودة بالميناء
portfolio	*maḥfaẓa, iḍbāra*	محفظة • اضبارة
portfolio (stocks and shares)	*maḥfaẓat al-awrāq al-māliyya*	محفظة الاوراق المالية
portfolio premium	*qisṭ al-iḍbāra*	قسط الاضبارة
port of destination	*mīnā' al-wuṣūl*	ميناء الوصول
port of discharge	*mīnā' at-tafrīgh*	ميناء التفريغ

port of embarkation	*mīnā' al-ibḥār*	ميناء الابحار
port of entry	*mīnā' al-dukhūl*	ميناء الدخول
port of loading	*mīnā' ash-shaḥn*	ميناء الشحن
port of shipment	*mīnā' ash-shaḥn*	ميناء الشحن
port of transit	*mīnā' at-tijāra 'l-ᶜābira*	ميناء التجارة العابرة
port regulations	*niẓām (lawā'iḥ) al-mīnā'*	نظام (لوائح) الميناء
post	*markaz, mawqiᶜ*	مركز. موقع
postal cheque	*shīk barīdī*	شيك بريدى
postal order	*idhn barīd*	اذن بريد
postal service	*khidmat al-barīd*	خدمة البريد
postal transfer	*taḥwīl barīdī*	تحويل بريدى
post and telecommunications	*maṣlaḥat al-barīd wa'l-ittiṣālāt al-baᶜīda*	مصلحة البريد والاتّصالات البعيدة
post-date	*yu'arrikh bi-tārīkh lāḥiq*	يؤرّخ بتاريخ لاحق
post-dated cheque	*shīk bi-tārīkh lāḥiq*	شيك بتاريخ لاحق
post office	*maktab barīd*	مكتب بريد
pound	*junayh istirlīnī, raṭl injilīzī*	جنيه استرلينى. رطل انكليزى
pound sterling	*junayh istirlīnī*	جنيه استرلينى
power of attorney	*tawkīl*	توكيل
power station	*maḥaṭṭat tawlīd kahrabā'*	محطّة توليد الكهرباء
precedent	*sābiqa qānūniyya*	سابقة قانونية
precious metal	*maᶜdin thamīn*	معدن ثمين

preconditioning stage	*marḥalat at-takayyuf*	مرحلة التكيّف
pre-date	*yu'arrikh bi-tārīkh sābiq*	يؤرّخ بتاريخ سابق
pre-determined costs	*takālīf muḥaddada muqaddaman*	تكاليف محدّدة مقدّما
preference shareholder	*musāhim mumtāz*	مساهم ممتاز
preference shares	*ashum mumtāza*	أسهم ممتازة
preferential duty	*ḍarība tafḍīliyya*	ضريبة تفضيلية
preferential rates	*mu^caddalāt tafḍīliyya*	معدّلات تفضيلية
preferential tariff	*at-ta^crifa 't-tafḍīliyya*	التعرفة التفضيلية
preferential trade agreement	*ittifāq tijārī bi-mu^cāmala tafḍīliyya*	اتّفاق تجارى بمعاملة تفضيلية
preferred creditor	*dā'in mumtāz*	دائن ممتاز
preferred position	*mawqi^c mufaḍḍal*	موقع مفضّل
preferred stock	*ashum mumtāza*	أسهم ممتازة
prejudicial to health	*ḍārr bi'ṣ-ṣiḥḥa*	ضارّ بالصحّة
preliminary audit	*tadqīq awwalī*	تدقيق أولى
preliminary decision	*qarār tamhīdī*	قرار تمهيدى
preliminary expenses	*nafaqāt awwaliyya*	نفقات أوّلية
preliminary investigation	*taḥqīq awwalī*	تحقيق اوّلى
premium bill of exchange	*kambiyāla mumtāza*	كمبيالة ممتازة
premium bond	*sanad ḥukūmī bi-jawā'iz bi'l-qur^ca*	سند حكومى بجوائز بالقرعة
premium (bonus)	*^cilāwa*	علاوة
premium discount	*takhfīḍ al-qisṭ*	تخفيض القسط

premium due	*qisṭ mustaḥiqq*	قسط مستحقّ
premium (insurance)	*qisṭ at-ta'mīn*	قسط التأمين
premium paid	*qisṭ maqbūḍ*	قسط مقبوض
premium (prize)	*jā'iza*	جائزة
premium reserve	*iḥtiyāṭī li-akhṭār jāriya*	احتياطى لاخطار جارية
pre-paid	*khāliṣ al-ujra*	خالص الأجرة
prepayment	*dafᶜ muqaddam*	دفع مقدّم
pre-production costs	*takālīf mā qabl al-intāj*	تكاليف ما قبل الانتاج
present value	*al-qīma 'l-ḥāliyya*	القيمة الحالية
present value method	*ṭarīqat al-qīma 'l-ḥāliyya*	طريقة القيمة الحالية
president	*ra'īs*	رئيس
pre-tax	*qabl khaṣm aḍ-ḍarība*	قبل خصم الضريبة
preventive maintenance	*ṣiyāna wiqā'iyya*	صيانة وقائية
preventive measures	*tadābīr wiqā'iyya*	تدابير وقائية
price	*siᶜr*	سعر
price control	*taḥakkum fi 'l-asᶜār*	تحكّم فى الاسعار
price, cost	*siᶜr at-taklifa*	سعر التكلفة
price cutting	*takhfīḍ al-asᶜār*	تخفيض الاسعار
price differentials	*furūq al-asᶜār*	فروق الاسعار
price fixing	*taḥdīd al-asᶜār*	تحديد الاسعار
price fluctuation	*taqallub al-asᶜār*	تقلّب الأسعار

price freeze	*tajmīd al-asᶜār*	تجميد الاسعار
price increase	*ziyādat as-siᶜr*	زيادة السعر
price index	*mu'ashshir al-asᶜār*	مؤشّر الاسعار
price inflation	*taḍakhkhum al-asᶜār*	تضخم الاسعار
price list	*qā'imat al-asᶜār*	قائمة الاسعار
price maintenance	*taḥdīd as-siᶜr*	تحديد السعر
price offered	*as-siᶜr al-maᶜrūḍ*	السعر المعروض
price reduction	*takhfīḍ as-siᶜr*	تخفيض السعر
price, retail	*siᶜr al-qaṭṭāᶜī*	سعر القطّاعى
prices and incomes policy	*siyāsat al-asᶜār wa'd-dukhūl*	سياسة الاسعار والدخول
price, selling	*siᶜr al-bayᶜ*	سعر البيع
price system	*irtifāᶜ as-siᶜr*	ارتفاع السعر
price system	*niẓām al-asᶜār*	نظام الاسعار
price variance	*ikhtilāf al-asᶜār*	اختلاف الاسعار
price war	*ḥarb al-asᶜār*	حرب الاسعار
pricing policy	*siyāsat at-tasᶜīr*	سياسة التسعير
pricing system	*niẓām at-tasᶜīr*	نظام التسعير
primary obligation	*iltizām awwalī*	التزام أوّلى
prime contractor	*al-muqāwil al-aṣlī*	المقاول الاصلى
principal	*ra'īsī, aṣlī*	رئيسى، أصلى
principle of indemnity	*mabda' at-taᶜwīḍ*	مبدأ التعويض

printed matter	*maṭbū^{c}āt*	مطبوعات
printer's error	*khaṭa' maṭba^{c}ī*	خطأ مطبعى
prior agreement	*ittifāq sābiq*	اتّفاق سابق
prior consultation	*tashāwur sābiq*	تشاور سابق
prior contract	*^{c}aqd sābiq*	عقد سابق
private arrangement	*taswiya khāṣṣa/widdiyya*	تسوية خاصّة/ودّية
private company	*sharika khāṣṣa*	شركة خاصّة
private documents	*wathā'iq khāṣṣa*	وثائق خاصّة
private enterprise	*mashrū^{c} khāṣṣ*	مشروع خاصّ
private insurance	*ta'mīn/ḍamān khāṣṣ*	تأمين/ضمان خاصّ
private interests	*maṣāliḥ khaṣṣa*	مصالح خاصّة
private limited company	*sharika khāṣṣa maḥdūda*	شركة خاصّة محدودة
private ownership	*milkiyya khāṣṣa*	ملكية خاصّة
private sale	*bay^{c} khāṣṣ*	بيع خاصّ
private sector	*qiṭā^{c} khāṣṣ*	قطاع خاصّ
privileged debt	*dayn mumtāz*	دين ممتاز
probability	*iḥtimāl*	احتمال
procedure	*ijrā'*	اجراء
procedure chart	*rasm bayānī li'l-ijrā'*	رسم بيانى للاجراء
proceedings	*ijrā^{c}āt, da^{c}wā*	اجراءات ، دعوى
proceedings of the court	*ijrā'āt al-maḥkama*	اجراءات المحكمة

proceeds of sales	*ḥaṣīlat al-mabīᶜāt*	حصيلة المبيعات
process	*ᶜamaliyya*	عملية
process chart	*rasm bayānī li'l-ᶜamaliyya*	رسم بيانى للعملية
procurement	*al-ḥuṣūl ᶜalā, tadbīr*	الحصول على، تدبير
produce	*maḥṣūl*	محصول
producer	*muntij*	منتج
producers' co-operative	*jamᶜiyyat taᶜāwun al-mintijīn*	جمعية تعاون المنتجين
produce, to	*yuntij*	ينتج
product	*muntaj*	منتج
product costing	*tathmīn al-muntajāt*	تثمين المنتجات
product diversification	*tanwīᶜ an-muntajāt*	تنويع المنتجات
production	*intāj*	انتاج
production area	*minṭaqat al-intāj*	منطقة الانتاج
production capacity	*ṭāqat al-intāj*	طاقة الانتاج
production centre	*markaz intāj*	مركز انتاج
production control	*murāqabat al-intāj*	مراقبة الانتاج
production costs	*takālīf al-intāj*	تكاليف الانتاج
production department	*qism al-intāj*	قسم الانتاج
production director	*mudīr al-intāj*	مدير الانتاج
production engineer	*muhandis al-intāj*	مهندس الانتاج
production line	*khaṭṭ al-intāj*	خطّ الانتاج

production manager	*mudīr al-intāj*	مدير الانتاج
production methods	*wasā'il al-intāj*	وسائل الانتاج
production planning	*takhṭīṭ al-intāj*	تخطيط الانتاج
production tax	*ḍarībat al-intāj*	ضريبة الانتاج
production unit	*waḥdat intāj*	وحدة انتاج
productivity	*al-intājiyya*	الانتاجية
productivity agreement	*ittifāq al-intājiyya*	اتّفاق الانتاجية
productivity bargaining	*musāwama intājiyya*	مساومة انتاجية
product mix	*mazīj al-muntajāt*	مزيج المنتجات
product planning	*takhṭīṭ al-muntajāt*	تخطيط المنتجات
profession	*mihna, ḥirfa*	مهنة • حرفة
professional fees	*at^{c}āb fanniyya*	أتعاب فنّية
professional liability insurance	*ta'mīn ḍidd al-mas'ūliyya 'l-mihniyya*	تأمين ضدّ المسؤولية المهنية
profit	*ribḥ*	ربح
profitability	*ar-ribḥiyya*	الربحية
profit and loss	*ar-ribḥ wa'l-khasāra*	الربح والخسارة
profit and loss account	*ḥisāb al-arbāḥ wa'l-khasā'ir*	حساب الارباح والخسائر
profit centre	*markaz al-arbāḥ*	مركز الارباح
profit margin	*ḥadd ar-ribḥ*	حدّ الربح
profit on investments	*arbāḥ at-tawẓīfāt al-māliyya*	ارباح التوظيفات المالية
profit sharing	*musāhama fi'larbāḥ*	مساهمة فى الارباح

profits tax	*ḍarībat al-arbāḥ*	ضريبة الارباح
profit variance	*inḥirāf ar-ribḥ*	انحراف الربح
programme	*barnāmaj, khiṭṭa*	برنامج، خطّة
programmed instruction	*at-taᶜlīm al-mubarmaj*	التعليم المبرمج
programmer	*wāḍiᶜ al-barāmij*	واضع البرامج
programming	*waḍᶜ al-barnāmaj*	وضع البرنامج
progress chart	*rasm bayān at-taqaddum*	رسم بيان التقدّم
progressive tax	*ḍarība taṣāᶜudiyya*	ضريبة تصاعدية
promissory note	*sanad idhnī, kambiyāla*	سند اذنى، كمبيالة
promissory note	*kambiyāla*	كمبيالة
promote sales, to	*yutājir, yurawwij*	يتاجر، يروّج
promotion	*tarqiya, tawīj*	ترقية ، ترويج
promotional activity	*nashāṭāt tashjīᶜ ash-sharika*	نشاطات تشجيع الشركة
promotion cost	*nafaqāt at-ta'sīs*	نفقات التأسيس
proof of loss	*ithbāt al-khasāra*	اثبات الخسارة
property, immovable	*amlāk ghayr manqūla*	املاك غير منقولة
property insurance	*ta'mīn ᶜala 'l-mumtalakāt*	تأمين على الممتلكات
property management	*idārat al-mumtalakāt*	ادارة الممتلكات
property, mortgaged	*amlāk marhūna*	املاك مرهونة
property, movable	*amlāk manqūla*	املاك منقولة
property, private	*milk khāṣṣ*	ملك خاصّ

property, public	*amlāk ᶜāmma*	املاك عامّة
property, real	*ᶜaqārāt thābita*	عقارات ثابتة
property tax	*ḍarībat ᶜaqār/mumtalakāt*	ضريبة عقار/ممتلكات
proprietary company	*ash-sharika 'l-mālika*	الشركة المالكة
proprietor	*mālik*	مالك
protected trade	*tijāra maḥmiyya*	تجارة محمية
protection	*ḥimāya, wiqāya*	حماية ، وقاية
protective policy	*siyāsat al-ḥimāya*	سياسة الحماية
protective tariff	*taᶜrifat al-ḥimāya 'l-jumrukiyya*	تعرفة الحماية الجمركية
protocol	*brutukoal, marāsim tashrīfāt*	بروتوكول ، مراسم تشريفات
prototype	*ṭirāz, mithāl*	طراز ، مثال
provisional agenda	*jadwal aᶜmāl mu'aqqat*	جدول أعمال موقّت
provisional budget	*mīzāniyya muᶜaqqata*	ميزانية مؤقّتة
provisional report	*taqrīr awwalī*	تقرير أوّلى
provision for depreciation	*mukhaṣṣaṣ al-istihlāk*	مخصّص الاستهلاك
public (a)	*ᶜāmm, ḥukūmī*	عام ، حكومى
publication	*nashr, nashra*	نشر ، نشرة
public auction	*mazād ᶜalanī*	مزاد علنى
public auditor	*murājiᶜ qānūnī*	مراجع قانونى
public corporation	*sharika/muᶜassasa ᶜāmma*	شركة/مؤسّسة عامّة
public demand	*at-ṭalab al-ᶜāmm/al-ḥukūmī*	الطلب العامّ/الحكومى

public domain	*amlāk ad-dawla 'l-ᶜāmma*	أملاك الدولة العامّة
public enterprise	*mashrūᶜ ᶜāmm*	مشروع عامّ
publicity	*iᶜlān*	اعلان
publicity manager	*mudīr ad-diᶜāya*	مدير الدعاية
public liability	*mas'ūliyya ᶜāmma*	مسؤولية عامّة
public liability insurance	*ta'mīn al-mas'ūliyya tijāh al-ghayr*	تأمين المسؤولية تجاه الغير
public nuisance	*izᶜāj ᶜāmm*	ازعاج عامّ
public opinion	*ar-ra'y al-ᶜāmm*	الرأى العام
public ownership	*milkiyya ᶜāmma*	ملكية عامّة
public relations	*ᶜalāqāt ᶜāmma*	علاقات عامّة
public relations officer	*mudīr al-ᶜalāqāt al-ᶜāmma*	مدير العلاقات العامّة
public sector	*qiṭāᶜ ᶜāmm*	قطاع عامّ
public services	*khadamāt ᶜāmma*	خدمات عامّة
public utility	*marfiq ᶜāmm*	مرفق عامّ
public works	*ashghāl ᶜāmma*	أشغال عامّة
publisher	*nāshir*	ناشر
punched card	*biṭāqa muthaqqaba*	بطاقة مثقّبة
punched-card system	*niẓām al-biṭāqāt al-muthaqqaba*	نظام البطاقات المثقّبة
punched tape	*sharīṭ muthaqqab*	شريط مثقّب
purchase	*shirā'*	شراء
purchase commitment	*iltizām bi'sh-shirā'*	التزام بالشراء

purchase money	*thaman ash-shirā' al-awwalī*	ثمن الشراء الاوّلى
purchase order	*ṭalab shirā'*	طلب شراء
purchase price	*thaman ash-shirā'*	ثمن الشراء
purchase records	*sijillāt al-mushtarayāt*	سجلّات المشتريات
purchase requisition	*ṭalab shirā'*	طلب شراء
purchase tax	*ḍarībat shirā'*	ضريبة شراء
purchasing agent	*wakīl shirā'*	وكيل شراء
purchasing power	*quwwa shirā'iyya*	قوّة شرائية

Q

qualification	*mu'ahhil, taḥaffuẓ, qayd, sharṭ*	مؤهّل، تحفّظ، قيد، شرط
qualified acceptance	*qabūl muqayyad*	قبول مقيّد
qualified approval	*taṣdīq muqayyad bi-sharṭ*	تصديق مقيّد بشرط
qualified expert	*khabīr mu'ahhal*	خبير مؤهّل
qualified to vote	*lahu ḥaqq at-taṣwīt*	له حقّ التصويت
qualifying examination	*imtiḥān li'l-ahliyya, imtiḥān al-qabūl*	امتحان للأهلية، امتحان القبول
qualitative analysis	*taḥlīl naw*^{c}*ī*	تحليل نوعى
quality	*naw*^{c}*iyya, naw*^{c}	نوعية، نوع
quality control	*murāqabat an-naw*^{c}*iyya*	مراقبة النوعية
quantify	*yuḥaddid al-kammiyya*	يحدّد الكمّية
quantitative analysis	*taḥlīl kammī*	تحليل كمّى
quantity	*miqdār, kammiyya*	مقدار، كمّية
quantity discount	*khaṣm al-kammiyya*	خصم الكمّية
quantity rebate	*khaṣm shirā' al-jumla*	خصم شراء الجملة

quarantine	*ḥajr ṣiḥḥī, ^{c}azl ṣiḥḥī*	حجر صحّى. عزل صحّى
quarterly	*faṣlī, rub^c sanawī*	فصلى. ربع سنوى
quarterly instalment	*qisṭ kull thalāthat shuhūr*	قسط كل ثلاثة شهور
quarterly payment	*duf^{c}a kull thalāthat shuhūr*	دفعة كل ثلاثة شهور
quarterly review	*majalla faṣliyya*	مجلّة فصلية
quasi contract	*shibh ^{c}aqd*	شبه عقد
quasi judicial	*shibh qaḍā'ī*	شبه قضائى
quasi partner	*bi-mathābat sharīk*	بمثابة شريك
quay	*raṣīf mīnā'*	رصيف ميناء
quayage	*rasm ar-raṣīf*	رسم الرصيف
quay dues	*rusūm raṣīf al-mīnā'*	رسوم رسيف الميناء
Queen's Counsel	*muhāmī min a^{c}lā daraja bi-birīṭāniya*	محام من أعلى درجة ببريطانيا
question	*su'āl, mas'ala, amr*	سؤال. مسألة . أمر
questionable	*mawḍi^c shakk*	موضع شك
questionnaire	*istibyān, istiftā'*	استبيان. استفتاء
question of fact	*mas'ala tata^{c}allaq bi-waqā'i^c ad-da^{c}wā*	مسألة تتعلّق بوقائع الدعوى
question of law	*mas'ala tata^{c}allaq bi'l-qanūn*	مسألة تتعلّق بالقانون
question of life or death	*qaḍiyyat ḥayāh aw mawt*	قضية حياة أو موت
question of time	*mas'alat waqt*	مسألة وقت
questions concerning	*masā'il tata^{c}allaq bi*	مسائل تتعلّق ب
question, that is the	*hādhā huwa 's-su'āl*	هذا هو السؤال

question, without	*dūna shakk*	دون شكّ
quick profit	*ribḥ sarī*^{c}	ربح سريع
quid pro quo	*al-mithl bi'l-mithl, muqābil*	المثل بالمثل. مقابل
quit, to	*yatruk, yughādir*	يترك . يغادر
quorum	*niṣāb qānūnī*	نصاب قانونى
quota	*ḥiṣṣa, kūta*	حصّة . كوتا
quota agreement	*ittifāq ḥiṣaṣ*	اتّفاق حصص
quota sampling	*mu*^{c}*āyana bi'l-ḥiṣṣa*	معاينة بالحصّة
quota share	*ḥiṣṣa nisbiyya*	حصّة نسبية
quotas, import	*ḥiṣaṣ istīrād*	حصص استيراد
quota system	*niẓām al-ḥiṣaṣ*	نظام الحصص
quotation	*tas*^{c}*īr, si*^{c}*r ma*^{c}*rūḍ*	تسعير. سعر معروض
quoted securities	*sanadāt musa*^{cc}*ara*	سندات مسعّرة

R

racial conflict	*nizā^c ^cunṣurī*	نزاع عنصری
racial integration	*idmāj ^cunṣurī*	ادماج عنصری
radioactive waste	*faḍalāt mushi^{cc}a*	فضلات مشعّة
radio broadcast	*idhā^ca*	اذاعة
radio station	*maḥaṭṭat idhā^ca*	محطّة اذاعة
raise a loan	*yaḥṣul ^calā qarḍ*	يحصل على قرض
raise an objection	*yuthīr i^ctirāḍ*	يثير اعتراضا
random sampling	*mu^cāyana ^cashwā'iyya*	معاينة عشوائية
range	*majāl, niṭāq*	مجال، نطاق
range of goods	*tashkīlat baḍā'i^c*	تشكيلة بضائع
rate	*nisba, mu^caddal, ujra*	نسبة ، معدّل ، أجرة
rate discrimination	*tamyīz fi'l-ujūr*	تمييز فى الاجور
rate of discount	*mu^caddal al-khaṣm*	معدّل الخصم
rate of exchange	*si^cr at-taḥwīl*	سعر التحويل

rate of increase	*nisbat az-ziyāda*	نسبة الزيادة
rate of interest	*si^c^r al-fā'ida*	سعر الفائدة
rate of pay	*mu'addal al-ajr*	معدّل الاجر
rate of return	*nisbat al-mardūd*	نسبة المردود
ratification	*ibrām, taṣdīq ^c^alā*	ابرام • تصديق على
rating	*taqdīr, taqyīm*	تقدير • تقييم
ratio	*nisba*	نسبة
rationalise	*yaj^c^aluh ma^c^qūl manṭiqī*	يجعله معقولا منطقيا
raw materials	*mawādd khām/awwaliyya*	موادّ خام / أوّلية
readjustment	*ta^c^dīl al-waḍ^c^*	تعديل الوضع
ready cash	*naqd sā'il*	نقد سائل
ready-made	*jāhiz*	جاهز
ready money	*māl jāhiz*	مال جاهز
real consumption	*istihlāk ḥaqīqī*	استهلاك حقيقى
real estate	*milk ^c^aqārī*	ملك عقارى
real estate tax	*ḍarība ^c^aqāriyya*	ضريبة عقارية
real income	*dakhl ḥaqīqī*	دخل حقيقى
realizable assets	*amwāl qābila li't-taṣarruf bihā*	اموال قابلة للتصرّف بها
realized profit	*ribḥ muḥaqqaq*	ربح محقّق
real property	*milk ^c^aqārī*	ملك عقارى
real time	*al-waqt al-ḥaqīqī*	الوقت الحقيقى

real value	*qīma ḥaqīqiyya*	قيمة حقيقية
ream	*ruzmat waraq*	رزمة ورق
reappraisal	*iᶜādat tathmīn/taqdīr/taqyīm*	اعادة تثمين/تقدير/تقييم
reasonable time	*mudda maᶜqūla*	مدّة معقولة
rebate	*takhfīḍ, tanzīl*	تخفيض٠ تنزيل
rebate of premium	*takhfīḍ qisṭ at-ta'mīn*	تخفيض قسط التأمين
recapitalisation	*iᶜādat takwīn ra'salmāl*	اعادة تكوين رأس المال
recapitulate	*yulakhkhiṣ*	يلخّص
receipt	*īṣāl، waṣl taslīm*	ايصال٠ وصل تسليم
receipts	*maqbūḍāt*	مقبوضات
received with thanks	*qubiḍa maᶜ ash-shukr*	قبض مع الشكر
receiver	*ḥāris qaḍā'ī*	حارس قضائى
receiver's bond	*kafālat al-ḥāris al-qaḍā'ī*	كفالة الحارس القضائى
reception	*istilām, istiqbāl*	استلام٠ استقبال
recession	*inkimāsh iqtiṣādī*	انكماش اقتصادى
reciprocal	*mutabādal*	متبادل
reciprocal agreement	*ittifāq mutabādal*	اتّفاق متبادل
reciprocal demands	*ṭalabāt mutabādala*	طلبات متبادلة
reciprocal insurance	*taᶜmīn mutabādal*	تأمين متبادل
reckless	*ṭā'ish, mutahawwir*	طائش٠ متهوّر
reclassification	*iᶜādat tasᶜīr/taṣnīf*	اعادة تسعير/تصنيف

recognition	*iᶜtirāf, taᶜarruf ᶜala*	اعتراف. تعرّف على
recognize	*yuqirr, yataᶜarraf ᶜalā*	يقرّ. يتعرّف على
recommendation	*tawṣiya, iqtirāḥ*	توصية . اقتراح
recompense	*jazā', taᶜwīḍ*	جزاء. تعويض
reconciliation	*taṭābuq ḥisāb, taswiya*	تطابق حساب. تسوية
reconciliation statement	*bayān muṭābaqa/taswia*	بيان مطابقة/تسوية
reconstruction of a company	*iᶜādat ta'sīs sharika*	اعادة تأسيس شركة
recorded delivery	*taslīm musajjal*	تسليم مسجّل
record figure	*raqm qiyāsī*	رقم قياسي
recording medium	*wasīlat tasjīl*	وسيلة تسجيل
records	*sijillāt*	سجلّات
recoup	*yaqtaṭiᶜ, yuᶜawwiḍ*	يقتطع . يعوّض
recoverable reserves	*iḥtiyāṭī yumkin istikhlāṣuh*	احتياطي يمكن استخلاصه
recovery costs	*taklifat istirdād*	تكلفة استرداد
recovery of damages	*taḥṣīl at-taᶜwīḍāt*	تحصيل التعويضات
recovery of debts	*istirdād ad-duyūn*	استرداد الديون
recovery of expenses	*istiᶜādat an-nafaqāt*	استعادة النفقات
recovery value	*al-qīma 'l-mustaradda*	القيمة المستردّة
recruiting programme	*barnāmaj istikhdām/tajnīd*	برنامج استخدام/تجنيد
recruitment	*istikhdām, tajnīd*	استخدام . تجنيد
recruit staff	*intiqā'/istikhdām al-muwaẓẓafīn*	انتقاء/استخدام الموظّفين

redeemable debentures	*sanadāt qābila li't-tasdīd*	سندات قابلة للتسديد
redeemable stock	*ashum qābila li'l-istirdād*	أسهم قابلة للاسترداد
redeem a mortgage	*yafukk rahn*	يفكّ رهنا
redemption dates	*tawārīkh al-istirdād*	تواريخ الاسترداد
redemption fund	*ṣundūq istihlāk ad-duyūn*	صندوق اسهلاك الديون
redemption yield	*ᶜā'id al-ashum al-mustahlaka*	عائد الاسهم المستهلكة
redeployment of labour	*iᶜādat tawzīᶜ al-yad al-ᶜāmila*	اعادة توزيع اليد العاملة
redirection	*iᶜādat irsāl barīdī*	اعادة ارسال بريدى
redistribution of income	*iᶜādat tazīᶜ ad-dakhl*	اعادة توزيع الدخل
redraft	*iᶜādat taḥrīr/saḥb*	اعادة تحرير/سحب
red tape	*ar-rūtīn al-ḥukūmī*	الروتين الحكومى
reduce costs	*yukhaffiḍ at-takālīf*	يخفّض التكاليف
reduced dividend	*sahm mukhaffaḍ ar-ribḥ*	سهم مخفّض الربح
reduced price	*siᶜr mukhaffaḍ*	سعر مخفّض
reduce the output	*yukhaffiḍ al-intāj*	يخفّض الانتاج
reduce the pressure	*yukhaffif aḍ-ḍaghṭ*	يخفّف الضغط
redundancy	*ziyāda ᶜan al-ḥāja*	زيادة عن الحاجة
redundancy payment	*taᶜwīḍ faṣl*	تعويض فصل
re-election	*iᶜādat intikhāb*	اعادة انتخاب
re-entry	*iᶜādat tasjīl*	اعادة تسجيل
re-establish	*yuᶜīd al-ᶜalāqāt*	يعيد العلاقات

re-examine	*yuᶜāyin/yurājiᶜ min jadīd*	يعاين/يراجع من جديد
re-export	*iᶜādat taṣdīr*	اعادة تصدير
referee	*ḥakam*	حكم
reference	*marjiᶜ*	مرجع
reference number	*raqm al-iḥāla*	رقم الاحالة
references	*marājiᶜ, maṣādir istiᶜlām*	مراجع ، مصادر استعلام
referendum	*istiftā' ᶜāmm*	استفتاء عامّ
refer to drawer	*irjiᶜ ila 's-sāḥib*	ارجع الى الساحب
refinery	*miṣfāh, maᶜmal takrīr*	مصفاة ، معمل تكرير
reform	*yuṣliḥ*	يصلح
refrigeration	*tabrīd*	تبريد
refrigerator	*thallāja*	ثلّاجة
refuel	*yuzawwid bi'l-waqūd*	يزوّد بالوقود
refund	*radd/istirdād māl*	ردّ/استرداد مال
refuse to accept	*yarfuḍ qabūl*	يرفض قبول
refuse to take delivery	*yarfuḍ istilām*	يرفض استلام
regain possession	*yastaᶜīd milkiyya*	يستعيد ملكية
regional market	*sūq iqlīmiyya*	سوق اقليمية
register	*sijill*	سجلّ
registered bond	*sanad ismī*	سند اسمى
registered capital	*ra'salmāl ismī*	رأس مال اسمى

registered company	*sharika musajjala*	شركة مسجّلة
registered letter	*risāla musajjala*	رسالة مسجّلة
registered mail	*barīd musajjal*	بريد مسجّل
registered office	*maqarr ash-sharika*	مقرّ الشركة
registered share certificate	*shahādat sahm ismī*	شهادة سهم اسمى
registered shareholder	*ḥāmil ashum shakhṣiyya*	حامل أسهم شخصية
registered tonnage	*ḥumūla musajjala*	حمولة مسجّلة
registered trade mark	*^{c}alāma tijāriyya musajjala*	علامة تجارية مسجّلة
register of members	*sijill al-a^{c}dā'*	سجلّ الأعضاء
registrar	*musajjil*	مسجّل
Registrar of Companies	*musajjil ash-sharikāt*	مسجّل الشركات
registration	*tasjīl*	تسجيل
registration	*tasjīl*	تسجيل
registration fee	*rasm tasjīl*	رسم تسجيل
registry office	*maktab al-aḥwāl al-madaniyya*	مكتب الاحوال المدنية
regulations	*lawā'iḥ, nuẓum*	لوائح ۰ نظم
reimburse	*yadfa^{c} lahu mā anfaqahu*	يدفع له ما أنفقه
reinstatement	*i^{c}ādat sarayān būlīṣat ta'mīn*	اعادة سريان بوليصة تأمين
reinsurance	*i^{c}ādat at-ta'mīn*	اعادة التأمين
reinsure	*yu^{c}īd ta'mīn*	يعيد تأمين
reinvest	*yu^{c}īd istithmār*	يعيد استثمار

reinvestment	*iᶜādat istithmār*	اعادة استثمار
reissue	*iṣdār jadīd*	اصدار جديد
related cost	*taklifa murtabiṭa*	تكلفة مرتبطة
relative prices	*asᶜār nisbiyya*	أسعار نسبية
release of mortgage	*fakk ar-rahn*	فكّ الرهن
remedy	*ijrā' li-ᶜilāj al-mawqif*	اجراء لعلاج الموقف
remit	*yursil māl, yuᶜfī*	يرسل مالا. يعفى
remittance	*taḥwīl mālī*	تحويل مالى
remittance advice	*ishᶜār taḥwīl*	اشعار تحويل
remittance in cash	*ad-dafᶜ naqdan*	الدفع نقدا
removal expenses	*nafaqāt naql athāth*	نفقات نقل اثاث
remove controls	*yulghi 'l-quyūd*	يلغى القيود
remuneration	*mukāfa'a, taᶜwīḍ*	مكافأة. تعويض
renegotiation	*iᶜādat at-tafāwuḍ*	اعادة التفاوض
renew	*yujaddid*	يجدّد
renewable contract	*ᶜaqd qābil li't-tajdīd*	عقد قابل للتجديد
renewable note	*kambiyālat tajdīd*	كمبيالة تجديد
renewal	*tajdīd*	تجديد
renewal bond	*sanad tajdīd*	سند تجديد
rent	*ījār*	ايجار
release	*ikhlā' ṭaraf, ibrā' dhimma*	اخلاء طرف

rental value	*qīma ījāriyya*	قيمة ايجارية
rent control	*murāqabat al-ījārāt*	مراقبة الايجارات
rent insurance	*ta'mīn ᶜala 'l-ījār*	تأمين على الايجار
reorganization	*iᶜādat tanẓīm*	اعادة تنظيم
reorganize management	*yuᶜīd tanẓīm al-idāra*	يعيد تنظيم الادارة
repatriation	*iᶜāda ila'l-waṭan*	اعادة الى الوطن
repayment	*dafᶜ, tasdīd*	دفع ، تسديد
replacement	*istibdāl*	استبدال
replacement costs	*takālīf al-ibdāl*	تكاليف الابدال
replacement method	*ṭarīqat al-iḥlāl*	طريقة الاحلال
replacement reserve	*iḥtiyāṭī ibdāl*	احتياطى ابدال
replacement value	*qīmat al-istibdāl*	قيمة الاستبدال
reply coupon	*qasīmat jawāb*	قسيمة جواب
reply-paid	*al-jawāb madfūᶜ*	الجواب مدفوع
report	*bayān, taqrīr*	بيان، تقرير
reporter	*muqaddim al-bayān/at-taqrīr*	مقدّم البيان/التقرير
reporting standards	*qawāᶜid iᶜdād at-taqārīr*	قواعد اعداد التقارير
repossess	*yastaridd*	يستردّ
representation	*bayān, iqrār, tamthīl*	بيان، اقرار، تمثيل
representative	*mumaththil*	ممثّل
reprint	*yuᶜīd ṭabᶜ*	يعيد طبع

reproduction cost	*taklifat iᶜādat al-intāj*	تكلفة اعادة الانتاج
repudiate	*yatakhallā ᶜan, yunkir*	يتخلّى عن. ينكر
requisition	*ṭalab, muṣādara*	طلب. مصادرة
resale	*iᶜādat al-bayᶜ*	اعادة البيع
resale price	*siᶜr iᶜādat al-bayᶜ*	سعر اعادة البيع
resale price maintenance	*muḥāfaẓa ᶜalā siᶜr al-bayᶜ*	محافظة على سعر البيع
resale value	*qīmat iᶜadat al-bayᶜ*	قيمة اعادة البيع
research	*baḥth*	بحث
research and development	*al-baḥth wa't-tanmiya*	البحث والتنمية
research cost	*taklifat al-abḥāth*	تكلفة الابحاث
research scientist	*ᶜālim mushtaghil bi'l-baḥth*	عالم مشتغل بالبحث
resell at a profit	*yabīᶜ thāniyatan bi-ribḥ*	يبيع ثانية بربح
reserve	*iḥtiyāṭī*	احتياطى
reserve account	*ḥisāb al-iḥtiyāṭī*	حساب الاحتياطى
reserve capital	*ra'smāl iḥtiyāṭī*	رأسمال احتياطى
reserve fund	*raṣīd al-iḥtiyāṭī*	رصيد الاحتياطى
reserve price	*siᶜr muḥaddad/at-taḥaffuẓ*	سعر محدّد/التحفّظ
residence	*iqāma*	اقامة
resident	*muqīm*	مقيم
residual	*mutabaqqī*	متبقّى
residual payment	*madfūᶜāt mutabaqqiya*	مدفوعات متبقية

residual value	*al-qīma 'l-mutabaqqiya*	القيمة المتبقّية
residuary legacy	*waṣiyyat radd*	وصية ردّ
residue	*al-bāqī*	الباقى
resign	*yastaqīl*	يستقيل
resignation	*istiqāla*	استقالة
resolution	*qarār*	قرار
resources	*mawārid, maṣādir*	موارد • مصادر
responsible	*mas'ūl*	مسؤول
responsible source	*maṣdar mas'ūl*	مصدر مسؤول
restock	*yuzawwid/yukhazzin min jadīd*	يزوّد/ يخزّن من جديد
restore	*yurammim, yuᶜīd ila 'l-aṣl*	يرمّم • يعيد الى الاصل
restraint of trade	*taqyīd at-tijāra*	تقييد التجارة
restriction on imports	*taqyīd al-istīrād*	تقييد الاستيراد
restrictive practices	*asālīb muqayyida*	أساليب مقيّدة
restrictive provisions	*aḥkām muqayyida*	أحكام مقيّدة
retail	*bayᶜ at-tajzi'a/al-qaṭṭāᶜī*	بيع التجزئة /القطّاعى
retail cost	*taklifat at-tajzi'a/al-qaṭṭāᶜī*	تكلفة التجزئة /القطّاعى
retailer	*maḥall bayᶜ at-tajzi'a, bā'iᶜ at-tajzi'a*	محلّ بيع التجزئة • بائع التجزئة
retail outlet	*sūq at-taṣrīf*	سوق التصريف القطّاعى
retail price	*siᶜr at-tajzi'a/al-qaṭṭāᶜī*	سعر التجزئة /القطّاعى
retail store	*matjar bayᶜ at-tajzi'a*	متجر بيع التجزئة

retail trade	*tajārat bay^c at-tajzi'a*	تجارة بيع التجزئة
retainer	*at^cāb muḥāmī*	أتعاب محام
retire	*yataqā^cad*	يتقاعد
retirement	*taqā^cud*	تقاعد
retirement age	*sinn at-taqā^cud*	سنّ التقاعد
retirement pay	*rātib at-taqā^cud*	راتب التقاعد
retiring partner	*sharīk munsaḥib*	شريك منسحب
retroactive	*bi-athar raj^cī*	بأثر رجعى
retrospective	*istirjā^cī*	استرجاعى
return on capital	*mardūd ar-ra'salmāl*	مردود الرأس مال
return on investment	*mardūd al-istithmār*	مردود الاستثمار
revaluation	*i^cādat taqyīm, raf^c qīmat ^cumla*	اعادة تقييم ، رفع قيمة عملة
revalue	*yu^cīd taqyīm*	يعيد تقييم
revenue	*īrād*	ايراد
revenue authorities	*maṣlaḥat aḍ-ḍarā'ib*	مصلحة الضرائب
revenue receipts	*maqbūḍāt īrādiyya*	مقبوضات ايرادية
revenue reserves	*iḥtiyaṭi 'l-īrād*	احتياطى الايراد
revocable credit	*i^ctimād qābil li'l-istirdād*	اعتماد قابل للاسترداد
revocable letter of credit	*kitāb i^ctimād qābil li'l-istirdād*	كتاب اعتماد قابل للاسترداد
revolving credit	*i^ctimād dawwār*	اعتماد دوّار
reward	*mukāfa'a*	مكافأة

rider	*mulḥaq tafsīrī*	ملحق تفسيرى
right of access	*ḥaqq ad-dukhūl/al-wuṣūl*	حقّ الدخول/الوصول
right of communication	*ḥaqq al-iṭṭilā^c*	حقّ الاطلاع
right of self-determination	*ḥaqq taqrīr al-maṣīr*	حقّ تقرير المصير
right of way	*ḥaqq al-murūr*	حقّ المرور
riot	*shaghab*	شغب
riparian rights	*ḥuqūq nahriyya*	حقوق نهرية
risk	*khaṭar, mukhāṭara*	خطر، مخاطرة
risk capital	*ra'salmāl dhū akhṭār*	رأس مال ذو أخطار
risk factor	*^{c}āmil al-khaṭar*	عامل الخطر
risk-taking	*mukhāṭara*	مخاطرة
risky	*yanṭawī ^{c}alā khaṭar*	ينطوى على خطر
rival demands	*ṭalabāt mutanāfisa*	طلبات متنافسة
rival supplies	*^{c}urūḍ mutanāfisa*	عروض متنافسة
robbery	*salb, nahb, qaṭ^c aṭ-ṭarīq*	سلب، نهب، قطع الطريق
rock bottom	*adnā mustawā*	أدنى مستوى
rolling stock	*mu^{c}iddāt sikak ḥadīd*	معدّات سكك حديد
rough draft	*muswadda*	مسودّة
royalty	*ray^c, itāwa*	ريع، اتاوة
royalty income	*dakhl ray^{c}ī*	دخل ريعى
run a business	*yudīr ^{c}amal*	يدير عمل

run into debt	*yaqa*ᶜ *fi'd-dayn*	يقع فى الدين
running expenses	*maṣārīf jāriya*	مصاريف جارية

S

sabotage	*takhrīb*	تخريب
sack (dismissal)	*ṭard, faṣl*	طرد ، فصل
sacrifice	*yuḍaḥḥī*	يضحّى
safe custody	*wadī^{c}a maḥrūsa*	وديعة محروسة
safe deposit box	*ṣundūq ḥadīd li-ḥifẓ al-wadā'i^c*	صندوق حديد لحفظ الودائع
safe deposit company	*sharikat ḥifẓ al-wadā'i^c*	شركة حفظ الودائع
safe estimate	*taqdīr maḍmūn*	تقدير مضمون
safekeeping	*ḥirāsa jayyida*	حراسة جيّدة
safety factor	*^{c}āmil as-salāma*	عامل السلامة
safety margin	*ḥadd al-amān*	حدّ الامان
salaried employee	*muwaẓẓaf bi-rātib*	موظّف براتب
salary	*rātib*	راتب
salary range	*sullam al-ujūr*	سلّم الاجور
sale	*bay^c, bay^c at-takhfīḍ*	بيع ، بيع التخفيض

saleable	*qābil li'l-bayᶜ*	قابل للبيع
saleable goods	*silaᶜ qābila li'l-bayᶜ*	سلع قابلة للبيع
sale and return	*bayᶜ bi-khiyār ar-radd*	بيع بخيار الردّ
sale by auction	*bayᶜ bi'l-mazād al-ᶜalanī*	بيع بالمزاد العلني
sale by description	*al-bayᶜ bi'l-waṣf*	البيع بالوصف
sale by private treaty	*bayᶜ widdī*	بيع ودّى
sale by sample	*bayᶜ bi'l-ᶜayyina*	بيع بالعيّنة
sale of goods	*bayᶜ al-baḍā'iᶜ*	بيع البضائع
sale on approval	*bayᶜ bi-sharṭ al-istiḥsān*	بيع بشرط الاستحسان
sale on consignment	*bayᶜ ᶜala 'l-ḥisāb*	بيع على الحساب
sale on credit	*al-bayᶜ bi'd-dayn*	البيع بالدين
sale or return	*silaᶜ tubāᶜ aw tuᶜād*	سلع تباع أو تعاد
sales agent	*wakīl al-bayᶜ*	وكيل البيع
sales branch	*farᶜal mabīᶜāt*	فرع المبيعات
sales budget	*mīzāniyyat al-mabīᶜāt*	ميزانية المبيعات
sales forecast	*tanabbu' bi'l-mabīᶜāt*	تنبّؤ بالمبيعات
sales index	*dalīl al-mabīᶜāt*	دليل المبيعات
sales invoice	*fātūrat al-mabīᶜāt*	فاتورة المبيعات
sales journal	*daftar yawmiyyat al-mabīᶜāt*	دفتر يومية المبيعات
sales ledger	*daftar 'ustādh al-mabīᶜāt*	دفتر أستاذ المبيعات
salesman	*bā'iᶜ*	بائع

sales management	*idārat al-mabī^{c}āt*	ادارة المبيعات
sales manager	*mudīr al-mabī^{c}āt*	مدير المبيعات
salesmanship	*fann al-bay^{c}*	فنّ البيع
sales order	*ṭalab mabī^{c}āt*	طلب مبيعات
sales policy	*siyāsat al-mabī^{c}āt*	سياسة المبيعات
sales potential	*imkāniyyat al-mabī^{c}āt*	امكانية المبيعات
sales promotion	*tarwīj al-mabī^{c}āt*	ترويج المبيعات
sales quota	*kūta 'l-mabī^{c}āt*	كوتا المبيعات
sales record	*sijill al-mabī^{c}āt*	سجلّ المبيعات
sales returns	*mardūdāt al-mabī^{c}āt*	مردودات المبيعات
sales revenue	*dakhl al-mabī^{c}āt*	دخل المبيعات
sales tax	*ḍarība ^{c}ala 'l-mabī^{c}āt*	ضريبة على المبيعات
sales territories	*manāṭiq al-bay^{c}*	مناطق البيع
salvage	*biḍā^{c}a munqatha*	بضاعة منقذة
salvage charges	*maṣārīf inqāth*	مصاريف انقاذ
salvage value	*qīmat al-mukhallajāt*	قيمة المخلّفات
sample	*^{c}ayyina*	عيّنة
sample signature	*tawqī^{c} numūdhajī*	توقيع نموذجى
sampling	*akhdh al-^{c}ayyināt, tawzī^{c} al-^{c}ayyināt majjānan*	أخذ العيّنات، توزيع العيّنات مجّانا
sampling error	*al-khaṭa' al-^{c}ayyinī*	الخطأ العيّنى

sanction	*yuṣādiq, ᶜuqūba*	يصادق، عقوبة
satisfaction	*riḍa, adā'*	رضى، أداء
save	*yuwaffir*	يوفّر
save labour, to	*yaqtaṣid fi'l-yad al-ᶜāmila*	يقتصد فى اليد العاملة
savings	*muddakharāt*	مدّخرات
savings account	*ḥisāb tawfīr*	حساب توفير
scare buying	*shirā' madhᶜūr*	شراء مذعور
schedule	*jadwal, jadwal zamanī*	جدول ، جدول زمنى
scheduled flight	*riḥla bi mawᶜid muḥaddad*	رحلة بموعد محدّد
scheduled territories	*manṭiqat al-istirlīnī*	منطقة الاسترلينى
schedules airline	*sharikat ṭayarān bi-riḥlāt muqarrara*	شركة طيران برحلات مقرّرة
scheme	*mashrūᶜ*	مشروع
scientific adviser	*mustashār ᶜilmī*	مستشار علمى
scientific management	*al-idāra 'l-ᶜilmiyya*	الادارة العلمية
scientific method	*aṭ-ṭarīqa 'l-ᶜilmiyya*	الطريقة العلمية
scoop	*sabq ṣaḥafī*	سبق صحفى
scrap	*khurda*	خردة
scrap value	*qīmat al-khurda*	قيمة الخردة
screening	*gharbala*	غربلة
sea bed	*qāᶜ al-baḥr*	قاع البحر
sea damage	*aḍrār al-baḥr*	أضرار البحر

sealed and delivered	*khutim wa bulligh, ushhid ʿalayh*	ختم وبلّغ ، أشهد عليه
seal of the company	*khitm ash-sharika*	ختم الشركة
search warrant	*amr taftīsh*	أمر تفتيش
seasonal adjustment	*taʿdīl mawsimī*	تعديل موسمى
seasonal articles	*mawādd mawsimiyya*	موادّ موسمية
seasonal drop	*inkhifāḍ mawsimī*	انخفاض موسمى
seasonal fluctuation	*taqallub mawsimī*	تقلّب موسمى
seasonal variation	*taghayyurāt mawsimiyya*	تغيرات موسمية
sea trade	*tijāra baḥriyya*	تجارة بحرية
seaworthy	*ṣāliḥ li'l-milāḥa*	صالح للملاحة
secondary boycott	*muqāṭaʿa thānawiyya*	مقاطعة ثانوية
secondary liability	*iltizām thānawī*	التزام ثانوى
second-class mail	*barīd daraja thāniya*	بريد درجة ثانية
second generation	*al-jīl ath-thānī*	الجيل الثانى
second-hand	*mustaʿmal*	مستعمل
second mortgage	*rahn thānī*	رهن ثان
seconds (imperfect goods)	*silaʿ daraja thāniya*	سلع درجة ثانية
secret	*sirrī*	سرّى
secretary	*sikritair, amīn sirr*	سكرتير ، أمين سرّ
secretary's office	*maktab as-sikritair*	مكتب السكرتير
secret partner	*sharīk khāfī*	شريك خفى

secret trust	*amāna sirriyya*	أمانة سرّية
secured credit	*i^{c}timād/qarḍ maḍmūn*	اعتماد/قرض مضمون
secured creditor	*dā'in maḍmūn*	دائن مضمون
secured debt	*dayn maḍmūn*	دين مضمون
secured loan	*qarḍ maḍmūn*	قرض مضمون
securities	*sanadāt māliyya*	سندات مالية
security	*waraqa māliyya, ḍamān*	ورقة مالية ، ضمان
security guard	*ḥāriṣ amn*	حارس أمن
security measures	*ijrā'āt amn*	اجراءات أمن
security officer	*ḍābiṭ al-amn*	ضابط الامن
seizure	*tawqī^{c} ḥajz, waḍ^{c} al-yad*	توقيع حجز ، وضع اليد
selection	*ikhtiyār, intiqā'*	اختيار ، انتقاء
self-employed	*ya^{c}mal li-ḥisābihi 'l-khāṣṣ*	يعمل لحسابه الخاصّ
self-service	*khidma dhātiyya*	خدمة ذاتية
sell	*yabī^{c}*	يبيع
sellers' market	*sūq al-bā'i^{c}īn*	سوق البائعين
seller's option	*ḥaqq khiyār al-bā'i^{c}*	حقّ خيار البائع
selling costs	*maṣrūfāt al-bay^{c}*	مصروفات البيع
selling price	*si^{c}r al-bay^{c}*	سعر البيع
sell off	*yabī^{c} li't-taṣfiya*	يبيع للتصفية
semi-skilled labour	*aydi ^{c}āmila shibh fanniyya*	أيد عاملة شبه فنّية

senior advisor	*mustashār aqdam*	مستشار أقدم
seniority	*asbaqiyya, awwaliyya*	أسبقية ، أوّلية
senior member	*al-ᶜuḍw al-aqdam*	العضو الاقدم
separate property	*amlāk mustaqilla*	أملاك مستقلّة
separate return	*bayān munfaṣil*	بيان منفصل
sequential sampling	*al-muᶜāyana 'l-mutaᶜāqiba*	المعاينة المتعاقبة
serial number	*raqam musalsal*	رقم مسلسل
servant	*khādim*	خادم
service bureau	*maktab khadamāt*	مكتب خدمات
service capacity	*ṭāqat al-khidma*	طاقة الخدمة
service charge	*rasm khidma*	رسم خدمة
service costs	*takālīf al-khadamāt*	تكاليف الخدمات
service department	*idārat al-khadamāt*	ادارة الخدمات
service trade	*tijārat al-khadamāt*	تجارة الخدمات
set of documents	*majmūᶜat wathā'iq*	مجموعة وثائق
set-off	*muqāṣṣa*	مقاصّة
settle a dispute	*yusawwī/yaḥsim nizāᶜ*	يسوّى/يحسم نزاعا
settlement	*taswiya*	تسوية
settlement account	*ḥisāb at-taṣfiya*	حساب التصفية
settlement price	*siᶜr al-ilghā'*	سعر الالغاء
severable	*qābil li't-tajzi'a*	قابل للتجزئة

several liability	*mas'ūliyya fardiyya*	مسؤولية فردية
severance pay	*taᶜwīḍ inhā' al-khidma*	تعويض انهاء الخدمة
shake-up	*taᶜdīl, taghyīr*	تعديل ، تغيير
share	*ḥiṣṣa, sahm*	حصّة ، سهم
share bonus	*ashum minḥa*	أسهم منحة
share certificate	*shahādat al-ashum*	شهادة الاسهم
shareholder	*musāhim*	مساهم
share market	*sūq al-ashum*	سوق الاسهم
share premium	*ᶜilāwat al-iṣdār*	علاوة الاصدار
share transfer	*taḥwīl ashum*	تحويل أسهم
shift	*nawba*	نوبة
shift differential	*ᶜilāwat an-nawba*	علاوة النوبة
ship-broker	*simsār baḥrī*	سمسار بحرى
shipbuilder	*bānī sufun*	بانى سفن
ship-building	*binā' as-sufun*	بناء السفن
shipbuilding yard	*ḥawḍ binā' as-sufun*	حوض بناء السفن
shipment	*shuḥna*	شحنة
ship owner	*mālik as-safīna*	مالك السفينة
shipper	*shāḥin*	شاحن
shipping	*shaḥn*	شحن
shipping agency	*wikālat shaḥn*	وكالة شحن

shipping charges	*maṣārīf shaḥn*	مصاريف شحن
shipping company	*sharikat milāḥa*	شركة ملاحة
shipping department	*qism ash-shaḥn*	قسم الشحن
shipping document	*mustanad ash-shaḥn*	مستند الشحن
shipping note	*rukhṣat shaḥn*	رخصة شحن
shipping office	*maktab ash-shaḥn*	مكتب الشحن
shipping order	*amr ash-shaḥn*	أمر الشحن
shipping port	*mīnā' taḥmīl/shaḥn*	ميناء تحميل
ship's articles	*ᶜaqd ᶜamal baḥḥāra*	عقد عمل بحّارة
ship's chandler	*muwarrid mu'an as-sufun*	مورّد مؤن السفن
ship's master	*qubṭān as-safīna*	قبطان السفينة
ship's papers	*awrāq al-bākhira*	اوراق الباخرة
shipwreck	*taḥaṭṭum as-safīna*	تحطّم السفينة
shop	*dukkān, matjar, warsha*	دكّان • متجر• ورشة
shop assistant	*mustakhdam fī ḥānūt*	مستخدم فى حانوت
shop floor workers	*ᶜummāl ᶜādiyyūn*	عمّال عاديون
shoplifter	*sāriq silaᶜ min ad-dakākīn*	سارق سلع من الدكاكين
shopping centre	*markaz tasawwuq*	مركز تسوّق
shop steward	*mandūb niqābī*	مندوب نقابى
shortage	*naqṣ*	نقص
short delivery	*taslīm nāqiṣ*	تسليم ناقص

shortfall	*naqṣ, ᶜawaz*	نقص، عوز
shorthanded	*nāqiṣ bi'l-yad al-ᶜāmila*	ناقص باليد العاملة
short haul	*naql li-masāfa qaṣīra*	نقل لمسافة قصيرة
short loans	*qurūḍ li-ajal qaṣīr*	قروض لاجل قصير
short-term	*li-ajal qaṣīr*	لاجل قصير
short-term credit	*iᶜtimād qaṣīr al-ajal*	اعتماد قصير الاجل
short-term insurance	*ta'mīn qaṣīr al-ajal*	تأمين قصير الاجل
short-term investment	*istithmār qaṣīr al-ajal*	استثمار قصير الاجل
short-term liabilities	*iltizāmāt qaṣīrat al-ajal*	التزامات قصيرة الاجل
short-term loan	*qarḍ qaṣīr al-ajal*	قرض قصير الاجل
short-term planning	*takhṭīṭ qaṣīr al-madā*	تخطيط قصير المدى
short weight	*wazn nāqiṣ*	وزن ناقص
shrinkage	*inkimāsh, taqalluṣ*	انكماش، تقلّص
shut down	*waqf al-ᶜamal*	وقف العمل
sick leave	*ijāza maraḍiyya*	اجازة مرضية
sickness benefit	*iᶜānat maraḍ*	اعانة مرض
sickness insurance	*ta'mīn ḍidd al-maraḍ*	تأمين ضدّ المرض
side line	*ᶜamal jānibī*	عمل جانبى
sign	*ᶜalāma, lāfita*	علامة، لافتة
sign a letter	*yuqqiᶜ risāla*	يوقّع رسالة
signature	*tawqīᶜ*	توقيع

sign on	*yataᶜāqad ᶜala 'stikhdām*	يتعاقد على استخدام
silent partner	*sharīk lā yudīr*	شريك لا يدير
silver standard	*ᶜiyār al-fiḍḍa*	عيار الفضّة
simple contract	*ᶜaqd ghayr rasmī*	عقد غير رسمى
simple interest	*fā'ida basīṭa*	فائدة بسيطة
single-entry	*qayd mufrad*	قيد مفرد
single premium	*qisṭ waḥīd*	قسط وحيد
single standard	*ᶜiyār mufrad li'n-naqd*	عيار مفرد للنقد
single tax	*ḍarība mufrada*	ضريبة مفردة
sinking fund reserve	*iḥtiyāṭī istihlāk al-qarḍ*	احتياطى استهلاك القرض
sit-down strike	*iḍrāb iᶜtiṣāmī*	اضراب اعتصامى
situations vacant	*waẓā'if khāliya*	وظائف خالية
situations wanted	*waẓā'if maṭlūba*	وظائف مطلوبة
skilled labour	*ᶜamal fannī*	عمل فنّى
skilled worker	*ᶜāmil fannī*	عامل فنّى
slander	*qadhf shafawī*	قذف شفوى
sliding scale	*miqyās inzilāqī*	مقياس انزلاقى
slowdown	*tabāṭu' fi'l-ᶜamal*	تباطؤ فى العمل
slow-moving stock	*biḍāᶜa kāsida*	بضاعة كاسدة
slump	*hubūṭ*	هبوط
slump in prices	*inkhifāḍ al-asᶜār*	انخفاض بالاسعار

small business	*mu'assasat aʿmāl ṣaghīra*	مؤسسة أعمال صغيرة
smuggling	*tahrīb*	تهريب
social insurance	*ta'mīn ijtimāʿī*	تأمين اجتماعى
social security	*ḍamān ijtimāʿī*	ضمان اجتماعى
social services	*khadamāt ijtimāʿiyya*	خدمات اجتماعية
software	*muʿṭayāt wa barāmij al-kumbyūtar*	معطيات وبرامج الكمبيوتر
solar energy	*aṭ-ṭāqa 'sh-shamsiyya*	الطاقة الشمسية
sold up	*mabīʿ*	مبيع
sole agent	*al-wakīl al-waḥīd*	الوكيل الوحيد
sole proprietor	*mālik fard*	مالك فرد
sole tenant	*musta'jir waḥīd*	مستأجر وحيد
solicitor	*muḥāmī (fī injiltira)*	محام (فى انجلترا)
source of income	*maṣdar īrād*	مصدر ايراد
space	*misāḥa, makān*	مساحة ، مكان
spare capital	*amwāl jāhiza*	اموال جاهزة
spare parts	*qiṭaʿ ghayār, ajzā' iḥtiyāṭiyya*	قطع غيار، أجزاء احتياطية
spare time	*waqt fā'iḍ*	وقت فائض
special agent	*wakīl khāṣṣ*	وكيل خاصّ
special agreement	*ittifāq khāṣṣ*	اتّفاق خاصّ
special conditions	*shurūṭ khāṣṣa*	شروط خاصّة
special contingency reserve	*iḥtiyāṭī khāṣṣ li'ṭ-ṭawāri'*	احتياطى خاصّ للطوارئ

special deposits	*wadā'iᶜ khāṣṣa*	ودائع خاصّة
special endorsement	*taẓhīr khāṣṣ*	تظهير خاصّ
specialist	*ikhṣā'ī, ikhtiṣāṣī*	اخصائى ، اختصاصى
specialization	*takhaṣṣuṣ*	تخصّص
special jurisdiction	*ikhtiṣāṣ muᶜayyan*	اختصاص معيّن
special licence	*taṣrīḥ khāṣṣ*	تصريح خاصّ
special partner	*sharīk khāṣṣ*	شريك خاصّ
special power	*wakāla khāṣṣa*	وكالة خاصّة
special price	*siᶜr khāṣṣ*	سعر خاصّ
special risk	*khaṭar khāṣṣ*	خطر خاصّ
specialty	*ᶜaqd rasmī*	عقد رسمى
specifications	*muwāṣafāt*	مواصفات
specific contracts	*ᶜuqūd musammāh*	عقود مسمّاة
specific duty	*rasm muᶜayyan*	رسم معيّن
specific performance	*tanfīdh muᶜayyan*	تنفيذ معين
specific tariff	*taᶜrifa muḥaddada*	تعرفة محدّدة
specimen signature	*namūdhaj imḍā'*	نموذج امضاء
speculation	*muḍāraba*	مضاربة
speculator	*muḍārib*	مضارب
sphere of influence	*dā'irat nufūdh*	دائرة نفوذ
split shift	*nawbat ᶜamal mujazza'a*	نوبة عمل مجزّأة

split up	*qismat as-sahm*	قسمة السهم
spokesman	*nāṭiq rasmī*	ناطق رسمى
sponsor	*kafīl, rāᶜī*	كفيل ٠ راعى
spot check	*taftīsh mufāji'*	تفتيش مفاجئ
spot transaction	*ṣafqa fawriyya*	صفقة فورية
stabilization	*tathbīt, istiqrār*	تثبيت.استقرار
staff administration	*idārat shu'ūn al-muwaẓẓafīn*	ادارة شؤون الموظفين
staff changes	*taghyīrāt fi'l-muwaẓẓafīn*	تغييرات فى الموظفين
staff committee	*lajnat shu'ūn al-muwaẓẓafīn*	لجنة شؤون الموظفين
staff council	*majlis al-muwaẓẓafīn*	مجلس الموظفين
staff manager	*mudīr shu'ūn al-muwaẓẓafīn*	مدير شؤون الموظفين
staff salaries	*rawātib al-muwaẓẓafīn*	رواتب الموظفين
stamp duty	*rasm aṭ-ṭābiᶜ*	رسم الطابع
stamp office	*maktab aṭ-ṭawābiᶜ*	مكتب الطوابع
stamp tax	*ḍarībat ṭawābiᶜ*	ضريبة طوابع
standard batch control	*al-murāqaba bi'd-dufaᶜāt al-qiyāsiyya*	المراقبة بالدفعات القياسية
standard costs	*takālīf qiyāṣiyya*	تكاليف قياسية
standardization	*tawḥīd al-qiyās*	توحيد القياس
standard of living	*mustawa 'l-maᶜīsha*	مستوى المعيشة
standard operating procedure	*uslūb at-tashghīl al-qiyāsī*	اسلوب التشغيل القياسى
standard performance	*al-adā' al-qiyāsī*	الاداء القياسى

standard procedures	*ijrā'āt muwaḥḥada*	اجراءات موحّدة
standard rate	*al-muᶜaddal al-asāsī*	المعدّل الاساسى
standard time	*al-waqt al-qiyāsī*	الوقت القياسى
standard unit	*waḥda qiyāsiyya*	وحدة قياسية
standard weight	*al-wazn al-qiyāsī*	الوزن القياسى
standing committee	*lajna dā'ima*	لجنة دائمة
starting date	*tārīkh al-bad'*	تاريخ البدء
state bank	*maṣrif ad-dawla/al-ḥukūma*	مصرف الدولة /الحكومة
statement of account	*bayān al-ḥisāb*	بيان الحساب
statement of expenses	*bayān bi'n-nafaqāt*	بيان بالنفقات
statistical quality control	*murāqabat an-nawᶜiyya 'l-iḥṣā'iyya*	مراقبة النوعية الاحصائية
statistical unit	*waḥda iḥṣā'iyya*	وحدة احصائية
statistics	*iḥṣā', iḥṣā'āt*	احصاء، احصاءات
statute	*qānūn barlamānī*	قانون برلمانى
statute of limitations	*qānūn at-taqādum*	قانون التقادم
statutory limitation	*at-taqādum al-qānūnī*	التقادم القانونى
steal	*yasriq*	يسرق
steel	*ṣulb, fūlādh*	صلب، فولاذ
steel-works	*maṣnaᶜ ṣulb*	مصنع صلب
sterling	*istirlīnī, miᶜyār al-fiḍḍa 'l-khāliṣa*	استرلينى، معيار الفضّة الخالصة
sterling area	*manṭiqat al-jinaih al-istirlīnī*	منطقة الجنيه الاسترلينى

stock	*sahm, baḍā'iᶜ*	سهم • بضائع
stock-broker	*simsār awrāq māliyya*	سمسار أوراق مالية
stock certificate	*shahādat as-sahm*	شهادة السهم
stock company	*sharika musāhama*	شركة مساهمة
stock control	*murāqat al-baḍā'iᶜ*	مراقبة البضائع
stock exchange	*sūq al-awrāq al-māliyya*	سوق الاوراق المالية
stockholder	*musāhim*	مساهم
stock in trade	*al-biḍāᶜa s-sā'ira,al-makhzūn*	البضاعة السائرة • المخزون
stock market	*sūq al-ashum al-māliyya*	سوق الاسهم المالية
stockpiling	*ikhtizān al-baḍā'iᶜ*	اختزان البضائع
stock-taking	*jard al-baḍā'iᶜ*	جرد البضائع
stock transfer	*naql milkiyyat as-sahm*	نقل ملكية السهم
stoppage	*tawaqquf, iḍrāb*	توقّف• اضراب
stop payment	*waqf ad-dafᶜ*	وقف الدفع
storage	*takhzīn*	تخزين
store, a	*maḥall tijārī*	محلّ تجارى
store, to	*yukhazzin*	يخزّن
storekeeper	*amīn makhzan, ṣāḥib matjar*	أمين مخزن• صاحب متجر
stowage	*tastīf al-baḍā'iᶜ, ujrat at-tastīf*	تستيف البضائع • اجرة التستيف
strategic planning	*at-takhṭīṭ al-istirātījī*	التخطيط الاستراتيجى
strike	*iḍrāb*	اضراب

strike, to	*yuḍrib ᶜan al-ᶜamal*	يضرب عن العمل
strike a bargain	*yaᶜqid ṣafqa*	يعقد صفقة
strikebreaker	*mufsid al-iḍrāb*	مفسد الاضراب
strong market	*sūq qawiyya*	سوق قوية
strong room	*ghurfat īdāᶜ manīᶜa*	غرفة ايداع منيعة
subcontract	*ᶜaqd min al-bāṭin*	عقد من الباطن
sub-editor	*sikritair taḥrīr*	سكرتير تحرير
subject to quota	*muḥaṣṣaṣ*	محصّص
sublease	*ᶜaqd Ījār min al-bāṭin*	عقد ايجار من الباطن
subpoena	*taklīf bi'l-ḥuḍūr*	تكليف بالحضور
subscribe	*yaktatib, yashtarik*	يكتتب ، يشترك
subscribed capital	*ar-ra's māl al-muktatab bihi*	الرأس مال المكتتب به
subscription	*iktitāb, ishtirāk*	اكتتاب ، اشتراك
subsidiary clause	*band thānawī*	بند ثانوى
subsidiary company	*sharika tābiᶜa*	شركة تابعة
subsidy	*iᶜāna*	اعانة
substantial damages	*aḍrār/taᶜwīḍāt kabīra*	أضرار/تعويضات كبيرة
substantiate a claim	*yuthbit ṣiḥḥat iddiᶜā'*	يثبت صحّة ادّعاء
subtenant	*musta'jir min al-bāṭin*	مستأجر من الباطن
succession tax	*ḍarībat al-mīrāth*	ضريبة الميراث
successor	*khalaf*	خلف

sue	*yuqāḍī*	يقاضى
suggestion scheme	*mashrūᶜ al-iqtirāḥāt*	مشروع الاقتراحات
sum insured	*al-mablagh al-maḍmūn*	المبلغ المضمون
summary	*mulakhkhaṣ*	ملخّص
sum up	*yajmaᶜ, yujmil*	يجمع • يجمل
sundry expenses	*nafaqāt mutanawwiᶜa*	نفقات متنوّعة
superannuation fund	*ṣundūq at-taqāᶜud*	صندوق التقاعد
superior court	*maḥkama ᶜulyā*	محكمة عليا
supermarket	*matjar kabīr bi khidma dhātiyya*	متجر كبير بخدمة ذاتية
super-tax	*ḍarība iḍāfiyya*	ضريبة اضافية
supervisor	*mushrif*	مشرف
supplementary agreement	*ittifāqiyya mukammila*	اتّفاقية مكمّلة
supplementary budget	*mizāniyya takmīliyya*	ميزانية تكميلية
supplementary report	*taqrīr takmīlī*	تقرير تكميلى
supplier	*muwarrid*	مورّد
supply	*imdādāt*	امدادات
supply and demand	*al-ᶜarḍ wa'ṭ-ṭalab*	العرض والطلب
surcharge	*ḍarība iḍāfiyya*	ضريبة اضافية
surety bond	*kafālat aḍ-ḍāmin*	كفالة الضامن
surplus	*fā'iḍ*	فائض
surplus capacity	*ṭāqa fā'iḍa*	طاقة فائضة

surplus profit	*ribḥ zā'id*	ربح زائد
surrender value	*qīmat at-tanāzul*	قيمة التنازل
surrender value of a policy	*qīmat shirā' ᶜaqd ta'mīn*	قيمة شراء عقد تأمين
surtax	*ḍarība iḍāfiyya*	ضريبة اضافية
survey	*masḥ, dirāsa*	مسح ، دراسة
survey certificate	*shahādat muᶜāyana*	شهادة معاينة
survey fee	*rasm muᶜāyana*	رسم معاينة
sustain heavy losses	*yatakabbad khasā'ir fādiḥa*	يتكبّد خسائر فادحة
sustain heavy losses	*yuᶜānī khasāra jasīma*	يعانى خسارة جسيمة

T

table	*jadwal, lā'iḥa*	جدول . لائحة
table of allowances	*jadwal ᶜalāwāt*	جدول علاوات/مخصّصات
table of contents	*fihris, jadwal al-muḥtawayāt*	فهرس. جدول المحتويات
taboo	*muḥarram*	محرّم
tabulating machine	*āla li-tanẓīm al-jadāwil*	آلة لتنظيم الجداول
tabulation	*tansīq fī jadāwil*	تنسيق فى جداول
tachograph	*ᶜaddād dawrāt musajjil*	عدّاد دورات مسجّل
tacit agreement	*ittifāq ḍimnī*	اتّفاق ضمنى
tacit approval	*muwāfaqa ḍimniyya*	موافقة ضمنية
tacit consent	*riḍā' ḍimnī*	رضاء ضمنى
take account of	*ya'khudh fi'l-ḥusbān*	يأخذ فى الحسبان
take advantage	*yaghtanim al-furṣa*	يغتنم الفرصة
take care of	*yaᶜtanī bi*	يعتنى ب
take for granted	*yaᶜtabar al-amr musallam bih*	يعتبر الامر مسلّما به

take-home pay	*ṣāfi 'r-rātib*	صافى الراتب
take into account	*ya'khudh fi'l-iᶜtibār*	يأخذ فى الاعتبار
take measures	*yattakhidh tadābīr/ijrā'āt*	يتّخذ تدابير/اجراءات
take office	*yatawallā manṣib/waẓīfa*	يتولّى منصبا/وظيفة
take out	*yasḥab*	يسحب
take-over	*yastawlī ᶜalā, yatawallā*	يستولى على ٠ يتولّى
takeover bid	*ᶜarḍ istīlā '/tawallī*	عرض استيلاء/تولّ
take part	*yashtarik, yusāhim*	يشترك ٠ يساهم
take precautions	*yattakhidh iḥtiyaṭāt*	يتّخذ احتياطات
take stock	*yajrud*	يجرد
take the chair	*yar'as jalsa*	يرأس جلسة
talks	*mubāḥathāt*	مباحثات
tally	*muṭābaqa, ᶜadd*	مطابقة ٠ عدّ
tangible asset	*aṣl malmūs*	أصل ملموس
tanker	*nāqilat bitrūl*	ناقلة بترول
tank, storage	*ṣahrīj at-takhzīn*	صهريج التخزين
tape	*sharīṭ*	شريط
tare	*wazn al-ghilāf/al-wiᶜā'*	وزن الغلاف/الوعاء
target	*hadaf*	هدف
target date	*tārīkh mustahdaf*	تاريخ مستهدف
target price	*siᶜr mustahdaf*	سعر مستهدف

tariff	*taᶜrifa*	تعرفة
tariff agreement	*ittifāq ᶜala 't-taᶜrifa*	اتّفاق على التعرفة
tariff barriers	*ḥawājiz jumrukiyya*	حواجز جمركية
tariff insurance	*taᶜrifat at-ta'mīn*	تعرفة التأمين
tariff laws	*al-qawānīn al-jumrukiyya*	القوانين الجمركية
tariff system	*niẓām at-taᶜrifa 'l-jumrukiyya*	نظام التعريفة الجمركية
tax	*ḍarība*	ضريبة
taxable income	*dakhl khāḍiᶜ li'ḍ-ḍarība*	دخل خاضع للضريبة
taxable profits	*arbāḥ khāḍiᶜa li'ḍ-ḍarība*	ارباح خاضعة للضريبة
taxable value	*al-qīma 'l-khāḍiᶜa li'ḍ-ḍarība*	القيمة الخاضعة للضريبة
taxable year	*as-sana 'ḍ-ḍarībiyya*	السنة الضريبية
tax accounting	*muḥāsabat aḍ-ḍarība*	محاسبة الضريبة
tax arrears	*muta'akhkhirāt aḍ-ḍarā'ib*	متأخّرات الضرائب
tax assessor	*muqaddir/rābiṭ aḍ-ḍarība*	مقدّر/رابط الضريبة
taxation	*farḍ aḍ-ḍarā'ib*	فرض الضرائب
tax avoidance	*tajannub dafᶜ aḍ-ḍarība*	تجنّب دفع الضريبة
tax certificate	*shahādat dafᶜ aḍ-ḍarā'ib*	شهادة دفع الضرائب
tax collection	*jibāyat/taḥṣīl aḍ-ḍarā'ib*	جباية/تحصيل الضرائب
tax collector	*jābī/muḥaṣṣil aḍ-ḍarā'ib*	جابى/محصّل الضرائب
tax consultant	*mustashār shu'ūn aḍ-ḍarā'ib*	مستشار شؤون الضرائب
tax credit	*iᶜtimād ḍarībī*	اعتماد ضريبى

tax cuts	*takhfīḍāt ḍarībiyya*	تخفيضات ضريبية
taxes	*ḍarā'ib, rusūm*	ضرائب، رسوم
taxes on profit	*ḍarā'ib al-arbāḥ*	ضرائب الارباح
tax exemption	*iᶜfā' min aḍ-ḍarā'ib*	اعفاء من الضرائب
tax-free allowances	*masmūḥāt muᶜfāh min aḍ-ḍarība*	مسموحات معفاه من الضريبة
tax incentives	*ḥawāfiz ḍarībiyya*	حوافز ضريبية
tax inspector	*ma'mūr ḍarā'ib*	مأمور ضرائب
tax law	*qānūn aḍ-ḍarība*	قانون الضريبة
tax limit	*al-ḥadd al-aqṣā li'ḍ-ḍarība*	الحدّ الاقصى للضريبة
tax office	*maktab taḥṣīl aḍ-ḍarā'ib*	مكتب تحصيل الضرائب
taxes on capital	*ḍarā'ib ra'salmāl*	ضرائب رأس المال
taxpayer	*dāfiᶜ aḍ-ḍarība, mukallaf*	دافع الضريبة ، مكلّف
tax planning	*at-takhṭīṭ aḍ-ḍarībī*	التخطيط الضريبى
tax rate	*nisbat aḍ-ḍarība*	نسبة الضريبة
tax rebate	*khaṣm min aḍ-ḍarība*	خصم من الضريبة
tax relief	*takhfīḍ ḍarībī*	تخفيض ضريبى
tax reserve	*iḥtiyāṭi 'ḍ-ḍarā'ib*	احتياطى الضرائب
tax, to	*yafriḍ ḍarība*	يفرض ضريبة
tax year	*as-sana 'ḍ-ḍarībiyya*	السنة الضريبية
team-work	*ᶜamal jamāᶜa*	عمل جماعة
technical ability	*qudra fanniyya*	قدرة فنّية

technical adviser	*mustashār fannī*	مستشار فنّى
technical assistance	*musāᶜada fanniyya*	مساعدة فنّية
technical committee	*lajna fanniyya*	لجنة فنّية
technical director	*mudīr fannī*	مدير فنّى
technical education	*at-taᶜlīm al-fannī*	التعليم الفنّى
technical point	*mas'ala fanniyya*	مسألة فنّية
technical training	*tadrīb fannī*	تدريب فنّى
technician	*fannī, khabīr fannī*	فنّى• خبير فنّى
technique	*uslūb, tiknīk*	أسلوب• تكنيك
technological change	*taghyīr tiknūlūjī*	تغيير تكنولوجى
technology	*tiknulūjya, taqniya*	تكنولوجيا• تقنية
telecode	*ramz baᶜīd*	رمز بعيد
telecommunication	*al-muwāṣalāt as-silkiyya wa'l-lāsilkiyya*	المواصلات السلكية واللاسلكية
telegram	*barqiyya*	برقية
telegraphic address	*al-ᶜunwān al-barqī*	العنوان البرقى
telegraphic money order	*ḥawāla barīdiyya tilighrāfiyya*	حوالة بريدية تلغرافية
telegraphic transfer	*taḥwīl mālī tilighrāfī*	تحويل مالى تلغرافى
telegraph office	*maktab al-barq/at-tilighrāf*	مكتب البرق/التلغراف
telephone	*hātif, tilifūn*	هاتف• تلفون
telephone answering service	*khidmat ar-radd ᶜala 't-tilifūn*	خدمة الردّ على التليفون
telephone directory	*dalīl al-hātif*	دليل الهاتف

telephone exchange	*baddālat/sintrāl al-hātif*	بدّالة/سنترال الهاتف
telephone operator	*ᶜāmil at-tilīfūn*	عامل التليفون
teleprinter	*mubriqa kātiba*	مبرقة كاتبة
telex	*tilix*	تلكس
teller	*ṣarrāf, jāmiᶜ al-aṣwāt*	صرّاف، جامع الاصوات
temporary	*mu'aqqat*	مؤقّت
temporary agreement	*ittifāqiyya mu'aqqata*	اتفاقية مؤقّتة
temporary assignment	*takhṣīṣ/taᶜyīn muᶜaqqat*	تخصيص/تعيين مؤقّت
temporary disablement	*ᶜajz mu'aqqat*	عجز مؤقّت
temporary injunction	*amr zajrī mu'aqqat*	أمر زجرى مؤقّت
temporary insurance	*ta'mīn/ḍamān mu'aqqat*	تأمين/ضمان مؤقّت
temporary measure	*tadbīr mu'aqqat*	تدبير موقّت
tenancy from year to year	*ijāra min sana ilā sana*	اجارة من سنة الى سنة
tenant	*musta'jir*	مستأجر
tenant for life	*musta'jir li-mada 'l-ḥayāh*	مستأجر لمدى الحياة
tender	*ᶜaṭā', ᶜarḍ*	عطاء، عرض
tender, invitation to	*ṭalab ᶜurūḍ/ᶜaṭā'āt*	طلب عروض/عطاءات
tentative agreement	*ittifāq tajrībī*	اتّفاق تجريبى
tentative suggestion	*muḥāwalat iqtirāḥ*	محاولة اقتراح
term	*sharṭ, mudda*	شرط، مدّة
term assurance	*ta'mīn muᶜaqqat*	تأمين مؤقّت على الحياة

terminal	*nihā'ī*	نهائى
terminate	*yunhī, yulghī*	ينهى. يلغى
terminate restrictions	*yulghi 'l-quyūd*	يلغى القيود
termination, notice of	*ikhṭār bi'l-intihā'*	اخطار بالانتهاء
termination of agreement	*inhā' al-ittifāq*	انهاء الاتّفاق
term insurance	*ta'mīn mawqūt*	تأمين موقوت
term of office	*muddat shaghl al-waẓīfa*	مدّة شغل الوظيفة
terms and conditions	*bunūd wa shurūṭ*	بنود وشروط
terms of delivery	*shurūṭ at-taslīm*	شروط التسليم
terms of payment	*shurūṭ ad-daf^{c}*	شروط الدفع
terms of sale	*shurūṭ al-bay^{c}*	شروط البيع
territorial limits	*ḥudūd iqlīmiyya*	حدود اقليمية
territorial waters	*al-miyāh al-iqlīmiyya*	المياه الاقليمية
terrorism	*irhāb*	ارهاب
test	*ikhtibār, faḥṣ*	اختبار. فحص
test-case	*qaḍiyya qad tuṣbiḥ sābiqa qānūniyya*	قضية قد تصبح سابقة قانونية
testimony	*shahāda*	شهادة
textile industry	*ṣinā^{c}at an-nasīj*	صناعة النسيج
textiles	*mansūjāt*	منسوجات
text of an amendment	*naṣṣ at-ta^{c}dīl*	نصّ التعديل
theft	*sariqa*	سرقة

thermal cracking	*at-taksīr al-ḥarārī*	التكسير الحراري
third party	*al-ghayr, ṭaraf thālith*	الغير • طرف ثالث
third-party insurance	*ta'mīn ḍidd al-ghayr*	تأمين ضدّ الغير
third-party liability	*iltizāmāt al-ghayr*	التزامات الغير
third world	*al-ᶜālam ath-thālith*	العالم الثالث
threat	*tahdīd*	تهديد
threat to peace	*tahdīd li's-silm*	تهديد للسلم
ticket	*tadhkara, biṭāqa*	تذكرة • بطاقة
ticket controller	*mufattish at-tadhākir*	مفتّش التذاكر
ticket holder	*ḥāmil at-tadhkara*	حامل التذكرة
tidal waters	*miyāh al-madd wa'l-jazr*	مياه المدّ والجزر
time and motion study	*dirāsat al-waqt wa'l-ḥaraka*	دراسة الوقت والحركة
time buying	*shirā' al-waqt*	شراء الوقت
time card	*biṭāqat ad-dawām*	بطاقة الدوام
time charter	*ta'jīl markab ḥasb al-waqt*	تأجيل مركب حسب الوقت
time factor	*ᶜāmil al-waqt*	عامل الوقت
timekeeper	*ḍābiṭ al-waqt*	ضابط الوقت
time-lag	*takhalluf zamanī*	تخلّف زمني
time-limit	*al-muhla*	المهلة
time paid for	*waqt yudfaᶜ ᶜanhu bilā ᶜamal*	وقت يدفع عنه بلا عمل
time rate	*ujrat al-waqt*	أجرة الوقت

time-saving	*tawfīr al-waqt*	توفير الوقت
time-table	*jadwal zamanī/mawāᶜīd*	جدول زمنى/مواعيد
title	*laqab, sanad tamalluk, haqq al-milkiyya*	لقب . حقّ الملكية . سند تملّك
token payment	*dufᶜa ramziyya*	دفعة رمزية
token strike	*iḍrāb ramzī*	اضراب رمزى
token strike	*iḍrāb ramzī (li't-taḥdhīr)*	اضراب رمزى (للتحذير)
tolerance	*tafāwut masmūḥ bihi*	تفاوت مسموح به
toll	*rasm, maks*	رسم . مكس
ton	*ṭinn*	طنّ
tonnage	*al-ḥumūla bi'ṭ-ṭinn*	الحمولة بالطنّ
tools	*adawāt, ālāt*	أدوات . آلات
topic of discussion	*mawḍūᶜ al-munāqasha*	موضوع المناقشة
top level manager	*mudīr min al-mustawa 'l-aᶜlā*	مدير من المستوى الاعلى
top management	*al-idāra 'l-ᶜulyā*	الادارة العليا
top secret	*sirrī jiddan*	سرّى جدّا
total account	*ḥisāb ijmālī*	حساب اجمالى
total amount	*al-miqdār al-kullī*	المقدار الكلّى
total cost	*majmūᶜ at-taklifa*	مجموع التكلفة
total disablement	*ᶜajz kullī*	عجز كلّى
total income	*dakhl ijmālī*	دخل اجمالى/كلّى
total loss	*al-khasāra 'l-kulliyya*	الخسارة الكلّية

total revenue	*rayᶜ kullī*	ريع كلّى
total surplus	*al-fā'iḍ al-ijmālī*	الفائض الاجمالى
total volume	*al-ḥajm al-kullī*	الحجم الكلّى
tourist agreement	*ittifāq siyāḥī*	اتّفاق سياحى
tourist office	*maktab siyāḥa*	مكتب سياحة
tourist trade	*tijārat/ḥirfat as-siyāḥa*	تجارة/حرفة السياحة
trade	*tijāra, mihna*	تجارة ، مهنة
trade agency	*wikāla tijāriyya*	وكالة تجارية
trade agreement	*ittifāqiyya tijāriyya*	اتّفاقية تجارية
trade association	*ittiḥād mihnī*	اتّحاد مهنى
trade balance	*al-mizān at-tijārī*	الميزان التجارى
trade barrier	*ḥājiz tijārī*	حاجز تجارى
trade bill	*kambiyāla tijāriyya*	كمبيالة تجارية
trade bloc	*kutla tijāriyya*	كتلة تجارية
trade controls	*al-quyūd ᶜala 't-tijāra*	القيود على التجارة
trade cycle	*dawra tijāriyya*	دورة تجارية
trade discount	*khaṣm tijārī*	خصم تجارى
trade discrimination	*tamyīz tijārī*	تمييز تجارى
trade dispute	*nizāᶜ tijārī*	نزاع تجارى
trade, domestic	*tijāra dākhiliyya*	تجارة داخلية
trade, export	*tijārat aṣ-ṣādir*	تجارة الصادر

trade, foreign	*tijāra khārijiyya*	تجارة خارجية
trade gap	*thaghra fi'l-mīzān at-tijārī*	ثغرة فى الميزان التجارى
trade in	*yubaddil silʿa qadīma*	يبدّل سلعة قديمة
trade, international	*tijāra dawliyya*	تجارة دولية
trade investments	*istithmārāt tijāriyya*	استثمارات تجارية
trade liability	*iltizām tijārī*	التزام تجارى
trademark	*ʿalāma tijāriyya*	علامة تجارية
trade name	*ism tijārī*	اسم تجارى
trade pattern	*namaṭ at-tijāra*	نمط التجارة
trade publication	*nashra mihniyya*	نشرة مهنية
trader	*tājir*	تاجر
trade relations	*ʿalāqāt tijāriyya*	علاقات تجارية
trade routes	*ṭuruq tijāriyya*	طرق تجارية
traders' credit	*iʿtimād at-tujjār*	اعتماد التجّار
trade secret	*sirr al-mihna*	سرّ المهنة
tradesman	*tājir, ḥirfī*	تاجر، حرفى
trade surplus	*mīzān tijārī rābiḥ*	ميزان تجارى رابح
trade union	*niqāba ʿummāliyya*	نقابة عمّالية
trading account	*ḥisāb al-mutājara*	حساب المتاجرة
trading assets	*uṣūl mustaghalla fi't-tijāra*	أصول مستغلّة فى التجارة
trading cheques	*shīkāt shirā'*	شيكات شراء

trading company	*sharika tijāriyya*	شركة تجارية
trading stamps	*ṭawābi^{c} tashjī^{c} al-mabī^{c}āt*	طوابع تشجيع المبيعات
trading year	*as-sana 't-tijāriyya*	السنة التجارية
traditional method	*uslūb taqlīdī, ṭarīqa taqlīdiyya*	أسلوب تقليدى • طريقة تقليدية
traditions	*taqālīd*	تقاليد
traffic	*ḥarakat al-baḍā'i^{c}*	حركة البضائع
traffic department	*qism ḥarakat al-baḍā'i^{c}*	قسم حركة البضائع
traffic management	*idārat ḥarakat al-baḍā'i^{c}*	ادارة حركة البضائع
traffic manager	*mudīr ḥarakat al-baḍā'i^{c}*	مدير حركة البضائع
traffic regulations	*anẓimat al-murūr*	أنظمة المرور
trainee	*mudarrab, taḥt at-tadrīb*	مدرّب • تحت التدريب
training	*tadrīb, tamrīn*	تدريب • تمرين
training, basic	*tadrīb asāsī*	تدريب أساسى
training department	*qism at-tadrīb*	قسم التدريب
training in industry	*at-tadrīb fi'ṣ-ṣinā^{c}a*	التدريب فى الصناعة
training, in-plant	*tadrīb dākhil al-maṣna^{c}*	تدريب داخل المصنع
train, to	*yudarrib*	يدرّب
transaction	*ṣafqa, mu^{c}āmala*	صفقة • معاملة
transferable	*qābil li't-taḥwīl/li'n-naql*	قابل للتحويل/للنقل
transferable securities	*sanadāt qābila li't-taḥwīl*	سندات قابلة للتحويل
transfer agent	*wakīl naql al-milkiyya*	وكيل نقل الملكية

transfer charge	*rasm at-taḥwīl*	رسم التحويل
transfer company	*sharikat naql amtiᶜa*	شركة نقل أمتعة
transfer deed	*ᶜaqd naql al-milkiyya*	عقد نقل الملكية
transfer duty	*rasm naql*	رسم نقل
transfer tax	*ḍarībat intiqāl*	ضريبة انتقال
transit	*tranzīt, murūr*	ترانزيت ، مرور
transit agreement	*ittifāq murūr*	اتّفاق مرور
transit fee	*rasm al-murūr*	رسم المرور
transitional period	*fatrat intiqāl*	فترة انتقال
transition stage	*marḥala intiqāliyya*	مرحلة انتقالية
transit permit	*taṣrīḥ al-murūr*	تصريح المرور
translator	*mutarjim*	مترجم
transmit	*jihāz irsāl*	جهاز ارسال
transport	*naql*	نقل
transport agent	*wakīl naql*	وكيل نقل
transport by air	*naql bi'l-jaww*	نقل بالجوّ
transport by road	*naql bi'l-barr*	نقل بالبرّ
transport by sea	*naql bi'l-baḥr*	نقل بالبحر
transport costs	*takālīf an-naql*	تكاليف النقل
transport tribunal	*maḥkamat an-naql*	محكمة النقل
travel agency	*wikālat siyāḥa*	وكالة سياحة

travel allowances	*mukhaṣṣaṣāt as-safar*	مخصّصات السفر
travel expenses	*nafaqāt as-safar*	نفقات السفر
travel guide	*dalīl as-safar*	دليل السفر
travel insurance	*ta'mīn as-safar*	تأمين السفر
travelling allowance	*badal as-safar*	بدل السفر
travelling salesman	*bā'iᶜ mutajawwil*	بائع متجوّل
traveller's cheque	*shīk siyāḥī*	شيك سياحى
treasurer	*amīn al-khazīna*	أمين الخزينة
treasury bond	*sanad ᶜala 'l-khazīna*	سند على الخزينة
Treasury Department	*wizārat al-khizāna*	وزارة الخزانة
treasury note	*sanad ᶜala 'l-khazīna*	سند على الخزينة
treaty	*ittifāqiyya, muᶜāhada*	اتّفاقية . معاهدة
treaty of alliance	*muᶜāhadat taḥāluf*	معاهدة تحالف
treaty of arbitration	*ittifāqiyyat taḥkīm*	اتّفاقية تحكيم
trend forecasting	*at-tanabbu' bi'l-ittijāh*	التنبّؤ بالاتّجاه
trend, market	*ittijāh as-sūq*	اتّجاه السوق
trespass	*taᶜaddī*	تعدّ
trial and error	*at-tajriba wa'l-khaṭa'*	التجربة والخطأ
trial balance	*mīzān al-ikhtibār*	ميزان الاختبار
trial judge	*qāḍī maḥkama ibtidā'iyya*	قاضى محكمة ابتدائية
trial lawyer	*muḥāmī murāfiᶜ fi'l-maḥākim*	محام مرافع فى المحاكم

tribunal	*maḥkama*	محكمة
tripartite alliance	*ḥilf thulāthī*	حلف ثلاثى
trouble-shooting	*taḥarri 'l-khalal*	تحرّى الخلل
truck	*ᶜarabat naql baḍā'iᶜ*	عربة نقل بضائع
truckage	*ujrat ᶜarabat an-naql*	اجرة عربة النقل
truckload	*ḥumūlat sayyārat naql*	حمولة سيّارة نقل
true copy	*ṣūra ṭibq al-aṣl*	صورة طبق الاصل
true rate	*muᶜaddal ṣaḥīḥ*	معدّل صحيح
trunk call	*ittiṣāl hātifī baᶜīd*	اتّصال هاتفى بعيد
trust	*ya'tamin*	تأتمن
turnover	*ḥajm al-ḥaraka 't-tijāriyya*	حجم الحركة التجارية
turnover tax	*ḍarībat jumlat al-mabīᶜāt*	ضريبة جملة المبيعات
two-tier systems	*niẓām as-siᶜrayn*	نظام السعرين
typify	*yumaththil, yarmiz ilā*	يمثّل • يرمز الى

U

ultimate end	*al-ghāya 'l-akhīra*	الغاية الاخيرة
ultimate truth	*al-ḥaqīqa 'l-asāsiyya*	الحقيقة الأساسية
ultra vires	*mutajāwiz li's-sulṭa 'l-mukhawwala*	متجاوز للسلطة المخوّلة
umpire	*ḥakam*	حكم
unacceptable	*ghayr maqbūl*	غير مقبول
unaccrued	*ghayr mustaḥiqq*	غير مستحقّ
unanimous approval	*muwāfaqa ijmā^ciyya*	موافقة اجماعية
unanimous vote	*taṣwīt bi'l-ijmā^c*	تصويت بالاجماع
unappropriated funds	*amwāl ghayr mukhaṣṣaṣa*	اموال غير مخصّصة
unauthorized	*bi-ghayr tafwīḍ/tarkhīṣ*	بغير تفويض/ترخيص
unavailable	*ghayr mutawaffir*	غير متوفّر
unavoidable	*lā yumkin tajannubuh*	لا يمكن تجنّبه
unavoidable accident	*ḥādith lā yumkin tajannubuh*	حادث لا يمكن تجنبه
unavoidable cost	*taklifa ḥatmiyya*	تكلفة حتمية

uncalled capital	*ra'smāl lam yuṭlab ba^{c}d*	رأسمال لم يطلب بعد
uncertified dividends	*arbāḥ lam yaṭlubhā aṣḥābhā*	أرباح لم يطلبها اصحابها
unclaimed goods	*baḍā'i^{c} lam yaṭlubha aṣḥābhā*	بضائع لم يطلبها أصحابها
unconditional	*ghayr mashrūṭ*	غير مشروط
unconfirmed	*ghayr muthbat, ghayr mu'akkad*	غير مثبت . غير مؤكّد
unconfirmed credit	*i^{c}timād ghayr muthabbat*	اعتماد غير مثبّت
undeniable	*lā yumkin inkāruh*	لا يمكن انكاره
underbid	*ya^{c}riḍ thamanan aqall*	يعرض ثمنا أقلّ
under-capacity	*dūna 'ṭ-ṭāqa*	دون الطاقة
undercharge	*yabī^{c} bi-si^{c}r nāqiṣ*	يبيع بسعر ناقص
underconsumption	*istihlāk munkhafiḍ*	استهلاك منخفض
undercut	*yabī^{c} bi-si^{c}r aqall*	يبيع بسعر اقلّ
underdeveloped	*mutakhallif*	متخلّف
underdeveloped areas	*manāṭiq mutakhallifa*	مناطق متخلّفة
under-developed nations	*al-'umam an-nāmiya*	الأمم النامية
under discussion	*taḥt al-baḥth*	تحت البحث
under-employed	*muwaẓẓaf qalīl al-^{c}amal*	موظّف قليل العمل
under-employment of resources	*quṣūr tawẓīf al-mawārid*	قصور توظيف الموارد
underestimate	*yuqaddir bi-aqall mina al-qīma*	يقدّر بأقلّ من القيمة
under examination	*taḥt al-ikhtibār*	تحت الاختبار
underinsurance	*ta'mīn bi-aqall min al-qīma*	تأمين بأقلّ من القيمة

underlease	*yu'ajjir min al-bāṭin*	يؤجّر من الباطن
underpayment	*dafᶜ nāqiṣ*	دفع ناقص
underproduction	*intāj mawādd thānawiyya*	انتاج موادّ ثانوية
under protest	*maᶜal-iḥtijāj*	مع الاحتجاج
undersea pipeline	*khaṭṭ anābīb taḥt saṭḥ al-baḥr*	خطّ أنابيب تحت سطح البحر
understaffed	*muftaqir li-muwaẓẓafīn*	مفتقر لموظّفين
understanding	*tafāhum*	تفاهم
undertaking	*taᶜahhud, mashrūᶜ*	تعهّد ، مشروع
undertaking, commercial	*munsha'a tijāriyya*	منشأة تجارية
under the counter	*khifya, bi-ṭarīqa ghayr mashrūᶜa*	خفية ، بطريقة غير مشروعة
under the law	*bi-muqtaḍa 'l-qānūn*	بمقتضى القانون
underutilization	*naqṣ istighlāl*	نقص استغلال
undervaluation	*taqyīm mukhaffaḍ, bakhs al-qīma*	تقييم مخفّض ، بخس القيمة
undervalue	*yunqiṣ qīmat*	ينقص قيمة
underwrite	*yaḍman al-iktitāb, yu'ammin*	يضمن الاكتتاب ، يؤمّن
underwriter	*ḍāmin, muktatib, mu'ammin*	ضامن ، مكتتب ، مؤمّن
underwriting	*ta'mīn, ḍamān, iktitāb*	تأمين ، ضمان ، اكتتاب
underwriting limit	*ḥudūd at-ta'mīn*	حدود التأمين
undesirable risk	*khaṭar ghayr marghūb fīh*	خطر غير مرغوب فيه
undischarged bankrupt	*muflis lam yuradd iᶜtibāruh*	مفلس لم يرد اعتباره
undistributed profits	*arbāḥ lam tuwazzaᶜ*	أرباح لم توزّع

undivided loyalty	*walā' ghayr mujazza'*	ولاء غير مجزّأ
undivided opinions	*ittifāq al-ārā'*	اتّفاق الآراء
undivided right	*ḥaqq ghayr mujazza'*	حق غير مجزّأ
undue influence	*ta'thīr mufriṭ, ta'thīr ghayr mashrūᶜ*	تأثير مفرط. تأثير غير مشروع
unearned income	*dakhl ghayr muktasab*	دخل غير مكتسب
unearned increment	*ziyāda ghayr muktasaba*	زيادة غير مكتسبة
unearned premium	*qisṭ ta'mīn ghayr muktasab*	قسط تأمين غير مكتسب
uneconomical	*ghayr iqtiṣādī*	غير اقتصادى
unemployed	*ᶜāṭil, ghayr muwaẓẓaf*	عاطل. غير موظّف
unemployment	*baṭāla*	بطالة
unemployment benefit	*iᶜānat biṭāla*	اعانة بطالة
unemployment compensation	*taᶜwīḍ biṭāla*	تعويض بطالة
unemployment insurance	*ta'mīn ḍidd al-biṭāla*	تأمين ضدّ البطالة
unenforceable	*lā yaqbal at-tanfīdh*	لا يقبل التنفيذ
unequivocal position	*mawqif ṣarīḥ*	موقف صريح
unexpired term	*muhla lam tantahi baᶜd*	مهلة لم تنته بعد
unfair competition	*munāfasa ghayr mashrūᶜa*	منافسة غير مشروعة
unfair trial	*muḥākama ghayr ᶜādila*	محاكمة غير عادلة
unfavourable balance of payment	*mīzān madfūᶜat fī ghayr ṣāliḥ al-balad*	ميزان مدفوعات فى غير صالح البلد
unfavourable balance of trade	*mīzān tijārī fī ghayr ṣāliḥ al-balad*	ميزان تجارى فى غير صالح البلد
unfinished product	*muntaj ghayr tāmm aṣ-ṣunᶜ*	منتج غير تامّ الصنع

unforeseen circumstances	*ẓurūf ṭāri'a/qāhira*	ظروف طارئة/قاهرة
unforeseen events	*ḥawādith mufāji'a*	حوادث مفاجئة
uniform costing	*ḥisāb at-takālīf al-munassaq*	حساب التكاليف المنسّق
uniform costs	*takālīf muwaḥḥada*	تكاليف موحّدة
uniform prices	*athmān muwaḥḥada*	اثمان موحّدة
unilateral contract	*^{c}aqd min jānib wāḥid*	عقد من جانب واحد
unilateral undertaking	*ta^{c}ahhud/mubāshara min jānib wāḥid*	تعهّد/مباشرة من جانب واحد
union	*ittiḥād, niqāba*	اتّحاد.نقابة
union contract	*^{c}aqd ma^{c}an-niqāba*	عقد مع النقابة
unissued stock	*ashum ghayr muṣdara*	أسهم غير مصدرة
unit cost	*taklifat al-waḥda 'l-intājiyya*	تكلفة الوحدة الانتاجية
unit cost	*taklifat al-waḥda*	تكلفة الوحدة
unit price	*si^{c}r al-waḥda*	سعر الوحدة
unit trust	*sharika tastathmir fī sharikāt ukhrā*	شركة تستثمر فى شركات أخرى
unity of purpose	*waḥdat al-gharaḍ*	وحدة الغرض
universal maintenance standards	*maqāyīs aṣ-ṣiyāna 'l-^{c}āmma*	مقاييس الصيانة العامّة
unjustifiable	*lā yumkin tabrīruh*	لا يمكن تبريره
unlawful act	*^{c}amal ghayr mashrū^{c}*	عمل غير مشروع
unlawful entry	*dukhūl ghayr mashrū^{c}*	دخول غير مشروع
unlimited	*ghayr maḥdūd*	غير محدود
unlimited company	*sharika dhāt mas'ūliyya ghayr maḥdūda*	شركة ذات مسؤولية غير محدودة

unlimited insurance	*ta'mīn ghayr maḥdūd*	تأمين غير محدود
unlimited liability	*mas'ūliyya ghayr maḥdūda*	مسؤولية غير محدودة
unlisted security	*sahm ghayr musaccar*	سهم غير مسعّر
unload	*yufrigh*	يفرغ
unofficial	*ghayr rasmī*	غير رسمى
unofficial strike	*iḍrāb ghayr rasmī*	اضراب غير رسمى
unpaid	*ghayr madfūc*	غير مدفوع
unpaid labour	*camal bilā ajr*	عمل بلا أجر
unpaid services	*khadamāt lā yudfac lahā*	خدمات لا يدفع لها
unproductive effort	*juhd lā yuntij*	جهد لا ينتج
unprofitable investment	*istithmār ghayr murbiḥ*	استثمار غير مربّح
unqualified	*ghayr mu'ahhal*	غير مؤهّل
unregistered	*ghayr musajjal*	غير مسجّل
unrestricted	*ghayr muqayyad*	غير مقيّد
unsaleable	*lā yumkin baycuh*	لا يمكن بيعه
unseaworthy	*ghayr ṣāliḥ li'l-milāḥa*	غير صالح للملاحة
unsecured credit	*ictimād ghayr maḍmūn*	اعتماد غير مضمون
unsecured debt	*dayn ghayr maḍmūn*	دين غير مضمون
unsecured loan	*qarḍ ghayr maḍmūn*	قرض غير مضمون
unskilled labour	*camal ghayr māhir*	عمل غير ماهر
unstable economy	*iqtiṣād muḍṭarib*	اقتصاد مضطرب

unused resources	mawārid ghayr mustaᶜmala	موارد غير مستعملة
unwritten law	qānūn ghayr mudawwan	قانون غير مدوّن
up-market	maḥall mustawā rāqī	محل مستوى راقى
upswing	ṣuᶜūd, intiᶜāsh	صعود ، انتعاش
up to date	ḥatta 'l-ān, ᶜaṣrī	حتّى الآن ، عصرى
upward mobility	tanaqqul ṣāᶜid	تنقّل صاعد
upward trend	ittijāh ṣāᶜid	اتّجاه صاعد
urgent need	ḥāja muliḥḥa	حاجة ملحّة
usage	ᶜurf, as-istiᶜmāl ash-shā'iᶜ	عرف،الاستعمال الشائع
use (n)	istiᶜmāl	استعمال
use , to	yastaᶜmil	يستعمل
user	muntafiᶜ	منتفع
usual hours of business	sāᶜāt ad-dawām	ساعات الدوام
usual terms	shurūṭ ᶜādiyya	شروط عادية
usury	ribā	ربا
usury laws	qawānīn ar-ribā	قوانين الربا
utilities, public	marāfiq ᶜāmma	مرافق عامّة
utility	manfaᶜa, nafᶜ	منفعة ، نفع
utility services	maṣāliḥ ᶜāmma	مصالح عامّة
utilizable assets	uṣūl qābila li'l-istiᶜmāl	أصول قابلة للاستعمال
utilization	istighlāl, intifāᶜ	استغلال، انتفاع

utmost good faith	*muntahā ḥusn an-niyya*	منتهى حسن النية

V

vacancy	*waẓīfa khāliya , farāgh*	وظيفة خالية • فراغ
vacant	*shāghir, khālin*	شاغر• خال
vacant possession	*waẓīfa/ḥiyāza shāghira*	وظيفة/حيازة شاغرة
vacate	*yukhlī, yughādir*	يخلى• يغادر
vacation	*ijāza, ᶜuṭla*	اجازة • عطلة
valid	*ṣaḥīḥ qānūnan*	صحيح قانونا
validate	*yuthbit ṣiḥḥat*	يثبت صحّة
validation certificate	*shahādat muṣādaqa*	شهادة مصادقة
valid contract	*ᶜaqd sharᶜī*	عقد • شرعى
validity	*sharᶜiyya, sarayān al-mafᶜūl*	شرعية • سريان المفعول
validity of a document	*sharᶜīyyat/sarayān wathīqa*	شرعية/سريان وثيقة
validity of contract	*ṣalāḥiyat al-ᶜaqd*	صلاحية العقد
validity period	*muddat aṣ-ṣalāḥiya*	مدّة الصلاحية
valid reason	*sabab maᶜqūl*	سبب معقول

valorization	*tathbīt as^c^ār as-sila^c^*	تثبيت أسعار السلع
valuable	*dhū qīma, qābil li't-taqyīm*	ذو قيمة . قابل للتقييم
valuable consideration	*^c^iwaḍ dhū qīma*	عوض ذو قيمة
valuables	*ashyā' thamīna*	اشياء ثمينة
valuation	*taqyīm*	تقييم
valuation	*tathmīn, taqdīr*	تثمين. تقدير
valuation of securities	*taqdīr qīmat al-awrāq al-māliyya*	تقدير قيمة الاوراق المالية
value	*qīma, thaman*	ثمن. قيمة
value-added tax (V.A.T.)	*ḍarībat al-qīma 'l-muḍāfa*	ضريبة القيمة المضافة
valuer	*muthammin*	مثمّن
variable	*mutaghayyir*	متغير
variable budget	*mīzāniyya mutaghayyira*	ميزانية متغيرة
variable budget	*mizāniyya marina*	ميزانية مرنة
variable cost	*taklifa mutaghayyira*	تكلفة متغيّرة
variable costing	*tathmīn mutaghayyir*	تثمين متغيّر
variable cost ratio	*nisbat at-taklifa 'l-mutaghayyira*	نسبة التكلفة المتغيّرة
variable costs	*takālīf mutaghayyira*	تكاليف متعيرة
variable element	*^c^unṣur mutaghayyir*	عنصر متغيّر
variable expense	*maṣrūfāt mutaghayyira*	مصروفات متغيرة
variable overheads	*maṣārīf ra'siyya mutaghayyira*	مصاريف رأسية متغيّرة
variable premium	*qisṭ mutaghayyir*	قسط متغيّر

variable returns	*ghalla mutaghayyira*	غلّة متغيّرة
variable risk	*khaṭar mutaghayyir*	خطر متغير
variable yield investments	*istithmārāt bi-mardūd mutaghayyir*	استثمارات بمردود متغيّر
variance	*ikhtilāf, tafāwut*	اختلاف ، تفاوت
variation of products	*tanawwu*^{c} *al-muntajāt*	تنوّع المنتجات
variety	*tashkīla, tanawwu*^{c}	تشكيلة ، تنوّع
vendee	*mushtarī*	مشترٍ
vending machine	*ālat bay*^{c}	آلة بيع
vendor	*bā'i*^{c}	بائع
vendor's lien	*ḥaqq al-bā'i*^{c} *fi'l-ḥajz*	حقّ البائع فى الحجز
venture	*mashrū*^{c}*, mughāmara*	مشروع ، مغامرة
venture capital	*raʾsmāl dhū akhṭār*	رأسمال ذو أخطار
venue	*ikhtiṣāṣ makānī, masraḥ al-ḥawādith*	اختصاص مكانى ، مسرح الحوادث
verbal	*shafahī*	شفهى
verbal agreement	*ittifāq shafahī*	اتّفاق شفهى
verbatim	*ḥarfiyyan, bi'n-naṣṣ*	حرفيا ، بالنصّ
verbatim report	*taqrīr ḥarfī kāmil*	تقرير حرفى كامل
verdict	*qarār al-muḥallafin, ḥukm*	قرار المحلّفين ، حكم
verification	*taḥaqquq, tathabbut*	تحقّق ، تثبّت
verification of accounts	*murāja*^{c}*at al-ḥisābāt*	مراجعة الحسابات
verification of debts	*taḥqīq ad-duyūn*	تحقيق الديون

verify	*yurājiᶜ, yataḥaqqaq min*	يراجع • يتحقّق من
verify an account	*yakshif ᶜalā ḥisāb*	يكشف على حساب
vertical integration	*takāmul ra'sī*	تكامل رأسى
vertical mobility	*taḥarrukiyya ra'siyya*	تحرّكية رأسية
vertical structure	*binya ra'siyya*	بنية رأسية
vested interest	*maṣlaḥa rāsikha*	مصلحة راسخة
veterinary services	*al-khadamāt al-bayṭariyya*	الخدمات البيطرية
veto	*vītū, ḥaqq ar-rafḍ*	فيتو • حقّ الرفض
via	*bi-ṭarīq*	بطريق
via airmail	*bi'l-barīd al-jawwī*	بالبريد الجوّى
viable economy	*iqtiṣād qādir ᶜala 'l-ḥayāh*	اقتصاد قادر على الحياة
vice-chairman	*nā'ib ra'īs (al-jalsa)*	نائب رئيس (الجلسة)
vice-president	*nā'ib ra'īs*	نائب رئيس
vice-versa	*wa'l-ᶜaks bi'l-ᶜaks*	والعكس بالعكس
violation	*naqḍ, mukhālafa, intihāk ḥurma*	نقض • مخالفة • انتهاك حرمة
violation of terms	*naqḍ ash-shurūṭ*	نقض الشروط
visa	*ta'shīra*	تأشيرة
visible exports	*ṣādirāt manẓūra*	صادرات منظورة
visible trade	*at-tijāra al-manẓūra*	التجارة المنظورة
visit	*ziyāra, tafaqqud*	زيارة • تفقّد
visitor's tax	*ḍarībat iqāma*	ضريبة اقامة

visual punch card	*biṭāqa muthaqqaba baṣariyya*	بطاقة مثقّبة بصرية
vital statistics	*iḥṣā'āt ḥayawiyya*	احصاءات حيوية
vocational training	*tadrīb mihanī*	تدريب مهنى
void	*bāṭil*	باطل
voidable contract	*ᶜaqd qābil li'l-ibṭāl*	عقد قابل للابطال
void contract	*ᶜaqd bāṭil*	عقد باطل
volume chart	*rasm bayānī li 'l-ḥajm*	رسم بيانى للحجم
volume cost	*kulfat al-ḥajm*	كلفة الحجم
volume discount	*khaṣm al-ḥajm*	خصم الحجم
volume of business	*ḥajm al-aᶜmāl*	حجم الاعمال
volume of production	*ḥajm al-intāj*	حجم الانتاج
voluntarily	*ṭawᶜan, ikhtiyāran*	طوعا ، اختيارا
voluntary	*ikhtiyārī, ṭawᶜī*	اختيارى ، طوعى
voluntary association	*irtibāṭ ikhtiyārī*	ارتباط اختيارى
voluntary bankruptcy	*iflās ikhtiyārī*	افلاس اختيارى
voluntary insurance	*ḍamān ṭawᶜī*	ضمان طوعى
voluntary liquidation	*taṣfiya ikhtiyāriyya*	تصفية اختيارية
voluntary winding up	*taṣfiya 'khtiyāriyya*	تصفية اختيارية
vote by ballot	*taṣwīt bi'l-iqtirāᶜ as-sirrī*	تصويت بالاقتراع السرّى
vote by proxy	*taṣwīt bi'n-niyāba*	تصويت بالنيابة
vote of confidence	*taṣwīt ᶜala 'th-thiqa*	تصويت على الثقة

voting	*taṣwīt*	تصويت
voting method	*ṭarīqat at-taṣwīt/al-intikhāb*	طريقة التصويت/ الانتخاب
voting paper	*waraqat intikhāb*	ورقة انتخاب
voting right	*ḥaqq at-taṣwīt*	حقّ التصويت
voting stock	*ashum li-ḥāmilihā ḥaqq at-taṣwīt*	أسهم لحاملها حقّ التصويت
voting system	*niẓām at-taṣwīt/al-intikhāb*	نظام التصويت/ الانتخاب
voucher	*mustanad ṣarf*	مستند صرف
vouch for	*yaḍman, yakful*	يضمن ٠ يكفل
voyage insurance	*ta'mīn ᶜalā safra*	تأمين على سفرة
voyage premium	*qisṭ ta'mīn ᶜalā safra*	قسط تأمين على سفرة
vulnerable position	*waḍᶜ muᶜarraḍ li't-tahdīd*	وضع معرض للتهديد

W

wage adjustment	*taᶜdīl al-'ujūr*	تعديل الاجور
wage and salary administration	*idārat al-'ujūr wa 'r-rawātib*	ادارة الاجور والرواتب
wage bracket	*sharīḥat al-ajr*	شريحة الأجر
wage council	*majlis al-'ujūr*	مجلس الأجور
wage differential	*farq al-'ujūr*	فرق الأجور
wage earner	*ᶜāmil bi'l-ajr*	عامل بالأجر
wage freeze	*tajmīd al-'ujūr*	تجميد الاجور
wage incentives	*ḥawāfiz ajriyya*	حوافز أجرية
wage inflation	*taḍakhkhum al-ujūr*	تضخم الاجور
wage policy	*siyāsat al-'ujūr*	سياسة الاجور
wage restraint	*ḍabṭ irtifāᶜ al-'ujūr*	ضبط ارتفاع الاجور
wages	*'ujūr*	أجور
wages board	*majlis al-'ujūr*	مجلس الأجور
wage scale	*sullam muᶜaddalāt al-'ujūr*	سلّم معدّلات الاجور

wages structure	*haykal al-'ujūr*	هيكل الأجور
wages tax	*ḍarība ᶜala 'l-'ujūr*	ضريبة على الاجور
waiting list	*qā'imat intiẓār*	قائمة انتظار
waiting period	*fatrat intiẓār*	فترة انتظار
waiting room	*ghurfat intiẓār*	غرفة انتظار
waive a claim, to	*yatanāzal ᶜan ḥaqq*	يتنازل عن حقّ
waiver clause	*sharṭ at-tanāzul*	شرط التنازل
walk-out	*iḍrāb mufāji'*	اضراب مفاجئ
walk out, to	*yuḍrib*	يضرب
warehouse	*mustawdaᶜ*	مستودع
warehouse charges	*nafaqāt al-khazn*	نفقات الخزن
warehouseman's lien	*ḥaqq ṣāḥib al-makhzan fi'l-ḥajz*	حقّ صاحب المخزن فى الحجز
warehouse receipt	*īṣāl al-mustawdaᶜ*	ايصال المستودع
warehousing	*takhzīn*	تخزين
wares	*baḍā'iᶜ, silaᶜ*	بضائع ، سلع
warpage dues	*rusūm jarr (ila'l-marsā)*	رسوم جرّ (الى المرسى)
warrant	*amr qaḍā'ī, ḍamān*	أمر قضائى، ضمان
warrant, to	*yaḍman*	يضمن
warranty	*ḍamān, taᶜahhud*	ضمان، تعهّد
warranty, breach of	*ikhlāl bi-ḍamān/bi-kafāla*	اخلال بضمان/بكفالة
warranty deed	*sanad ḍamān*	سند ضمان

warranty, express	*kafāla ṣarīḥa*	كفالة صريحة
warranty, implied	*kafāla ḍimniyya*	كفالة ضمنية
wastage	*khasāra, talaf*	خسارة ، تلف
waste	*tabdīd, faḍalāt*	تبديد ، فضلات
waste, to	*yubaddid*	يبدد
wasting asset	*aṣl mutanāqiṣ*	اصل متناقص
water	*mā'*	ماء
water damage	*ḍarar al-mā', taᶜwīḍ ᶜan ḍarar al-mā'*	ضرر الماء ، تعويض عن ضرر الماء
water installations	*munsha'āt mā'iyya*	منشآت مائية
water level	*mustawa 'l-mā'*	مستوى الماء
water pollution	*talwīth al-miyāh*	تلويث المياه
water-power	*quwwat al-mā'*	قوّة الماء
water supply	*at-tazwīd bi'l-mā'*	التزويد بالماء
watertight	*lā yanfudh minhu 'l-mā'*	لاينفذ منه الماء
water transport	*an-naql al-mā'ī*	النقل المائى
waterway	*ṭarīq milāḥa*	طريق ملاحة
wave of depression	*mawjat rukūd*	موجة ركود
waybill	*bayān al-baḍā'iᶜ al-mashḥūna barran,*	بيان البضائع المشحونة برّا
weak market	*sūq ḍaᶜīfa*	سوق ضعيفة
wealth	*tharwa, māl*	ثروة ، مال
wealth tax	*ḍarībat ath-tharwa*	ضريبة الثروة

wear and tear	*bilā nājim ᶜan al-istiᶜmāl*	بلى ناجم عن الاستعمال
weather permitting	*maᶜ manākh mulā'im*	مع مناخ ملائم
week	*'usbūᶜ*	أسبوع
weekly	*'usbūᶜiyyan*	أسبوعيا
weekly payment	*dafᶜa 'usbūᶜiyya*	دفعة أسبوعية
weekly report	*taqrīr 'usbūᶜī*	تقرير أسبوعى
weekly return	*ᶜā'id 'usbūᶜī*	عائد أسبوعى
weekly wage	*ajr 'usbūᶜī*	أجر أسبوعى
weighted average	*al-wasaṭ al-murajjaḥ*	الوسط المرجّح
weighting	*tarjīḥ*	ترجيح
weights and measures	*al-mawāzīn wa'l-makāyīl*	الموازين والمكاييل
welfare department	*qism ar-rafāhiya*	قسم الرفاهية
welfare management	*idārat at-tarfīh*	ادارة الترفيه
welfare state	*dawlat ar-rafāhiya*	دولة الرفاهية
welfare worker	*murshid ijtimāᶜī*	مرشد اجتماعى
wet goods	*sila' sā'ila*	سلع سائلة
wharf	*raṣīf taḥmīl /tafrīgh as-sufun*	رصيف تحميل ، تفريغ السفن
wharfage	*rasm istkhdām ar-raṣīf*	رسم استخدام الرصيف
white collar worker	*muwaẓẓaf (min ghayr dhawi 'l-ḥuraf)*	موظّف (من غير ذوى الحرف)
whole life insurance	*ta'mīn madaᶜl-ḥayāh*	تأمين مدى الحياة
whole life policy	*būlīṣat ta'mīn mada 'l-ḥayāh*	بوليصة تأمين مدى الحياة

wholesale	*bay*^{c} *bi'l-jumla*	بيع بالجملة
wholesale dealer	*tajir jumla*	تاجر جملة
wholesale price	*si'r al-jumla*	سعر الجملة
wholesaler	*bā'i*^{c} *bi'l-jumla*	بائع بالجملة
wholesale trade	*tijārat al-jumla*	تجارة الجملة
whole-time working	^{c}*amal bi-dawām kāmil*	عمل بدوام كامل
widow's insurance	*ta'mīn armala*	تأمين ارملة
widow's pension	*ma*^{c}*āsh al-arāmil*	معاش الارامل
wildcat	*bi'r istikshāfiyya*	بئر استكشافية
wildcat strike	*iḍrāb ghayr mashrū*^{c}	اضراب غير مشروع
wilful negligence	*ihmāl mufta*^{c}*al*	اهمال مفتعل
will	*waṣiyya*	وصية
willing party	*aṭ-ṭaraf ar-rāghib*	الطرف الراغب
windfall	*kasb mufāji'*	كسب مفاجئ
windfall profit	*ribḥ ghayr mutawaqqa*^{c}	ربح غير متوقّع
winding up	*taṣfiya*	تصفية
winding up order	*amr taṣfiya*	امر تصفية
window-dressing	*taḥrīf al-ḥaqā'iq (al-māliyya)*	تحريف الحقائق (المالية)
wind up	*yuṣaffī*	يصفّى
with all faults	*ma*^{c} *kull al-*^{c}*uyūb*	مع كل العيوب
withdrawal	*saḥb*	سحب

withdraw an action	*yasḥab da'wā/shakwā*	يسحب دعوى/شكوى
withdraw from a deal	*yansaḥib min ṣafqa*	ينسحب من صفقة
withholding	*iqtiṭā*^{c}*, iḥtibās*	اقتطاع ، احتباس
withholding tax exemption	*i*^{c}*fā' min aḍ-ḍarība 'l-muqtaṭa*^{c}*a*	اعفاء من الضريبة المقتطعة
withholding the truth	*ikhfā' al-ḥaqīqa*	اخفاء الحقيقة
within a limited time	*fī waqt muḥaddad*	فى وقت محدّد
with interest	*ma*^{c}*a 'l-fā'ida*	مع الفائدة
within the law	*fī niṭāq al-qānūn*	فى نطاق القانون
without delay	*bi-dūn ta'khīr*	بدون تأخير
without prejudice	*dūna'l-ikhlāl bi-ḥaqq, dūna ta*^{c}*aṣṣub*	دون الاخلال بحقّ ، دون تعصّب
without reserve	*bidūn taḥaffuẓ*	بدون تحفّظ
witness	*shāhid, shahāda*	شاهد ، شهادة
witness box	*maḥall wuqūf ash-shāhid*	محلّ وقوف الشاهد
witness, to	*yashhad*	يشهد
women's wages	*'ujūr an-nisā'*	اجور النساء
work	^{c}*amal, shughl*	عمل ، شغل
workability	*imkāniyyat at-tanfīdh*	امكانية التنفيذ
work cycle	*dawrat al-*^{c}*amal*	دورة العمل
worker	^{c}*āmil, mustakhdam*	عامل ، مستخدم
work force	*al-quwwa 'l-*^{c}*āmila*	القوة العاملة
working agreement	*ittifāqiyyat al-*^{c}*amal*	اتّفاقية العمل

working assets	*'uṣūl ᶜāmila*	أصول عاملة
working capital	*ra'smāl ᶜāmil*	رأسمال عامل
working class	*aṭ-ṭabaqa l-ᶜāmila*	الطبقة العاملة
working conditions	*ẓurūf al-ᶜamal*	ظروف العمل
working day	*yawm al-ᶜamal*	يوم العمل
working expenses	*maṣārīf at-tashghīl*	مصاريف التشغيل
working hours	*sāᶜāt al-ᶜamal*	ساعات العمل
working papers	*awrāq ᶜamal*	أوراق عمل
working party	*lajnat khubarā' (li-dirāsat shay')*	لجنة خبراء (لدراسة شيء)
working population	*ash-shaᶜb al-ᶜāmil*	الشعب العامل
working time	*waqt al-ᶜamal*	وقت العمل
work in progress	*aᶜmāl taḥt at-tanfīdh*	أعمال تحت التنفيذ
workload	*ḥiml al-ᶜamal*	حمل العمل
workman	*ᶜāmil*	عامل
workmanship	*ṣanᶜa, maḥārat aṣ-ṣināᶜa*	صنعة • مهارة الصناعة
work measurement	*qiyās al-ᶜamal*	قياس العمل
workmen's accident insurance	*ta'mīn ḥawādith al-ᶜummāl*	تأمين حوادث العمّال
workmen's compensation	*taᶜwīḍ al-ᶜummāl*	تعويض العمّال
workmen's compensation acts	*qawānīn taᶜwīḍ al-ᶜummāl*	قوانين تعويض العمّال
workmen's compensation insurance	*ta'mīn taᶜwīḍ iṣābāt al-ᶜamal*	تأمين تعويض اصابات العمل
work out	*yaḥsib, yadrus*	يحسب • يدرس

work permit	*taṣrīh ᶜamal, ijāzat ᶜamal*	تصريح عمل. اجازة عمل
work programme	*birnāmaj ᶜamal*	برنامج عمل
works	*wirash, maṣāniᶜ*	ورش. مصانع
works engineer	*muhandis al-wirash*	مهندس الورش
works foreman	*mulāhiẓ al-ᶜummāl*	ملاحظ العمّال
workshop	*warsha*	ورشة
work simplification	*tabsīṭ al-aᶜmāl*	تبسيط الاعمال
works manager	*mudīr al-maṣnaᶜ*	مدير المصنع
works regulations	*niẓām al-maṣnaᶜ*	نظام المصنع
work study	*dirāsat al-ᶜamal*	دراسة العمل
work, to	*yaᶜmal*	يعمل
work to rule	*tabṭiʾat al-ᶜamal*	تبطئة العمل
World Bank	*al-bank ad-dawlī*	البنك الدولى
world consumption	*al-istihlāk al-ᶜālamī*	الاستهلاك العالمى
world economy	*al-iqtiṣād al-ᶜālamī*	الاقتصاد العالمى
world markets	*aswāq ᶜālamiyya*	أسواق عالمية
world trade	*at-tijāra 'd-dawliyya/al-ᶜālamiyya*	التجارة الدولية/العالمية
worldwide	*dhā'iᶜ al-intishār*	ذائع الانتشار
world-wide policy	*būlīṣa ᶜālamiyya*	بوليصة عالمية
writ	*amr qaḍā'i*	أمر قضائى
write a letter	*yaktub risāla*	يكتب رسالة

write down	*yukhaffiḍ qīmat al-biḍāʿa*	يخفّض قيمة البضاعة
write off	*yashṭub dayn, yashṭub ḥisāb*	يشطب دين أوحساب
write up	*yuḥarrir*	يحرّر
writing, to confirm in	*yu'akkid kitābiyyan*	يؤكّد كتابيا
writ of attachment	*amr ḥajz*	أمر حجز
writ of execution	*amr tanfīdh ḥukm*	أمر تنفيذ حكم
writ of summons	*amr ḥuḍūr*	أمر حضور
written consent	*muwāfaqa kitābiyya*	موافقة كتابية
written contract	*ʿaqd maktūb*	عقد مكتوب
written statement	*taṣrīḥ maktūb*	تصريح مكتوب
wrong address	*ʿunwān khaṭa'*	عنوان خطأ
wrong delivery	*taslīm khaṭa'*	تسليم خطأ
wrongful	*jā'ir, ẓālim*	جائر، ظالم
wrongful act	*taṣarruf khaṭa'*	تصرّف خطأ
wrongful dismissal	*ṭard jā'ir*	طرد جائر
wrought iron	*ḥadīd muṭāwiʿ*	حديد مطاوع

X

xerox process	*ᶜamaliyyat taṣwīr az-zīrūx*	عملية تصوير الزيروكس
X-ray, an	*ṣūrat ashiᶜᶜat iks*	صورة أشعّة إكس
X-ray analysis	*taḥlīl bi-ashiᶜᶜat iks*	تحليل بأشعّة إكس
X-ray examination	*faḥṣ bi-ashiᶜᶜat iks*	فحص بأشعّة إكس
X-ray machine	*makanat ashiᶜᶜat iks*	مكنة أشعّة إكس
X-rays	*ashiᶜᶜat iks*	أشعّة إكس
X-ray therapy	*ᶜilāj ashiᶜᶜat iks*	علاج أشعّة إكس
X-ray, to	*yuṣawwara bi ashiᶜᶜat iks*	يصوّر بأشعّة إكس

Y

yard (measurement)	*yārda*	ياردة
yardstick	*mi^{c}yār, miqyās*	معيار. مقياس
year	*sana, ^{c}ām*	سنة . عام
year book	*ad-dalīl/al-kitāb as-sanawī*	الدليل/الكتاب السنوى
year-end	*nihāyat as-sana*	نهاية السنة
year-end dividend	*ḥiṣṣat arbāḥ nihāyat as-sana*	حصّة أرباح نهاية السنة
year-end inventory	*qā'imat/biḍā^{c}at jard ākhir as-sana*	قائمة/بضاعة جرد آخر السنة
year free of premium	*sanat ta'mīn mu^{c}fāh min al-qisṭ*	سنة تأمين معفاة من القسط
yearly income	*dakhl sanawī*	دخل سنوى
yearly premium	*qisṭ sanawī*	قسط سنوى
year of acceptance	*sanat al-qabūl, sanat al-iktitāb*	سنة القبول. سنة الاكتتاب
year of assessment	*sanat at-taqdīr aḍ-ḍarībī, sanat at-taklīf aḍ-ḍarībī*	سنة التقدير الضريبى، سنة التكليف الضريبى
yield, to	*yughill*	يغلّ

Z

Z chart	*ar-rasm al-bayáni 'Z'*	الرسم البيانى " Z "
zero error	*in*^{c}*idām al-khaṭa'*	انعدام الخطأ
zero defects	*in*^{c}*idām al-*^{c}*uyūb*	انعدام العيوب
zero hour	*sā*^{c}*at aṣ-ṣifr*	ساعة الصفر
zero rating	*at-taqdīr bi-ṣifr*	التقدير بصفر
zone	*minṭaqa*	منطقة
zone, free	*minṭaqa ḥurra*	منطقة حرّة
zone pricing	*tas*^{c}*īr ḥasb al-minṭaqa*	تسعير حسب المنطقة
zone, to	*yuqassim ila manāṭiq*	يقسّم الى مناطق

COUNTRIES & CURRENCIES

1. *The plural of a currency is obtained by adding āt at the end of the word. Thus:*

   dīnār becomes dīnārāt (dinars)

   junayh becomes junayhāt (pounds)

   riyāl becomes riyālāt (riyals), and so on.

2. *The adjective of the country concerned is added after such words as dīnār, dūlār, riyāl, i.e. dinār ᶜirāqi, dūlār amrīkī, riyāl suᶜūdī (an Iraqi dinar, etc). Naturally when talking to people in the country concerned there is no need for the adjective.*

Afghanistan	*afghānistān*	أفغانستان
afghani	*afghānī*	أفغانى
Albania	*albānyā*	ألبانيا
lek	*lik*	ليك
Algeria	*al-jazā'ir*	الجزائر
dinar	*dīnār jazā'irī*	دينار جزائرى
Angola	*angūlā*	أنجولا
kwanza	*kwānzā*	كوانزا
Argentina	*al-arjantīn*	الارجنتين
peso	*bīzo arjantīnī*	بيزو ارجنتينى
Australia	*istirālīya*	استراليا
Australian dollar	*dūlār istirālī*	دولار استرالى
Austria	*an-nimsā*	النمسا
schilling	*shilin nimsāwī*	شلن نمساوى

Bahamas	*bahāma*	بهاما
Bahamian dollar	*dūlār bahāmī*	دولار بهامى
Bahrain	*al-baḥrain*	البحرين
dinar	*dīnār baḥrānī*	دينار بحرانى

Bangladesh	*banghlādish*	بانغلاديش
taka	*tākā*	تاكا
Barbados	*barbādūs*	بربادوس
Barbados dollar	*dūlār barbādūsī*	دولار بربادوسى
Belgium	*baljīkā*	بلجيكا
Belgian franc	*frank baljīkī*	فرنك بلجيكى
Bermuda	*birmūdā*	برميودا
Bermuda dollar	*dūlār birmūdī*	دولار برميودى
Bolivia	*būlīfyā*	بوليفيا
peso	*bīzū būlīfī*	بيزو بوليفى
Botswana	*būtswāna*	بوتسوانا
pula	*būlā*	بولا
Brazil	*al-barāzīl*	البرازيل
cruzeiro	*krūzīrū*	كروزيرو
Bulgaria	*bulghāryā*	بلغاريا
lev	*lif*	ليف
Burma	*burmā*	بورما
kyat	*kyāt*	كيات

Canada	*kanada*	كندا
Canadian dollar	*dūlār kanadī*	دولار كندى
Chile	*shīlī*	شيلى
Chilian peso	*bīzū shīlī*	بيزو شيلى
China	*aṣ-ṣīn ash-shaᶜbiyya*	الصين الشعبية
renminbi Yuan	*rinminbi yuwān*	رنمينبى يوان
Colombia	*kūlūmbyā*	كولومبيا
Colombian peso	*bīzū kūlūmbiyya*	بيزو كولومبية
Costa Rica	*kustārīkā*	كستا ريكا
colon	*kūlūn*	كولون
Cuba	*kūbā*	كوبا
Cuban peso	*bīzū kūbiyya*	بيزو كوبية
Cyprus	*Qubruṣ*	قبرص
Cyprus pound	*junayh qubruṣī*	جنيه قبرصى
Czechoslovakia	*tshīkūslūfākyā*	تشيكوسلوفاكيا
koruna (crown)	*kurūnā tshīkiyya*	كرونا تشيكية
Denmark	*ad-dinmārk*	الدنمارك
Danish kroner	*krūn dinmārkī*	كرون دنماركى

Dominican Republic	*jumhūriyyat ad-dūminikān*	جمهورية الدومنيكان
Dominican peso	*bīzū dūminikān*	بيزو دومنيكان
Ecuador	*ikwādūr*	اكوادور
sucre	*sūkr*	سوكر
Egypt	*miṣr*	مصر
Egyptian pound	*junayh miṣrī*	جنيه مصرى
Ethiopia	*ithyūbyā*	اثيوبيا
Ethiopian dollar	*dūlār ithyūbī*	دولار اثيوبى
	birr	
Finland	*finlanda*	فنلندة
markka	*marka*	ماركة
France	*faransā*	فرنسا
French franc	*frank faransī*	فرنك فرنسى

Gambia	*ghāmbyā*	غامبيا
dalasa	*dālasā*	دالسا
Germany (East)	*almānya 'sh-sharqiyya*	المانيا الشرقية
Ostmark	*mārk sharqī*	مارك شرقى
Germany (West)	*almānya 'l-gharbiyya*	المانيا الغربية
Deutsch mark	*mark gharbī*	مارك غربى
Ghana	*ghānā*	غانا
cedi	*sīdī*	سيدى
Greece	*al-yūnān*	اليونان
drachma	*drakhmā*	دراخما
Hong Kong	*hūngh kūngh*	هونغ كونغ
Hong Kong dollar	*dūlār hūngh-kūngh*	دولار هونغ كونغ
Hungary	*al-majar*	المجر
forint	*fūrint*	فورنت

Iceland	*ayslānda*	ايسلاندة
Icelandic krona	*kurūnā ayslandiyya*	كرونا ايسلاندية
India	*al-hind*	الهند
Indian rupee	*rūbiyya hindiyya*	روبية هندية
Indonesia	*indūnīsyā*	اندونيسيا
rupiah	*rūbiyya indūnīsiyya*	روبية اندونيسية
Iran	*īrān*	ايران
riyal	*riyāl īrānī*	ريال ايرانى
Iraq	*al-ᶜirāq*	العراق
Iraqi dinar	*dīnār ᶜirāqī*	دينار عراقى
Irish Republic	*jumhūriyyat irlanda*	جمهورية ايرلندة
Irish pound	*junayh irlandī*	جنيه ايرلندى
Italy	*iṭālyā*	ايطاليا
lira	*līra iṭāliyya*	ليرة ايطالية
Jamaica	*jamaykā*	جامايكا
Jamaican dollar	*dūlār jamaykī*	دولار جامايكى
Japan	*al-yābān*	اليابان
yen	*yin yābānī*	ين يابانى

Jordan	*al-urdun*	الاردن
Jordanian dinar	*dīnār urdunī*	دينار أردنى
Kenya	*kinyā*	كينيا
Kenya shilling	*shilin kīnī*	شلن كينى
Korea (North)	*kurya 'sh-shamāliyya*	كوريا الشمالية
won	*won*	ون
Korea (South)	*kurya 'l-janūbiyya*	كوريا الجنوبية
won	*won*	ون
Kuwait	*al-kuwayt*	الكويت
Kuwaiti dinar	*dīnār kuwaytī*	دينار كويتى
Lebanon	*lubnān*	لبنان
Lebanese pound	*līra lubnāniyya*	ليرة لبنانية
Liberia	*laybīryā*	ليبيريا
Liberian dollar	*dūlār laybīrī*	دولار لايبيرى

Libya	*lībyā*	ليبيا
Libyan dinar	*dīnār lībī*	دينار ليبى
Luxembourg	*lūksumbūrgh*	لكسمبورغ
Luxembourg franc	*frank luksumburghī*	فرانك لكسمبورغى
Malta	*malṭā*	مالطا
Maltese pound	*junayh malṭī*	جنيه مالطى
Malaysia	*mālīzyā*	ماليزيا
Malaysian dollar	*dūlār mālīzī*	دولار ماليزى
Mexico	*al-maksīk*	المكسيك
Mexican peso	*bīzū maksīkī*	بيزو ماكسيكى
Morocco	*al-maghrib*	المغرب
dirham	*dirham maghrībī*	درهم مغربى
Netherlands	*hūlanda*	هولندة
guilder	*kîldār*	كيلدر

New Zealand	*nyūzīlanda*	نيوزيلندة
New Zealand dollar	*dūlār nyūzīlandī*	دولار نيوزيلندى
Nicaragua	*nīkaraghwa*	نيكاراغوا
cordoba	*kūrdūbā*	كوردوبا
Nigeria	*nayjīryā*	نيجيريا
naira	*nāyrā*	نايرا
Norway	*an-nurwīj*	النرويج
Norway kroner	*krūn nurwījī*	كرون نرويجى
Oman, Sultanate of	*salṭanat ᶜumān*	سلطنة عمان
Omani riyal	*riyāl ᶜumānī*	ريال عمانى
Pakistan	*bākistān*	باكستان
Pakistani rupee	*rūbiyya bākistāniyya*	روبية باكستانية
Panama	*banamā*	بناما
balboa	*balbowa*	بالبوا

Paraguay	*barāghwāy*	باراغواى
guarani	*ghārānī*	غارانى
Peru	*bīrū*	بيرو
sol	*ṣul*	صول
Philippines	*al-filibbīn*	الفليبين
Philippine peso	*bīzū filibbīnī*	بيزو فليبينى
Poland	*būlanda*	بولندا
ziloty	*zilūtī*	زلوتى
Portugal	*al-burtughāl*	البرتغال
Portuguese escudo	*iskūdū*	ايسكودو
Qatar	*qaṭar*	قطر
Qatari riyal	*riyāl qaṭarī*	ريال قطرى
Rumania	*rūmānyā*	رومانيا
leu	*lū*	لو

Salvador, El	*as-salfādūr*	السلفادور
colon	*cūlūn*	كولون
Saudi Arabia	*al-mamlaka 'l-ᶜarabiyya 's-suᶜūdiyya*	المملكة العربية السعودية
riyal	*riyāl suᶜūdī*	ريال سعودى
Shri Lanka	*sīrī lānkā*	سيريلانكا
Shri Lankan rupee	*rūbiyyat sīrī lānkā*	روبية سيريلانكا
Singapore	*singhāfūrā*	سنغافورة
Singapore dollar	*dūlār singhāfūrī*	دولار سنغافورى
South Africa	*janūb ifrīqyā*	جنوب افريقيا
rand	*rand*	راند
Spain	*asbānyā*	اسبانيا
peseta	*bīzītā*	بيزيتا
Sudan	*as-sūdān*	السودان
Sudanese pound	*junayh sūdānī*	جنيه سودانى
Sweden	*as-suwīd*	السويد
Swedish kroner	*kurūn swīdī*	كرون سويدى
Switzerland	*swisrā*	سويسرا
Swiss franc	*frank swisrī*	فرانك سويسرى
Syria	*sūryā*	سوريا
Syrian pound	*līra sūriyya*	ليرة سورية

Taiwan	*taywān*	تايوان
Taiwan dollar	*dūlār taywānī*	دولار تايوانى
Thailand	*táyland*	تايلاند
baht	*baht*	باهت
Tunisia	*tūnis*	تونس
Tunisian dinar	*dīnār tūnusī*	دينار تونسى
Turkey	*turkyā*	تركيا
Turkish lira	*līra turkiyya*	ليرة تركية

Uganda	*ughanda*	اوغندا
Uganda shilling	*shilin ughandī*	شلن اوغندى
United Arab Emirates	*al-imārāt al-ᶜarabiyya 'l-muttaḥida*	الامارات العربية المتحدة
U.A.E.dirham	*dirham al-imārāt*	درهم الامارات
United Kingdom	*al-mamlakat al-muttaḥida*	المملكة المتّحدة
pound sterling	*junayh istirlīnī*	جنيه استرلينى
United States of America	*al-wilāyāt al-muttaḥida 'l-amrīkiyya*	الولايات المتّحدة الامريكية
United States dollar	*dūlār amrīkī*	دولار أمريكى
Uruguay	*urughwāy*	اوروغواى
Uruguay peso	*bīzū urughway*	بيزو اوروغواى

U.S.S.R. (Russia)	*rūsyā*	روسيا
rouble	*rūbl*	روبل
Venezuela	*finizwīlā*	فنزويلا
bolivar	*būlifār*	بوليفار
Vietnam	*fiyitnām*	فيتنام
dong	*dungh*	دونغ
Yemen (North)	*al-yaman ash-shamāliyya*	اليمن الشمالية
riyal	*riyāl yamanī*	ريال يمنى
Yemen (South)	*al-yaman al-janūbiyya*	اليمن الجنوبية
South Yemen dinar	*dīnār yamanī*	دينار يمنى
Yugoslavia	*yūghuslāfyā*	يوغوسلافيا
Yugoslav dinar	*dīnār yūghuslāfī*	دينار يوغوسلافى

Zimbabwe	*zimbabwi*	زمبابوی
Zimbabwe dollar	*dūlār zimbabwī*	دولار زمبابوی